THE POLITICS OF THE
SOUTH AFRICA RUN

THE POLITICS OF THE SOUTH AFRICA RUN

European Shipping and Pretoria

G. R. BERRIDGE

CLARENDON PRESS · OXFORD
1987

Oxford University Press, Walton Street, Oxford OX2 6DP

Oxford New York Toronto
Delhi Bombay Calcutta Madras Karachi
Petaling Jaya Singapore Hong Kong Tokyo
Nairobi Dar es Salaam Cape Town
Melbourne Auckland
and associated companies in
Beirut Berlin Ibadan Nicosia

Oxford is a trade mark of Oxford University Press

Published in the United States
by Oxford University Press, New York

British Library Cataloguing in Publication Data
Berridge, G. R.
The politics of the South Africa run:
European shipping and Pretoria.
1. South Africa—Commercial policy—
History—20th century 2. South Africa
—Politics and government—1978–
I. Title
382'.0968 HF1613.4
ISBN 0-19-827484-X

Library of Congress Cataloging in Publication Data
Berridge, Geoff.
The politics of the South Africa run.
Bibliography: p.
Includes index.
1. Merchant marine—South Africa—History.
2. Merchant marine—Europe—History. 3. Shipping
conferences—History. 4. Union-Castle Mail Steamship
Company—History. I. Title.
HE903.4.B47 1987 387.5'004 87–1600
ISBN 0-19-827484-X

Set by Hope Services, Abingdon
Printed in Great Britain
at the University Press, Oxford
by David Stanford
Printer to the University

For my daughter,
Cathy

PREFACE

THIS book grew out of a general interest in international political economy and earlier work on Anglo-South African relations. I had the idea that if I could penetrate the dealings of the Union-Castle Line with the South African government then I might simultaneously open a new window on South Africa's relations with foreign capital, throw some light on the general question of corporate–government relations from an unusual angle (shipping lines are not normally thought of as 'multinational corporations'), and obtain more information on South Africa's gold sales policy (the mail ships carried the bullion)—a policy which in *Economic Power in Anglo-South African Diplomacy* (London, 1981) I had claimed was politically inspired. In the event, I soon discovered that the story of Union-Castle's relations with South Africa was really the story of the South African Conference's relations with South Africa, and that this was much more significant than I had ever imagined. A vast private archive was also generously opened up to me, first to the end of 1970 and then to the end of 1977. As a result, I became absorbed in the post-war history of the Conference and quite lost sight of my early interest in gold. What follows will help to determine whether or not I was right to follow this course.

I was given access to Conference papers on the understanding that I would show the manuscript of the final work to the present Conference Chairman, N. M. Forster, and take seriously any alterations which he might suggest; he understood that this did not amount to a veto. In practice, he asked for only a few—largely on the grounds that they affect continuing business—and I have made all of them. They are not of any great significance. I should add that this does not mean to say that he accepts all of my analysis, which would be untrue.

In addition to N. M. Forster, to whom my debt is immense, I would like to thank once more all of the other people who have helped me in one way or another with this book, but in particular the following: Lord Cayzer, Professor J. E. Spence, Jack Holgate, Don Small, A. E. Lemon, Jack Nicholl, Neil Sempill, George Young, Pixie Young, Captain Frank Marriott, W. E. Luke, Jackie Kalley, June Foster, Vivian Solomon, H. D. Rengger, and the participants in the Commonwealth History Seminar at Nuffield College. My colleagues in the Department of Politics at Leicester have borne well my eccentric interest in 'ships', and I am particularly grateful to John Hoffman for alerting me to the 'radical approach to power', the (slender) implications of which for this study I discuss in the Conclusion. My wife Sheila has been very patient throughout the whole business and has been of great assistance in translating Afrikaans documents into English. I am also grateful to my mother for typing out the manuscript, to Nicola Pike of OUP for expert editing, and to Henry Hardy of OUP for labouring with such good humour over the vexed problem of the title.

I would also like to take this opportunity to thank the following institutions for financial assistance with my research, which included a visit to South Africa in 1982: the British Academy, the Nuffield Foundation, and the University of Leicester (Research Board).

The formal title of the conference in the Europe–South Africa trade has gone through a number of changes and is today the 'Europe South & South-East African Conference Lines'. However, for most of its history it has been referred to simply as 'the South African Conference', and that is the style which I have employed. Sometimes I also refer to it as 'the Conference' or 'the Lines'. For the sake of clarity, I refer throughout to 'the Southbound trade' and 'the Northbound trade', although it was customary until the mid-1950s to describe the former as 'the Outward trade' and the latter as 'the Homeward trade'.

G.R.B

Leicester, 1986

CONTENTS

LIST OF TABLES

ABBREVIATIONS

ASSOCOM	Association of Chambers of Commerce
B & C	The British & Commonwealth Shipping Company Limited
BNEC	British National Export Council
CACT	Conference (Europe/SA) Archives, Cape Town
c.a.f.	currency adjustment factor
CAL	Conference (Europe/SA) Archives, London
Cayz. H.	Cayzer House, London (head office of the B & C Group)
CBI	Confederation of British Industries
CCN	Companhia Colonial de Navegaçao
CENSA	Council of European and Japanese National Shipowners' Associations
CFM	Caminhos de Ferro de Moçambique (Mozambique Railways)
CGM	Compagnie Générale Maritime
CMB	Compagnie Maritime Belge
CNN	Companhia Nacional de Navegaçao
CPTM	Companhia Portuguesa de Transportes Maritimos (known latterly as 'CTM')
CSG	Consultative Shipping Group
DOAL	Deutsche Ost-Afrika Linie
DSR	Deutsche Seereederei
EANSL	East Africa National Shipping Line
ECL	Enterprise Container Lines
EHCL	Ellerman Harrison Container Line
EIN	Empresa Insulana de Navegaçao
EPB	Executive Planning Board
ESC	European National Shippers' Councils
FCI	Federated Chamber of Industries
FRELIMO	Frente de Libertaçao de Moçambique (Front for the Liberation of Mozambique)

GATT	General Agreement on Tariffs and Trade
Greenwich	National Maritime Museum, Greenwich
IDC	Industrial Development Corporation
ISCOR	South African Iron and Steel Corporation
JSP	Jadranska Slobodna Plovidba
NFC	National Finance Corporation
OAU	Organization of African Unity
OCL	Overseas Containers Limited
OFA	Ocean Freight Agreement
PFG	Portuguese Flag Group
POL	Polish Ocean Lines
PPECB	Perishable Products Export Control Board
PRO	Public Record Office, Kew
SA Shipping News	*The South African Shipping News and Fishing Industry Review*
SAA	South African Airways
SAAU	South African Agricultural Union
SACD	South African Cargo Depots (subsequently known as South African Container Depots)
SAECS	Southern Africa Europe Container Service
Safcon	South African Conference Lines
SAR&H	South African Railways and Harbours Administration
U-C DM	Union-Castle Directors' Meetings (minute books)
UKSATA	United Kingdom–South Africa Trade Association
UNCTAD	United Nations Conference on Trade and Development

INTRODUCTION

As a result of recent historical research, our understanding of the relationship between the multinational corporation and the state is much more subtle today than it was a decade or so ago.[1] There is now ample evidence that the political influence which multinationals exert over both their home and host states varies enormously and is often severely limited. This is partly because of the independent sources of strength of the state and partly because of the continuing vigour of the ideology of nationalism. Nevertheless, the myth of the political omnipotence of the multinational corporation remains a potent one, for the scope of its operations, the scale of its resources, and the economic significance of its activities make it easy to sustain the myth by impressionistic argument and evocative metaphor—the long-tentacled 'octopus' being an old favourite.[2] This is one reason for the continuing need for historical studies such as this book, and particularly for those which can throw light on the manner in which the multinational is sometimes used by the state as an instrument of foreign policy.[3]

If there remains a general need for further historical research on the political role of the multinational, this is, however, especially urgent in the case of multinationals with major investments in South Africa. There are three main reasons for this. In the first place, the activities of these companies within South Africa are widely believed to 'support apartheid', though the character of this support is often left couched in the most general terms. Secondly, lobbying by multinationals is held by many to account for the reluctance shown by their home governments

[1] For example, C. F. Bergsten et al., *American Multinationals and American Interests* (Washington DC, 1978); D. K. Fieldhouse, *Unilever Overseas: The Anatomy of a Multinational, 1895–1965* (London, 1978); S. D. Krasner, *Defending the National Interest: Raw Materials Investments and U.S. Foreign Policy* (Princeton, 1978); and L. Turner, *Oil Companies in the International System*, 2nd edn. (London, 1980).

[2] Classic examples of this genre are R. Jenkins, *Exploitation: The World Power Structure and the Inequality of Nations* (London, 1970); and R. J. Barnet and R. E. Muller, *Global Reach: The Power of the Multinational Corporations* (London, 1975).

[3] The need for further research in this area has been emphasized both by Klaus Knorr in 'International Economic Leverage and its Uses', in K. Knorr and F. N. Trager (eds.), *Economic Issues and National Security* (Lawrence, Kan., 1977); and by R. S. Olson in his 'Economic Coercion in World Politics', *World Politics*, 31.4, July 1979.

in Western Europe and North America to put serious pressure on Pretoria for domestic reform, though the evidence for this conclusion is invariably conspicuous by its absence. Finally, in South Africa's present crisis, and notwithstanding the last point, multinationals are likely to remain under pressure to get out of the Republic, or at least to use such influence as they have to hasten the National Party government along the road of reform; thus the character of their existing relationships with the South African government is of the greatest practical, as well as historical, significance.

The international shipping lines serving South Africa have never figured in the debate about the role of multinationals in the Republic, any more than liner companies in general have featured in the general political argument about multinational corporations (though their *economic* consequences have received much attention from the United Nations Conference on Trade and Development—UNCTAD). Both omissions no doubt have something to do with the notorious secrecy of the shipping industry and the consequent difficulty of uncovering reliable source material. However, it seems likely that the main reason is that the international shipping line—like the international airline—has characteristics which minimize opportunities for dramatic confrontations with the state and even make it conventional to exclude it from the category 'multinational' altogether, namely: the mobility of its major capital units, and its tendency to employ its own nationals (or at any rate not the nationals of the countries at the foreign ends of its trades). The result is that neither expropriation of assets nor 'exploitation' of employees is an issue. But in other respects the relationship between a liner company and a state which wants an efficient shipping service for its trades is identical to the relationship between a more conventional multinational and a state which wants factories, mines, or plantations established on its territory. Besides, liner companies sometimes invest heavily abroad in shore facilities and in shipping-related activities—a phenomenon greatly advanced by containerization—and may even be part of a conglomerate which engages in foreign direct investment in altogether unrelated spheres. Furthermore, one of the very features of the liner company which has tended to render it politically uninteresting, that is, its relative immunity from expropriation, would also seem to give it a source of strength *vis-à-vis* the state which is not available to the ordinary multinational. For all of these reasons, it is unwise to omit the liner company from the general debate about the political role of the multinational corporation, and no less unwise to omit it from the debate about the political and economic significance of multinationals to South Africa.

The economy of South Africa is unusually dependent on foreign trade in general[4] and on trade with Western Europe in particular, and this trade has been threatened by sanctions since the early 1960s. As a result, it is not surprising that the liner companies in the Europe–South Africa trade—organized into a 'conference' whose 'range' covers the United Kingdom, Scandinavia, the Baltic, the North Continent (Hamburg/le Havre), and the Mediterranean at the European end, and, at the southern end, extends from Walvis Bay round to Chinde in Mozambique (thus including the important ports of Maputo and Beira)—should have received a great deal of government attention in Pretoria. What is surprising, however, is just how important the relationship between the liner companies in this trade and the South African government has proved to be—to the Republic's economy, to its defences against sanctions, and (albeit in a lesser degree) to its foreign policy.

The detailed account which I shall provide of the relationship between European shipping capital and the South African government begins in 1944, four and a half years before the Nationalists came to power. This makes possible an illuminating contrast with the pre-Nationalist era. However, in order to set the scene it is necessary to go back much further, because by 1944 the essence of the relationship— which was merely to take on exaggerated form under the Nationalists—had already been long established.

The Origins of the 'Ocean Freight Agreement'

Despite their invulnerability to expropriation and the organization of their trade in a 'closed conference'—as cartels with controlled memberships are known in the shipping world—the liner companies which serve the Europe–South Africa trade (see Appendix I) suffer a measure of government control which is not only unique among the trades serving South Africa, but seems to have few close parallels in any other trade in the world outside those serving the United States.[5] This control is formally detailed in a public, long-term contract known

---

[4] J. Nattrass, *The South African Economy: Its Growth and Change* (Cape Town, 1981), 268.

[5] UNCTAD Secretariat, *The Regulation of Liner Conferences*, TD/104/Rev. 1 (New York, 1972).

as the 'Ocean Freight Agreement' (OFA), which has historically been supplemented by private understandings contained in 'supporting letters'. What was in effect the first OFA was concluded in 1912, while the last one was signed in 1977 and remains in force until the end of 1991.

In 1912 a settlement was reached to a prolonged crisis in relations between the 'South African Conference'—as the conference in the trade with Europe was commonly known—and the South African government which had been brought to a head the previous year by the new Union Parliament's Post Office Administration and Shipping Combinations Discouragement Act. Under this Act, no shipping line offering deferred rebates[6] or similar rewards for exclusive support would be eligible to compete for the prized contract awarded by the government for the carriage of mails between Britain and South Africa: the so-called 'Mail Contract'. The settlement which followed passage of the Post Office Act consisted of three notionally separate agreements: a 'Mail Contract'; a government 'Freight Contract' (Southbound); and a 'Homeward Produce Agreement' (Northbound). But in effect they represented a package deal (the last two coming to be known collectively in subsequent negotiations as the 'Ocean Freight Agreement'). For their part, the Conference Lines, represented in the negotiations solely by the Union-Castle Line, agreed to make significant reductions in the freight rates for South Africa's agricultural exports and to abolish the controversial deferred rebate. In return, the government finally awarded the Mail Contract to Union-Castle once more (negotiations had been going on intermittently since late in 1908), and agreed to give the Lines a virtual monopoly on government cargo for the unprecedentedly extended period of five years.[7]

This was the bargain which was at the heart of the settlement of 1912, and it is significant because the principles—substantive and procedural—which both shaped it and were clarified by it established

[6] The deferred rebate is a device whereby a conference shipper is paid a rebate on a given shipment at some future date *provided* that he has remained loyal to the conference in the interim. It has been the classic means of securing a hold on shippers since its introduction by the Calcutta Conference in 1877: V. E. Solomon, *The South African Shipping Question, 1886–1914* (Cape Town, 1982), p. xxi. I have also leaned heavily on this authoritative work for other aspects of my analysis of the 1912 settlement. In addition, see Solomon's 'The "Open Market" in South African Shipping: A Forgotten Controversy', *The South African Journal of Economics*, 47.3, 1979.

[7] Hitherto government freight contracts had been extended for 3 years at the most. The new Mail Contract was to last for 10 years and at the beginning of the negotiations Union-Castle had sought the same period for the Freight Contract.

the characteristic flavour of Conference-government relations until the early 1960s and, in very important respects, down to the present day. These principles were as follows. Firstly, the Lines should hold an almost complete monopoly on government cargo. Secondly, freight rates on South Africa's agricultural exports should be low. Thirdly, the Lines should recoup losses suffered in the Northbound trade by charging high rates on Southbound consumer and capital goods. Fourthly, stripped of the protection afforded by the deferred rebate (except in Southern Mozambique, where the writ of the Post Office Act obviously did not run), and nominally operating in a free market, the Lines should prevent the disruption to the trade which would be caused by the intrusion of non-Conference shipping lines ('outsiders') by nurturing the vague but potent idea that the South African Conference was under the protection of the South African government. Finally, these substantive norms should be guaranteed by the following procedural rules: direct Union-Castle control of all negotiations with the South African government on behalf of the Conference; government control—either direct or indirect—of all important negotiations with the Conference on the South African side; and, on the well-founded premiss that Union-Castle needed the Mail Contract more than the government needed Union-Castle to accept it, and with the proviso that this rule was operated more explicitly after the Second World War than before it, the *linking* of negotiations on new Mail Contracts and new Ocean Freight Agreements in order that Union-Castle and, by extension, the Conference as a whole, could be made to pay for the Mail Contract by concessions on freight rates.

In the 1920s there were two further landmarks in the extension of government influence over the South African Conference. The first was the creation in 1926 of the Perishable Products Export Control Board (PPECB), and the second was the formation in 1929 of the South African Shipping Board. The PPECB was created in order to organize storage of Union perishables (mainly fruit) at the ports and to negotiate with the shipowners on the terms of their shipment. It came under the authority of the Minister of Railways and was to inject a certain amount of grit—as well as expertise—into the government's negotiations with the Lines, especially in the 1960s and 1970s. The PPECB became a party in its own right to the OFA when the Agreement was renewed at the beginning of 1928.[8] As for the

[8] On the origins and work of the PPECB, see *SA Shipping News*, Aug. 1965 and Oct. 1976.

Shipping Board, this was also a statutory body created under the Minister of Railways,[9] but its formation was far more significant. As evidence of the government's determination to keep the Conference in check, the Shipping Board was given the power to recommend fines against shipowners who refused to disclose information which it thought they should divulge.[10] The Lines came under no serious pressure from the Shipping Board over the next few years,[11] but after the Second World War it was to become a heavy weapon indeed in the hands of the government.

The Dominance of Union-Castle over the Conference

It is not difficult to understand why the South African government traditionally should have taken such a close interest in the shipping services which carried the Europe–South Africa trade: as mentioned earlier, foreign trade—dominated by Britain and Continental Europe—has always been very important to the South African economy. Nor is it surprising that this government interest should have increased in the early 1960s, when politically inspired interference in South Africa's trade appeared to be a very real threat. However, the existence of strong motives for government intervention in the Europe–South Africa trade does not in itself explain why the government should have been so successful in their pursuit. Why, then, was the Conference so vulnerable? The explanation is not complicated: the Union-Castle Line, a major British liner company, was extremely dependent on the South Africa trade, and Union-Castle dominated the South African Conference.

Not only was Union-Castle almost wholly dependent upon the South Africa trade,[12] but it was both directly and indirectly at the mercy of *the government* for a significant proportion of its earnings. Union-Castle had held the Mail Contract from South Africa since the

---

[9] In Sept. 1944 responsibility for the Shipping Board was transferred to the Minister of Economic Development, subsequently known as the Minister of Economic Affairs: 'The South African Shipping Board: Its Creation and Functions', *Commerce & Industry*, Feb. 1948.

[10] Ibid.

[11] CAL, 'South African Shipping Board', 22 Mar. 1950.

[12] For the early history of the Union-Castle Line and its umbilical connection with South Africa, see the house account by M. Murray, *Union-Castle Chronicle, 1853–1953* (London, 1953).

nineteenth century,[13] and was thereby provided not only with an annual subsidy but also with berthing priority for the mail ships in South Africa's sometimes congested ports; this made the mail line popular with passengers and shippers alike, and the object of considerable envy on the part of other lines. Furthermore, Union-Castle shipped south substantial quantities of government cargo purchased in Britain and Continental Europe.[14] For these reasons the authorities in South Africa, especially after they were strengthened by Union in 1910,[15] obtained a powerful hold over the Union-Castle Line.

If the South African government held great sway over Union-Castle, the Fenchurch Street company had an equally firm grip on the South African Conference, which had, indeed, been formed on its initiative in 1883.[16] (Union-Castle influence was also paramount in the adjacent conferences: Europe–East Africa, Europe–Lobito, Europe–Mauritius, and UK–Port Sudan.) Initially composed exclusively of British lines, the inter-war period witnessed an influx of lines from Europe and Scandinavia (see Appendix I). Nevertheless, the South African Conference remained firmly in the control of the Union-Castle Line.

The Chairman of the South African Conference always came from Union-Castle, and the Conference Secretariat, opened in 1908, was always housed and staffed by Union-Castle (though its expenses were shared among the Lines in proportion to their interest in the trade). In deference to the Company's large and vital stake in the commerce with South Africa—and because any other course would have led to the collapse of the Conference and a suicidal freight war—Union-Castle was always allowed to have its way on issues of major principle at 'Joint Meetings' (where policy decisions were taken[17]), albeit after a certain amount of grumbling from the other lines. And in case there should be any backsliding in execution, and because it ran the machinery of the Conference in any case, Union-Castle always handled negotiations

[13] Union-Castle was formed in 1900 when Donald Currie's Castle Line took over the Union Line. Previously the Mail Contract had been held by the Union Line and then shared between the rival companies.

[14] Government cargo was estimated at only 10% of total Conference carryings in 1911 (Solomon, *The South African Shipping Question*, 236), but it grew considerably after the First World War with the expansion of South Africa's state and semi-state sectors.

[15] Ibid., 237.   [16] Ibid., 6.

[17] These were the meetings of senior representatives of the member lines, and were so called in order to distinguish them from the caucus meetings of the British Lines which continued after the influx of Continental lines in the inter-war period.

with the South African authorities on behalf of the Conference as a
whole as well as on its own account, that is to say, on freight matters as
well as on the Mail Contract.

This remained the general position in the closing stages of the
Second World War. Despite the dilution of the British character of the
Conference by the entry of the 'Continental Lines', the South African
Conference remained very much the private property of Union-Castle.

It is important to add, too, that the man who was both Chairman and
Managing Director of the Company at this time, Sir Vernon
Thomson, was not a man to be diffident in advancing his proprietary
rights.

By 1944, Stanley Barr, a Union-Castle Assistant Manager, had
already been Chairman of the South African Conference for almost a
decade, but it was Sir Vernon Thomson who actually took the chair at
Joint Meetings. Sir Vernon was a great power in the shipping world.
He had joined Union-Castle in 1932 and, having been largely
responsible for restoring the fortunes of the Company after its
damaging association with Lord Kylsant's Royal Mail Steam Packet
group in the early part of the century,[18] reached the top shortly before
the outbreak of war. At this point, when the Union-Castle Line, along
with the rest of Britain's merchant marine, fell under the control of the
British government, Sir Vernon was appointed Principal Shipping
Adviser and Controller of Commercial Shipping at the Ministry of
War Transport, a position of great influence which he held until April
1946. He was inflexible and notoriously autocratic; he was also good-
looking. In short, he was the very personification of that elegant
hauteur for which Union-Castle had become a byword both within the
Conference and in South Africa itself. This was the man who, at the
beginning of 1944, found time amid his ministerial work to give
thought to the post-war needs of his company and the shipping
conference over which it so grandly presided.

[18] Murray, chap. 18; and E. Green and M. Moss, *A Business of National Importance:
The Royal Mail Shipping Group, 1902–1937* (London, 1982), chaps. 8 and 9.

I

'PARTNERSHIP' WITH SMUTS
1944-1948

THE current Ocean Freight Agreement was due to expire at the end of 1944, but the Mail Contract continued to run until the end of 1946. Nevertheless, at the beginning of 1944 Union-Castle was as anxious to secure early renewal of the latter as it was to obtain an extension of the former. The tide of the war had turned by this time and it was clear to the Company that it would not be long before decisions would have to be taken on the replacement of the costly tonnage which had been lost during requisition.[1] Mail ships had always been expensive and they were hardly likely to be less so once the war had ended and every shipping company was besieging the yards with orders for replacements. As a result, Union-Castle had no intention of committing itself to buying new vessels until it had a firm guarantee from the Union government that it would be able to find profitable employment for them for many years to come. This applied to the Company's fruit ships as well, which were custom-built for the South Africa trade. It is also reasonable to suppose that Fenchurch Street was at the least mildly perturbed by the stirring of nationalist attitudes towards shipping apparent in the Union at this time, and calculated that the sooner its position in the South Africa trade was re-established the better.

The years between the two world wars had witnessed a marked growth of nationalism in shipping across the world,[2] but South Africa itself had been largely unaffected.[3] During this period the only ocean-going tonnage on the South African register had been the handful of vessels run by the Railways and Harbours Administration (SAR&H), mainly to transport sleepers from Australia, and as late as March 1943

---

[1] Almost a third of the Company's tonnage was lost during the war, including 2 of the 8 vessels in the mail fleet: M. Murray, *Union-Castle Chronicle, 1853–1953* (London, 1953), 264 f.

[2] S. G. Sturmey, *British Shipping and World Competition* (London, 1962), chap. 5.

[3] C. Verburgh, *Ontwikkeling en Vooruitsigte van die Suid-Afrikaanse Handelskeepvaart* (Stellenbosch, 1966), chap. 1.3.

a government-appointed Shipping Commission advised against the expansion of this small state fleet. Clearly impressed by the vigorous representations of the influential Cape Town Chamber of Commerce, on the Shipping and Freights Committee of which the Conference Lines were of course represented,[4] the Commission maintained that shipping services to and from South Africa to all quarters of the globe, mostly under the British flag, had been adequate to the country's needs and efficiently operated.[5] However, in his Annual Report for 1942–3 the General Manager of the SAR&H disagreed with the Shipping Commission's conclusion, and his call for an expansion of the state fleet was supported by the Nationalists, the Labour Party, and some members of the United Party in Parliament.[6] It was also no secret that the Minister of Transport, Claud Sturrock, was also in favour of a more assertive shipping policy for South Africa.[7]

The problem for Union-Castle and the other lines in the Conference was, of course, that the British government's requisition of the vessels serving South Africa had demonstrated to the Union both the general point that a national merchant fleet is of enormous value in times of national emergency and the particular point that South Africa's shipping services were extremely vulnerable when Britain was at war. The fact that the Union had also been at war on Britain's side (by a narrow parliamentary majority) did not detract from this point. Neither of these lessons was entirely lost on the Shipping Commission itself and, as a result, its hostility to an enlarged *state* fleet did not prevent it from suggesting (rather coyly) that benefits would accrue to Britain as well as South Africa if some of the private tonnage serving the Union were to be transferred to the South African register.[8] In 1943 and 1944, therefore, it must have been obvious to the Union-Castle Line's agents in the Union that the movement for a South African merchant marine—either in the hands of the state, or private enterprise, or divided between the two—was likely to grow, and that this could ultimately present the Conference with serious competition, especially for government cargo and the Mail Contract.

It was against this background that Union-Castle decided to approach the Union government in early 1944 and attempt to tie it

---

[4] Cape Archives, CC 3/1/2/1/1/17.
[5] Union of South Africa, *Interim Report of the Shipping Commission* (Pretoria, 1945).
[6] *Fairplay*, 23 Mar. 1944.·
[7] *SA Shipping News*, Jan. 1946.
[8] *Interim Report*, paras. 124–7.

down to new long-term commitments.[9] Within the parameters
established by the settlement of 1912 and not substantially amended
since, Sir Vernon Thomson must have anticipated reasonably generous
treatment from the government, at that time firmly in the hands of
General Smuts. Relations with Pretoria were judged by the Company
to be excellent. This is not altogether surprising. The war had fostered
a collaborative spirit, there was a good personal relationship between
Sir Vernon and General Smuts, and the reputation of the Company in
South Africa was high. Shortly before the war started Union-Castle
had completed the total reconstruction of its mail fleet and reduced the
voyage time between Southampton and Cape Town from seventeen to
fourteen days.[10] Furthermore, during the war the Company had
responded promptly to government requests with substantial financial
contributions to its propaganda campaign against pro-Nazi—or at any
rate anti-government—elements in the Afrikaner population: £1,000
for the 'Union Unity Fund' in early 1940,[11] and a further £1,000 for
the *Suiderste* newspaper two years later.[12]

Sir Vernon Thomson's hopes for the forthcoming negotiations were
not disappointed. By May 1944 the Shipping Board had recommended
the extension of the Ocean Freight Agreement,[13] and by the end of
June the Minister of Transport had agreed that it should run on until
the end of 1946 and continue thereafter on a year-to-year basis.[14]
Meanwhile, it seems clear that during a meeting between Sir Vernon
and Smuts in London on 5 June the Union-Castle Line was assured of
renewal of the Mail Contract, provided terms satisfactory to the Union
government could be negotiated.[15] Later in the year Smuts suggested
that Sir Vernon should travel to South Africa to conduct the
negotiations in March 1945.[16]

At the beginning of 1945 the signs for the renewal of the Mail
Contract were thus looking remarkably good. Nevertheless, the
expectation that Union-Castle would have to make certain concessions
in the Mail Contract to the increasingly assertive national mood in
shipping matters was reinforced on 28 February, when the Minister of
Transport told the House of Assembly that the government was

[9] Cayz. H., U-C DM, 25 Jan. 1944, min. 7692.   [10] Murray, 200 f.
[11] Cayz. H., U-C DM, 16 Jan. 1940, min. 6874.
[12] Ibid., 20 Jan. 1942, min. 7293; and 17 Feb. 1942, min. 7315.
[13] CAL, Safcon, Minute Book 41, 27 June 1944, min. 12711.
[14] CAL, Sturrock/U-C Cape Town Agency correspondence, June–Aug. 1944.
[15] Cayz. H., U-C DM, 14 June 1944, min. 7764.
[16] Ibid., 19 Dec. 1944, min. 7873.

determined to do what it could 'to put South Africa on the sea. . . . In any negotiations with the shipping companies in the future', Sturrock continued, 'we shall, I hope, be more exacting in the demands we make to ensure that South African shipping interests are protected'.[17] On top of this, Sir Vernon also learned, shortly before his departure for the Union, that the government would probably take the opportunity to extract better terms under the OFA—in spite of the recently agreed extension of this particular contract—as a further price for renewal of the Mail Contract.[18]

The New Mail Contract and the New OFA

On 5 March 1945 Sir Vernon Thomson arrived in South Africa (ominously for the Union-Castle Line, by air). The following morning he was greeted by Smuts, and in the afternoon the negotiations began. As foreseen, the Mail Contract was not to be concluded unless *simultaneous* consideration was also given to the renegotiation of the OFA, which was to be 'linked' in the additional sense that it would run concurrently with the Mail Contract.[19] Sir Vernon registered a mild objection to this procedure, asking for the Mail Contract to be discussed first, but when this was resisted by the government he wisely decided not to make an issue of it.

Although he did not take part in any of the detailed discussions, Sturrock attempted to establish their tone at the beginning by repeating—though more diffidently—the theme which he had introduced in the House of Assembly in February: South Africa's new maritime aspirations. He hastened to add, however, that the corollary of this envisaged by the government was not a weakening of South Africa's links with the Union-Castle Line but a strengthening of them. 'Anything that we approach you with today will be with the best of intentions,' said the Minister of Transport, 'without any desire to drive a hard bargain but to make the Union-Castle Company not only a British but also a South African Company.' What the government wanted was the gradual growth of a genuine 'partnership'.

The negotiations, though occasionally complex, did not last long. By

[17] House of Assembly Debates, c. 2515.
[18] Cayz. H., U-C DM, 20 Feb. 1945, min. 7909.
[19] Unless otherwise indicated, the following account of these negotiations is based on CAL, South African Ocean Mail Service Contract and Ocean Freight Agreement: Conference between the Union Government and the Union-Castle Mail Steamship Co. Ltd., 1945 [verbatim transcript].

4 April the two sides had signed a new Mail Contract and a new Ocean Freight Agreement, both of which were to run for ten years from 1 January 1947. It is true that the new OFA, unlike its predecessor, had a 'break clause', which provided that in the event of failure to reach an understanding on any matter regarding which 'unforeseeen difficulties' had arisen, either party could terminate the Agreement on eighteen months' notice, but this was not really a defeat for Sir Vernon since, like the government negotiators, he was aware that at this juncture the future of the freight markets was unusually difficult to predict and he was no more anxious than they were to give too many hostages to fortune. Moreover, he rejected out of hand a half-hearted attempt by the government to have an identical clause inserted in the Mail Contract (the future of mail shipment being relatively clearer), observing that, 'There is not the remotest possibility of my agreeing to make a Mail Contract which is liable to be terminated at 18 months notice.' As a result, it is clear that Sir Vernon had broadly achieved his main objective: the early commitment of the government for a lengthy period to the shipping services of the Conference Lines in general and the Union-Castle Line in particular. His company had thus been provided with the confidence to commence its post-war replacement programme at once.

Sir Vernon had reason to be pleased with the details of the two contracts as well. Certainly, concessions had been made in the Mail Contract to nationalist sentiment and the new spirit of 'partnership', but these were not of any great moment. F. J. du Toit, the Secretary for Commerce, who took a leading part in the early stages of the negotiations, soon seemed reconciled to being able to do little more than 'sugar the pill' and put in the odd 'lightning conductor' for Parliament, where he was apprehensive of the reaction to these contracts. Amongst these concessions were Union-Castle's highly qualified 'special undertakings', *inter alia*, to employ a 20 per cent minimum of South Africans in its ships, and to register certain cargo vessels in the Union. In the absence of a genuine 'break clause', the Company also airily agreed to entertain 'discussions' on the Mail Contract in the event of unforeseen difficulties arising. As regards the OFA, Sir Vernon allowed the government to press on him an amendment to the 1934 Freight Agreement in order to obscure—rather than eliminate—what its own lawyers regarded as a clear contravention of the Post Office Act, 1911, namely, the contract rate system, which had been introduced by the Lines as an alternative tie on shippers following the agreement in 1912 to scrap the deferred rebate.[20] He also accepted an increase in the categories of government cargo to be carried at the low, 'basis rate' tariff. Lastly, he agreed that the Lines would not—in order to fight any future outsiders—*reduce* Southbound rates to such an extent that the protection they presently afforded the Union's infant industries would be eroded, though this only made public what had been agreed in confidential correspondence supporting the 1934 Agreement,[21] and was in any case neutralized as far as the Lines were concerned by the promise which Sir Vernon extracted from the government to look favourably on the placing of freight-dumping duties on goods competitive with Union goods which were shipped by outsiders to South Africa at cut rates.[22]

So, the price which Sir Vernon had been required to pay for the early renewal of the two contracts was obviously not high. Since, in addition, he was granted the increase in the annual mail service subsidy for which he had asked, from £228,000 to £300,000, it is not surprising that he was warmly received on his return to Fenchurch Street. The enthusiasm felt by the Union-Castle Board for Sir Vernon's achievements was also extended to the Company's Chief Agent in the Union, A. M. Campbell, who was awarded a special honorarium of £1,000.[23]

In the South African House of Assembly, however, the two new contracts were given a different reception. The long-term commitments to the Lines when it was still difficult to see the shape of the future, the heavy qualifications with which the 'special undertakings' in the Mail Contract were hedged around, the realization that this contract had not been put out to tender, the discouraging implications of both agreements for the development of a national merchant marine, and the fact that the benefits to the Lines were more tangible than those to the Union, all helped to arouse great hostility to the contracts—as du

[20] This system of carrying at a lower tariff the cargo of shippers who agreed to ship exclusively with the Conference had only been introduced in the wool trade (though it was subsequently extended to other commodities in the Northbound trade). Nevertheless, the Department of Justice felt that it produced a result 'falling squarely within the mischief which . . . Parliament was at pains to discourage in the Post Office Act, 1911', and advised the government that it could not validly enter into a new Mail Contract with Union-Castle while this practice, wrongly condoned in the 1934 Agreement, continued: CACT, Secretary for Justice to Secretary for Commerce, 10 Mar. 1945, Confidential Memorandum, CT 121/1945.
[21] CAL, Pirow to Gibb, 8 Feb. 1934.
[22] CAL, Waterson/Thomson correspondence, 4 Apr. 1945.
[23] Cayz. H., U-C DM, 17 Apr. 1945, min. 7396.

Toit had feared. Neither were the critics confined to the ranks of the Nationalist opposition, but contained amongst their number government back-benchers as well. Indeed, in the House of Assembly (there was also a debate in the Senate) only one back-bencher spoke in unqualified support of the agreements in the course of a lengthy debate.

According to the Nationalist MP, P. O. Sauer, Union-Castle had become 'the spoiled child of the Governments of the Union'.[24] The predominant theme of the critics, however, was that the government had simply been duped by the clever British shipping magnates. And when the government had to invoke the Company's good service record and its high reputation in the shipping world to justify the trust in its probity and good intentions on which both contracts rested at key points, one member had the poor taste to observe that 'One of their chairmen got two years some time ago'.[25]

Despite these attacks, both agreements emerged from the House of Assembly intact, on 29 May, although they were passed by a comparatively unenthusiastic vote of 60 to 32.[26] On 8 June they were passed by the Senate as well. Sir Vernon was home and dry. Or was he?

The problem for Union-Castle with these agreements—especially the OFA—lay in the uncertainty of the future. The argument that government satisfaction from the working of the contracts rested less on watertight wording than on the continuation of goodwill in Fenchurch Street cut the other way as well. This applied particularly to freight rates, on which the new OFA was able to say little, since these were still controlled by the British Ministry of War Transport and it was impossible to foresee when normal conditions would return. As a result, the Lines were to be allowed to charge the wartime rates current on 1 January 1947, provided these did not exceed the merchants' tariff prevailing on 1 January 1927.[27] Subsequently, adjustments would depend on *mutual* agreement, failing which either

[24] *House of Assembly Debates*, c. 8367 (29 May 1945).
[25] Ibid., c. 8387 (29 May 1945). This was a reference to Lord Kylsant, who in 1931 was found guilty of issuing a false prospectus for Union-Castle's parent company at that time, the Royal Mail Steam Packet Company. On this episode, see Murray, 186–90; and E. Green and M. Moss, *A Business of National Importance: The Royal Mail Shipping Group, 1902–1937* (London, 1982), chap. 7.
[26] A number of United Party members abstained from the final vote, *Cape Times*, 30 May 1945.
[27] OFA, 4 Apr. 1945, cll. 4 and 23(a).

party could terminate the OFA on eighteen months' notice. But what if the friendly attitude in Pretoria should disappear and the government should ask for an unreasonable reduction in the general tariff, or, alternatively, refuse to entertain a Conference request for a reasonable increase? How could Union-Castle jeopardize the future of the Mail Contract by resorting to the 'break clause' in the OFA?

In 1945, however, basking in the goodwill of General Smuts and with no suspicion that his government might be heading for extinction, Union-Castle seems to have given little thought to the possibility of a future impasse with the Union. And who can blame it? For its profitable relationship with South Africa was further consolidated by negotiations later in the year, though this time they were conducted only indirectly with the Union government. These discussions concerned the shipment of gold bullion from South Africa to Britain in the Company's vessels.

The Re-negotiation of the 1926 Gold Freight Agreement

Though it had been rendered 'temporarily non-operative' following requisition at the beginning of the war, Union-Castle had an agreement with the South African banks and gold-mining companies for the shipment of bullion to Britain dating from 1926. This provided, *inter alia*, for the shipment of all of South Africa's gold to Britain in the mail ships at a freight rate of 6s. 6d. per cent of the value of gold at the standard price of 85s. per fine ounce.[28] Since the Gold Freight Agreement had generated an annual average net freight earning which in the 1930s had amounted to about £150,000,[29] it is not surprising that the Company was anxious to resuscitate it as soon as possible after the war ended. As a result, it contrived to join negotiations on bullion shipping arrangements which took place in autumn 1945 between the Ministry of War Transport and the Bank of England, which at that time was responsible for buying Union gold from the SA Reserve Bank and then for arranging its Northbound shipment.[30] By the middle of November agreement between the Company and the Bank had been reached, though the Ministry was to remain the beneficiary while Union-Castle vessels were still formally under its control. (It was not

[28] CAL, Union-Castle Agreement Book 2, 34.
[29] Cayz. H., U-C DM, 14 Jan. 1932, min. 4769, 25 Jan. 1935, min. 5582, and 10 Nov. 1938, min. 6570.
[30] Ibid., 23 Oct. 1945, min. 8029.

altogether a handicap to the Company that its Deputy Chairman, Sir Ernest Harvey, who conducted the negotiations, should have been Deputy Governor of the Bank before joining Union-Castle in 1936[31].)

Under the new Gold Freight Agreement negotiated by Sir Ernest Harvey, Union-Castle was granted the right to ship all the gold purchased by the Bank of England in South Africa in 1946, at the rate of 5s. per cent of its value in sterling; £100m. worth was mentioned. Special bullion rooms were to be provided in all vessels carrying gold. The Agreement was renewable annually.[32]

The Union-Castle Board was delighted with this new Agreement. Not only were the terms good, but the friendly attitude of the Bank of England and the Bank's confidence in the continuation of its own arrangements with the SA Reserve Bank (communicated privately to Sir Ernest) suggested that there was every prospect in the new Agreement of a 'substantial source of revenue for the future'.[33] Indeed there was! The shipment of £100m. worth of gold in 1946 at 5s. per cent promised gross revenue of a quarter of a million pounds. In the event, the Agreement lasted until the beginning of 1948, when, as we shall see, it was renegotiated once more.

The Birth of the South African Merchant Marine

The Union-Castle Line had been determined not to lose any opportunity in 1945 to restore its own position and that of the Conference Lines in general in the South Africa trade, and it was entitled to feel satisfied with the results of its labours. Nevertheless, if the Company had assumed that as the corollary of this it would forestall, or at least significantly retard, the creation of a South African merchant marine—as many critics of the new Mail Contract and the new OFA had claimed—then in this respect it was doomed to disappointment. Indeed, the pace of this agitation was, if anything, increased by the reaction against the new contracts, although some of its energy was spent on an internal argument over the issue of state control versus private enterprise.

However, partly as a result of the continuing hostility of the

[31] Sir Ernest had spent his entire career in the Bank of England prior to joining Union-Castle. He entered the Bank in 1885 and was appointed Deputy Governor in 1929.
[32] Cayz. H., U-C DM, 27 Nov. 1945, min. 8047; and CAL, Barr (U-C) to Gurney (Bank of England), 7 Nov. 1945, and Gurney to Barr, 16 Nov. 1945.
[33] Cayz. H., U-C DM, 27 Nov. 1945, min. 8047.

Association of Chambers of Commerce (ASSOCOM),[34] and partly as a result of the scarcity of second-hand tonnage suitable for the state fleet and the horror of Sturrock's advisers at the price of new ships,[35] during the course of 1946 the argument for state shipping in South Africa was lost, and the field was left to private enterprise. Thereafter, patriotic sentiment, high freight rates, the perennial unpopularity of the shipping conferences, and the certainty of government favour, all contributed to an unprecedented rush of private capital into South African shipping.[36] In February 1946 South African Lines was launched, and this was followed in June by the announcement of plans for the formation of the South African Marine Corporation and the Alpha South African Steamship Company.[37] These were only the most prominent of the new companies.

However, as shipping became more competitive again in the later 1940s, the South African companies established in the preceding decade began to disappear. Indeed, by 1953 the Union's merchant fleet had shrunk from a peak of 175,743 gross tons in 1950 to only 119,986 gross tons, which was less than it had been in 1947 (see Appendix II), and by the following year only three of the twenty companies which had been established after 1941 were left.[38] Nevertheless, it was apparent to the established lines of the Conference that, under all the froth of 1946 and 1947, there was some fairly strong beer. In particular, it was clear from the beginning that 'Safmarine', as the South African Marine Corporation came to be called, was a serious concern.

Safmarine was formed as the result of an agreement between the prominent South African industrialist, Dr H. J. van der Bijl, and an American shipping line, the States Marine Corporation. The Company was conceived as a merger of South African capital (supplied by Anglo-American Corporation and Anglo-Transvaal Consolidated) and American expertise. Air Chief Marshal Sir Arthur 'Bomber' Harris, a friend of the President of States Marine and a native of Southern Africa, was appointed Safmarine's first Managing Director.

---

[34] *SA Shipping News*, Apr. 1946.
[35] Union of South Africa, South African Railways, *Report of the Overseas Mission (1946)* (Johannesburg, 31 Mar. 1947), chap. 1.
[36] Verburgh, 24–7.
[37] Of the Alpha Line's first six directors, one was Morris Kentridge, an MP who had been critical of the Mail Contract in the ratification debate, and another was the Nationalist MP, J. F. T. Naude.
[38] Verburgh, 33.

'It is evident', said the *South African Shipping News* in July 1946, '. . . that Safmarine is a considerable undertaking, holding the promise of giving the Union its first powerful indigenous shipping concern.' In 1947, with three 'Victory' ships purchased from the US Maritime Commission, Safmarine began a regular service between South Africa and North America.[39]

It is true that the South African flag lines formed in this period did not announce any immediate intention of entering the Europe–South Africa trade. Rather, their interests were to be principally in the trades with the United States, South America, and the rest of Africa. Nevertheless, in view of the pre-eminence of the trade with Europe in the Union's overseas trade as a whole, it was probably regarded as only a matter of time by the Conference before one of these companies, at least, made a bid to enter this trade.

In March 1946 Union-Castle decided to give the name *Pretoria Castle* to one of the two new mail ships which had been ordered following the conclusion of the Mail Contract, and later in the year it transferred two recently acquired cargo-passenger vessels to South African registry. These were also given South African names: the *Good Hope Castle* and the *Drakensberg Castle*.[40] It remained to be seen whether these gestures to nationalism would be sufficient. In the birth of South Africa's merchant marine in these years there was a rather dangerous straw in an otherwise fair wind for the South African Conference.

The Special Immigrant Service

The war had ended in August 1945, there was an enormous world demand for shipping, and Union-Castle's dominant position in the Europe–South Africa trade had been guaranteed once more by the various agreements negotiated during the course of the year. Nevertheless, it was clear that it would be a considerable time before the Company would be able to resume its normal pattern of sailings to the Union and thus exploit its alluring opportunities to the full.

Almost one-third of the Union-Castle fleet had been lost during the war, and it was obvious that a substantial period would have to elapse

---

[39] On the origins of Safmarine, see Verburgh, 27 f.; and B. D. Ingpen, *South African Merchant Ships* (Cape Town, 1979), 45–7.

[40] It should be noted, though, that the decision to name some of the Company's vessels after South African castles had been taken in 1937: Murray, 204 f.

before this tonnage was fully replaced. Moreover, in spite of the fact that the Ministry of War Transport proposed to make a 'special effort' to release the Company's surviving ships as soon as possible[41]—probably because of the importance of restoring British exports to South Africa in the context of the gold and dollar shortage, rather than because of any special influence on the part of Sir Vernon Thomson—the government's need for troop-ships after the end of hostilities was so great that it was not planned to release the first vessel until June 1946 and the last until the end of 1947 (see Appendix IV). Furthermore, the ships had all been gutted and in some cases changed beyond all recognition during their war service,[42] which meant that a further six months, on average, had to be allowed for their reconversion in the yards.[43]

In these frustrating circumstances, it was apparent to Union-Castle that it would be the end of 1946 before it would be possible to contemplate the resumption of the regular mail service to South Africa, and that even then the majority of sailings would have to be provided by fast cargo-passenger vessels. Apart from immediate considerations of profit, it was of the greatest importance to the Company to be able to restore the mail service by the date of the commencement of the new Contract (1 January 1947) in order to prevent further criticism in the Union that its vessels always put British before South African interests. It was also important that mail ships should replace cargo-passenger ships as quickly as possible for reasons of prestige. In view of all this, it is not surprising that Union-Castle should have been extremely concerned when it learned, in the second half of 1946, that the British government was being subjected to strong pressure from Pretoria to agree to a scheme which would result in even more delay to the resumption of the full mail service. This scheme, which followed from the announcement by General Smuts of a new policy to encourage European (especially British) emigration to South Africa—partly for economic and social but also for electoral reasons[44]—consisted of a proposal that the mail ships *Carnarvon Castle*, *Winchester Castle*, and *Arundel Castle* should be released from government service immediately and made available 'in their present condition' for the

---

[41] PRO, Provision of Shipping for Emigration to South Africa, MT 73/23.
[42] The *Pretoria Castle* (I) had been converted into an aircraft carrier.
[43] PRO, MT 73/23.
[44] On the immigration policy of Smuts, see J. Stone, *Colonist or Uitlander? A Study of the British Immigrant in South Africa* (Oxford, 1973), 129 ff.

conveyance of emigrants to the Union. This proposal produced a complicated sequence of negotiations between September 1946 and February 1947, in which the Dominions Office was aligned with the South African government on one side, and the Ministry of Transport and the War Office (neither of which liked this proposal at all) were aligned on the other. The Union-Castle Line, which liked the proposal even less, but valued its good relations with General Smuts to such a degree that it could not bring itself to say so, gave the strong appearance of wishing to be on both sides at the same time.

Smuts announced his new policy to encourage immigration into South Africa on 14 August 1946, and it was soon clear that he not only attached the greatest importance to it but regarded it as very much his personal policy.[45] However, among other problems confronting large-scale immigration into the Union, there was the acute shortage of passenger shipping caused, amongst other things, by wartime losses, the continued requisition of vessels, and the backlog in applications for berths back to South Africa which had built up during and immediately after the war.[46] Thus great pressure would have to be brought on the British government for shipping if the new policy was to have even a chance of success. And this pressure would have to be all the greater since Smuts did not intend to be satisfied with an allotment of berths on ordinary passenger vessels; he wanted entire ships turned over to the immigrant traffic, in the hope that this would maximize the flow and permit better control of its character.[47]

Evidence of the reaction of Sir Vernon Thomson to the sudden desire of the Smuts government for settler ships from his fleet is only slender. His view at first seems to have been that if the Ministry of Transport was prepared to see mail ships used for this purpose *while they were still under requisition*, then this was largely its own concern. However, they should be released to the Company for reconversion on the dates already agreed with the Ministry (see Appendix IV), otherwise they would miss their turns in the shipyards.[48] In any event, the South Africans were clearly under the impression that Sir Vernon was on their side, and on 21 September the South African High

[45] This at any rate was the opinion expressed in the reports sent to London from the British High Commission in Pretoria, e.g. PRO, Maclennan to Head, 22 Aug. 1946, and 8 Nov. 1946, DO35/1135.
[46] G. H. Nicholls, *South Africa In My Time* (London, 1961), 406.
[47] Central Archives Depot, Pretoria, SA Immigration Council, Bull. 1, Dec. 1947, K201.
[48] PRO, MT 73/23.

Commissioner, Heaton Nicholls, stated their case to Alfred Barnes, Minister of Transport in the Attlee government. His letter carried clear echoes of the Mail Contract debate in the House of Assembly. Having described the dimensions of the problem, the High Commissioner formally requested release of the *Carnarvon Castle*, the *Winchester Castle*, and the *Arundel Castle*, in their present condition. As troop-ships, he pointed out, they could carry between 1,200 and 1,400 passengers instead of the 800 or so which would be all they could manage in normal circumstances. He concluded strongly:

> We are fortified in making our request for this because although these three vessels are on the British Register they were built solely for the South Africa run. The Union Castle Company is subsidised by the Union Government and the ships were built and maintained out of the profits accruing from the South Africa service. South Africa is almost wholly dependent upon the passenger service provided by the Union Castle Company and it is considered that the United Kingdom Government has no permanent right to retain these ships when they are so badly needed on the South Africa run.[49]

Against the background of the national shipping fever currently gripping South Africa, this sort of argument must have impressed Sir Vernon Thomson. The Ministry of Transport was not altogether unmoved either, and Union-Castle was accordingly informed that it was prepared to release the *Winchester Castle* and the *Carnarvon Castle* (but not the *Arundel Castle*). However, they were to be run in the immigrant traffic for owner's account, and the Ministry indicated that the Company would have to take its chances in finding space in the shipyards for reconversion when the vessels were no longer required for immigrants; in other words, these two vessels would lose their places in the queue.[50] Union-Castle declined to accept them on these terms,[51] and Barnes was obliged to reply to Heaton Nicholls that his request was denied.[52]

Over the following months South Africa House kept up the pressure on both Sir Vernon and the Ministry, though it was convinced that the latter was the major stumbling-block. By January 1947 it had made a small dent in the British position: the *Carnarvon Castle* would be released to carry emigrants for its next three voyages before being

[49] Ibid.
[50] Ibid., Note of Miss G. M. Richards, 27 Sept. 1946.
[51] PRO, MT 73/23.
[52] He explained that there were many competing claims on few ships and that the South African route was already better served than any other: PRO, 11 Oct. 1946, MT 73/23.

taken in hand for reconversion.[53] But this was hardly going to transport sufficient loyal Britons to deliver Smuts from Afrikanerdom, and the South Africans replied that if the Ministry were not more forthcoming they would be obliged to look elsewhere. Already the Alpha Line had announced that it would place the three cargo-passenger ships which it was planning to buy at the disposal of the Union government,[54] and now South Africa House warned that it was holding an offer from the Greek shipowner, E. P. Nomikos.[55] A week later General De Villiers, Chairman of the recently created Immigration Council, informed Barnes, at a meeting at the Ministry urgently solicited by the High Commission, that he was going on to Holland and Sweden and would seek shipping there if he could not get satisfaction from Britain.[56]

Sir Vernon Thomson was by now no doubt impressed by the importance which Smuts attached to his immigration policy, and also alarmed at the implications of government-sanctioned outsiders intruding into the sphere of the South African Conference. As a result, he had reconciled himself to the need to put one or more mail ships into the immigrant trade.[57] Nevertheless, Sir Vernon's lukewarm attitude was not lost on the Ministry, and Barnes, on whom the general demand for shipping space had not lessened, was not anxious to assume the responsibility for meeting South Africa's full request. At the meeting with De Villiers on 23 January he put the Union off once more, indicating merely that he would look into the availability of the *Arundel Castle*. He also suggested, however, that De Villiers should take his case to the Dominions Secretary, Lord Addison,[58] who had a long-standing friendship with Smuts and a well-established sensitivity to the South African point of view.[59]

The Union's pressure for settler ships now moved rapidly into a higher gear. Following Barnes's advice, De Villiers immediately enlisted the support of Addison, and, more or less simultaneously, Smuts himself cabled directly to Attlee, asking for all three ships and adding that, 'Vernon Thomson is anxious to help in every way possible and is indeed willing to come out and discuss matter with us at short notice but can do nothing until he can get these ships'.[60] To increase

[53] PRO, Barr to Keenlyside, 31 Dec. 1946, MT 73/23.
[54] *SA Shipping News*, Dec. 1946.   [55] PRO, MT 73/23.
[56] PRO, Kemball-Cook to Keenlyside and Weston, 23 Jan. 1947, MT 73/24.
[57] PRO, Meyer to Weston, 4 Jan. 1947, MT 73/23.
[58] PRO, Kemball-Cook to Keenlyside and Weston, 23 Jan. 1947, MT 73/24.
[59] K. and J. Morgan, *Portrait of a Progressive: The Political Career of Christopher, Viscount Addison* (Oxford, 1980), 246 f.   [60] PRO, 27 Jan. 1947, MT 73/23.

the pressure, this appeal was made public. Attlee at once asked Barnes to 'look into this request as a matter of urgency'.[61]

In the face of this offensive, the Ministry of Transport capitulated. At first, it is true, it demanded an inter-departmental meeting to agree the general principles at stake prior to further direct discussions with the South Africans, but although the Dominions Secretary had reluctantly agreed to this it never happened.[62] Instead, as Addison had always preferred, there was a 'quick, friendly discussion' with the South Africans at the Dominions Office, on 13 February, followed by another one on the evening of the same day at South Africa House, the latter also attended by Sir Vernon Thomson. The result was what Union-Castle came to call the 'Special Immigrant Service'.

Under the agreement reached on 13 February the South Africans were to get two of the three mail ships for which they had asked, with the strong possibility that the third, the *Arundel Castle*, would follow when it was relinquished by the War Office in October. The *Winchester Castle* and the *Carnarvon Castle* would sail in the Immigrant Service until 'sometime early next year', whereupon—following a promise from Harland & Wolff that space could be found for them in 1948—they would be withdrawn for reconversion.[63] (This had allayed the Union-Castle fear that their reconversion would be postponed indefinitely.[64]) On 22 February Attlee was able to cable the good news to Smuts,[65] and in the middle of the year the Special Immigrant Service was inaugurated.

This was not the end of Smut's pressure for more shipping on Union-Castle and the Ministry of Transport, for the general demand for passenger berths to South Africa increased rather than diminished during 1947. As a result, Sir Vernon agreed at the end of the year to prolong the commitment of the *Winchester Castle* and the *Carnarvon Castle* to the Immigrant Service for most of 1948, while the Ministry agreed to release the *Arundel Castle*.[66] At a conference with Smuts in South Africa in March 1948 Sir Vernon further agreed to provide up

[61] PRO, Prime Minister's Minute, M. 59/47, 27 Jan. 1947, MT 73/23.
[62] PRO, Weston to Hampden, 3 Feb. 1947, MT 73/23, and Addison to Barnes, 6 Feb. 1947, MT 73/24.
[63] PRO, Weston to Sir Vernon Thomson, 15 Feb. 1947, MT 73/24.
[64] PRO, Hampden to Weston, 7 Feb. 1947, MT 73/24, Robson (SRD) to Kemball-Cook, 15 Feb. 1947, MT 73/24, and Weston to Machtig, 17 Feb. 1947, MT 73/24.
[65] PRO, MT 73/24.
[66] Cayz. H., U-C DM, 27 Jan. 1948, min. 8521. However, the *Arundel Castle* was not to be allowed to enter the mail service until April 1948; it would remain in it until March 1949.

to 50 per cent of the tourist- and cabin-class capacity of the mail ships in the general service for immigrants, to order a one-class vessel just for the immigrant traffic (which became the *Bloemfontein Castle*), and, until this was delivered, to keep on one of the mail ships presently in the Special Immigrant Service.[67] Sir Vernon had come quite a long way since September 1946.

The Special Immigrant Service was a serious impediment to Union-Castle's efforts to restore the full mail service at the earliest opportunity, as Heaton Nicholls himself acknowledged.[68] But even with the support of the British Ministry of Transport, it was one which the Company was unable to remove in the face of the importance attached by Smuts to his new immigration policy. Moreover, if Sir Vernon had resisted the plan he would have played straight into the hands of shipping nationalists in the Union, for he would have drawn attention once more to the lesson learned in the war that only a national merchant marine can give priority to national interests. If, therefore, the early renewal of the Mail Contract and the OFA had demonstrated Union-Castle's influence on the South African government in those negotiations involving a strong sense of common interest, the introduction of the Special Immigrant Service was the first major post-war illustration of the fact that Union-Castle was likely to come off worst when this was lacking.

Intimations of Difficulties ahead

There were other intimations of serious difficulties ahead before the Smuts government fell in May 1948. In the middle of 1947, after the new OFA had been in operation for only half a year, the SA Shipping Board, from which the spirit of 1945 already seemed to have evaporated, served notice on the Conference of its intention to veto any rate increase proposed in London.[69] Though the new OFA certainly restated what was by now the considerable influence of the government over freight rates in the trade, only the most obtuse or tendentious reading of it could support the Board's interpretation, particularly in regard to rates on non-government Southbound cargo. The dispute lasted until early 1948 when the Shipping Board

---

[67] Ibid., 27 Apr. 1948, min. 8565.
[68] Nicholls, 407.
[69] CAL, Frye (Chairman of the Shipping Board) to Mackenzie (Acting Representative of the Conference Lines in South Africa), 15 Sept. 1947.

retreated,[70] but it was an ill omen for the South African Conference. So too, for Union-Castle, was the Bank of England's insistence, against the background of the threat of air competition, that the gold freight should be reduced from 5s. to 4s. per cent of the sterling value of gold, even if the Company could afford to be complacent about this in 1948 in view of the greatly increased quantities of gold which the Bank undertook to ship in that year.[71] For the moment, however, and notwithstanding the Special Immigrant Service, these remained only intimations of difficulties ahead. On the whole, the relations between the Conference and the Smuts government were excellent and as a result Union-Castle went from strength to strength after the war.

All of Union-Castle's cargo vessels were derequisitioned on 2 March 1946, and by the middle of 1948 almost all of its passenger vessels were back on their normal routes. In the second half of 1947 the two new mail ships which had been ordered following the signing of the new Mail Contract in 1945 were launched in Belfast. In 1947, and especially in 1948, the financial crisis in Britain meant that the Bank of England had to ship far more gold from the Union than it had anticipated.[72] Coinciding with the continuation of extremely high freight rates, these developments ensured that Union-Castle made exceptionally high profits, increasing from £½m. in 1946 to almost £2m. in 1947.[73]

Sir Vernon Thomson struck a cautious note in reporting these results and explaining the modest dividend which his Board had decided to declare. 'Experience shows', he told the Company's shareholders in June 1948, 'that shipping has periods of prosperity and of depression.' The best course, he continued, was therefore to pay a 'reasonable, steady dividend through good periods and bad', and to build up reserves in the good times against the inevitable return of adversity.[74] In developing this theme, it is possible that Sir Vernon had in mind not only the influence of the market on Union-Castle earnings, but also that of political sentiment in Pretoria towards the

[70] CAL, Thomson to Frye, 29 Oct. 1947; and Safcon, Minute Book 45, 17 Feb. 1948.
    [71] The new Gold Freight Agreement was concluded in January. Under it the Bank agreed to ship a minimum of £150m. worth of gold during 1948. The Agreement was to last for one year: Cayz. H., U-C DM, 17 Feb. 1948, min. 8538.
    [72] In 1948 £250m. worth of gold was shipped before the end of November: ibid., 23 Nov. 1948, min. 8693.
    [73] ' "Golden Run" Makes Millions', Daily Express, 19 May 1948.
    [74] The Times, 14 June 1948.

Company and the shipping conference which it led. For the good times since the war had been in some measure attributable to the favour which the Company had found with the Smuts government, and just two weeks before the Annual General Meeting at which Sir Vernon had made these remarks, that government had been ousted by Dr Malan's Herenigde Nasionale Party, in alliance with N. C. Havenga's small Afrikaner Party. The 'Nationalists', as they were called by English-speakers, were not, of course, well known for their fondness for the 'British connection', nor for their fondness for capitalism, even though, following the Broederbond-inspired economic *volkskongres* of October 1939, they had refined their attitude to one of supporting the capture of South African capitalism from the English and operating it in the interests of the Afrikaners.[75] In the light of the Nationalists' hostility to Britain and their attachment to *volkskapitalisme*, it had come as no surprise when they voted solidly against the ratification of the Mail Contract in the House of Assembly in 1945, and took the opportunity of that debate to say some most unkind things about the Union-Castle Line and the South African Conference in general.

[75] T. D. Moodie, *The Rise of Afrikanerdom* (London, 1975), 203–7; and B. Bunting, *The Rise of the South African Reich*, rev. edn. (Harmondsworth, 1969), 376 ff.

2

COLLISION WITH THE NATIONALISTS
1948-1955

FOLLOWING the South African general election, Dr Malan's Nationalists had formed a new government on 4 June. The news was received in Fenchurch Street with grave misgiving. Not only had a pro-Commonwealth government with which it had established excellent relations been replaced by an Afrikaner nationalist government widely believed to be replete with crypto-Nazis, but Cabinet portfolios which had an intimate bearing on the Company's interests had been given to men who were likely to adopt a particularly hostile attitude to the British-dominated South African Conference. Thus Dr T. E. Dönges and P. O. Sauer, both of whom had attacked the Mail Contract in the House of Assembly debate in 1945, became Minister of Posts and Telegraphs (as well as Minister of the Interior) and Minister of Transport, respectively, while the combative Eric Louw became Minister of Economic Development.[1] In the circumstances, the Company decided that it would have to make a special effort to establish good relations with the government which had now become its 'partner' in South Africa.[2]

Fortunately for the mail line, the *Pretoria Castle* was due to make its maiden voyage to South Africa in late July. The arrival in Table Bay of the first of the mail ships to be built after the war was bound to attract considerable public attention and would be majestic evidence of the Company's commitment to the South Africa trade. Sir Vernon rightly saw that making an event of this would bolster Union-Castle prestige in South Africa and present a first-class opportunity to win over the new government.[3] As a result, he himself sailed on the *Pretoria Castle*, and on its arrival in Table Bay in August he entertained on board two hundred of the most prominent members of South African national

---

[1] The designation of this portfolio was changed to 'Economic Affairs' on 27 August 1949.
[2] Cayz. H., U-C DM, 22 June 1948, min. 8603.
[3] Ibid., 22 June 1948, min. 8614.

life, amongst them Dr Malan and ten of the twelve members of his Cabinet. Sir Vernon's move was a success. In a toast to the *Pretoria Castle* at this reception even Paul Sauer felt obliged to concede that Union-Castle had served South Africa as well as it had served its shareholders.[4] On his return to England, having had further meetings with Malan and the new Ministers whose portfolios had a bearing on the Company's business, Sir Vernon was able to tell the Union-Castle Board that 'The relationships established with the Union Ministers from the Prime Minister downwards were most cordial and entirely satisfactory'.[5]

The unexpectedly good start to relations between Union-Castle and the Nationalist government was not, of course, simply a result of Sir Vernon Thomson's adroit diplomatic exploitation of the maiden voyage of the *Pretoria Castle* and the accompanying distribution of Company largess (also employed at this juncture to insure against the return of General Smuts).[6] It was more especially an expression of the general— and much remarked—correctness with which Malan approached the previously reviled 'British connection' after the election,[7] a correctness based on some very weighty considerations. These included the slender parliamentary majority achieved by his electoral alliance and its embrace of Havenga's small but more moderate Afrikaner Party;[8] Malan's 'great regard' for Britain's Foreign Secretary, Ernest Bevin, and his strong desire for participation in the West's gestating cold war security arrangements, in which Bevin was playing the leading role;[9] the awareness of his new government of South Africa's enormous dependence on commercial and financial dealings with Britain; and, not least, the acute sense shared by most South Africans of the continuing paramountcy of British power in the greater part of Africa to the north of their borders—especially over the High Commission

[4] *Cape Times*, 19 Aug. 1948.
[5] Cayz. H., U-C DM, 14 Sept. 1948, min. 8650.
[6] Smuts was provided by Sir Vernon Thomson with free board at Union-Castle's luxurious Mount Nelson Hotel in Cape Town during the short parliamentary session from August until October 1948, though, of course, this was friendship as well as insurance: J. Van Der Poel (ed.), *Selections from the Smuts Papers*, 8, Aug. 1945–Oct. 1950 (Cambridge, 1973), 223.
[7] E.g. D. Geldenhuys, 'The South African National Party and the British Government (1939–1961)', *Politikon*, 5.1, June 1978.
[8] N. M. Stultz, *Afrikaner Politics in South Africa, 1934–1948* (London, 1974), 145 f.
[9] R. Ovendale, 'The South African Policy of the British Labour government, 1947–51', *International Affairs*, 59.1, Winter 1982–3, 47.

Territories, which Malan, like his predecessors, hoped Britain would transfer to the Union.[10] Nor had the attitude of the Labour government in Britain to the new government in South Africa given Malan any incentive to make good earlier promises of hostility towards the 'British connection'. Though cautious in its response to Malan's proposals for South Africa's inclusion in the Western defence system, Attlee's government was sensitive to Britain's powerful reasons for preserving friendly relations with Pretoria and, as Ovendale points out, was responsible for establishing the general character of Britain's South African policy for the greater part of the post-war period: friendly relations qualified by informal pressure for racial reform.[11]

There was, however, another reason for the good start to relations between Union-Castle and Malan's new government. This was the ironic coincidence of interest between them on the most important item on the agenda of Sir Vernon Thomson's visit to South Africa in August 1948: the Special Immigrant Service.

Terminating the Special Immigrant Service

The Nationalists rightly believed that the main point of Smuts's immigration policy had been to strengthen the English-speaking population in the Union vis-à-vis the Afrikaner population. It came as no surprise, therefore, when one of their first acts in government was to suspend the immigration programme[12] and demand—shortly before Sir Vernon was due to sail for South Africa in late July—that Union-Castle should bring the Special Immigrant Service to an end 'with immediate effect'.[13] However, since it hampered the full restoration of the mail service, the Union-Castle Line had never liked the Special Immigrant Service from the beginning and had had to be badgered into it by Smuts and his allies in the Dominions Office. Fenchurch Street could thus happily reply that the ending of this service suited it very well.

It is true that this coincidence of interest between Union-Castle and Malan's new government was the source of some chagrin to the South African Minister responsible, Dr Dönges, who, prior to Sir Vernon's

[10] Ibid.   [11] Ibid.
[12] J. Stone, *Colonist or Uitlander? A Study of the British Immigrant in South Africa* (London, 1962), 134 ff.
[13] Cayz. H., U-C DM., 20 July 1948, min. 8629.

visit to the Union, gratuitously informed him that he would have his way on this issue whether it suited Union-Castle's interests or not.[14] It is also true that the Company wanted a more orderly winding-down of the service than the Minister seemed to have in mind. Nevertheless, following Sir Vernon's arrival, Dr Dönges appears to have recovered from his frustration at finding himself on the same side as Union-Castle and, in the negotiations which followed, agreement on an orderly termination was reached. The price of this, though, was that Sir Vernon had to agree to release the government from any remaining financial obligations in regard to the settler ships and co-operate in stricter 'screening' of remaining emigrants.[15] Later in 1948, with stricter screening introduced and plans afoot to lengthen the residency requirement for the naturalization (and thus entitlement to vote) of British subjects from two to five years,[16] the Nationalist government became less anxious about the Special Immigrant Service and actually asked Union-Castle to keep the *Arundel Castle* in the Service for a short period beyond the agreed end of its tour in March 1949. The Company fell in with this request, and the vessel was not withdrawn until 20 May 1949.

Louw Forces the South African Flag into the Conference

The Malan government might have been anxious to remain on good terms with the British government, but its prickly Nationalist Ministers could not be expected to remain indifferent when it appeared that the British-dominated South African Conference Lines were standing in the way of national aspirations; nor did they. Indeed, by the middle of 1949 what had passed for a honeymoon period between the government and the Conference was brought to an end when the latter turned down the first application for membership to be received from what purported to be a South African flag line. The crisis between Fenchurch Street and Pretoria to which this led—the first of many in subsequent years—was finally resolved in January 1950, but only at the cost of significant concessions by the Lines.

It had probably always been realized that it was just a matter of time before one or more of the companies in South Africa's new ocean-going marine would make a bid to enter the trade between Europe and

---

[14] Ibid.
[15] Ibid., 14 Sept. 1948, min. 8651; and *Cape Times*, 17 and 19 Aug. 1948.
[16] J. Barber, *South Africa's Foreign Policy, 1945–1970* (London, 1973), 51 f.

the Union, and that the election of the Nationalists had brought this nearer. Although shipping was clearly not a priority of the Malan government (it did not become an important target of *volkskapitalisme* for another decade), the desire of the Smuts government to make at least some impression on South Africa's total dependence on foreign—and especially British—shipping was inherited by Malan and given a hard new ideological edge. Support for indigenous against foreign capital—in shipping as in other sectors of the economy—was now forthcoming, not merely because it was considered patriotic duty, or because it was thought that it would help the balance of payments, or for reasons of national security; such support, particularly where the foreign capital concerned was British, was also considered to be a blow against 'imperial domination'.[17] In view of this, and in view of the obvious anxiety of Union-Castle to ingratiate itself with the Nationalist government, it is at first glance surprising that the Lines turned down so abruptly the first South African application for membership when it came—from South African Lines (usually known as 'SALines')—in early 1949.[18]

The South African Conference, however, had cause enough to reject the application from SALines. Firstly, there was the automatic hostility of the Lines to *any* new applicant, since the trade in their view was already fully tonnaged. Secondly, there was the influence in SALines of the Greek shipowner, Eugenides, who was disliked by the Conference because of his behaviour in other waters.[19] Thirdly, there was the belief that the predominance of foreign capital in SALines would enable the Conference to persuade the government that it was not really a 'South African' company anyway.[20] Fourthly, SALines had hardly behaved as a model supplicant: it had announced its intention to commence sailings before being accepted into the Conference, and it had refused the customary request for a balance sheet.[21] Finally, and without doubt the main reason for the rebuff of SALines, was the

[17] J. E. Spence, *Republic under Pressure: A Study of South African Foreign Policy* (London, 1965), 29-34; and G. Berridge, *Economic Power in Anglo-South African Diplomacy: Simonstown, Sharpeville and After* (London, 1981), 17 f.

[18] Cayz. H., U-C DM, 24 May 1949, min 8834, and 16 June 1949, min. 8858. On the origins of SALines and the development of its service, see B. D. Ingpen, *South African Merchant Ships* (Cape Town, 1979), 44 f.

[19] Greenwich, Joint Meeting Minutes, 2 Nov. 1949.

[20] At this point, Union-Castle information was that only 20% of its equity was South African, the remainder being held principally by Greek and Swedish interests: Cayz. H., U-C DM, 24 May 1949, min. 8834, and 16 June 1949, min. 8858.

[21] Ibid., 16 June 1949, min. 8858.

failure of the Union government to indicate its support for the Company at the time of its first application. At a meeting of the British Lines' caucus on 2 June, Sir Vernon had stated that Union-Castle would not fight the Union government to keep the South African flag out of the trade, and it was agreed that if the government gave its support to SALines then the Conference attitude would have to change.[22] A little over a fortnight later the government rectified its omission.

On 18 June Sir Vernon Thomson was invited to South Africa House in London to learn the contents of a telegram from Eric Louw, the Union's aggressive Minister of Economic Development. In this Louw stated that the SALines application had the government's fullest support and that he was concerned at the hostile attitude of the Conference. He added, subtly, that 'The Government understood that . . . it was proposed to raise the question in the House on the second reading of the Undue Restraint of Trade Bill, with a view to exploring whether Shipping could not be brought under the provisions of the Bill'.[23]

It is not surprising that Eric Louw gave forceful backing to the SALines application. Even as a young business man, many years earlier, he had attacked South Africa's dependence on British shipping and urged the creation of a national fleet.[24] Furthermore, if the shortage of South African capital in SALines rendered it something less than the perfect spearhead for a campaign to take the Union flag into the all-important Europe–South Africa trade, the Company possessed other attributes which were likely to arouse Louw's sympathies. For one thing, SALines was now closely linked to the Deutsche Ost-Afrika Linie (DOAL),[25] a Conference member whose rights had lapsed during the war, and for a variety of political and economic reasons Louw was keen to refurbish South Africa's German connection;[26] and for another, SALines was the only South African line at this time to employ exclusively white crews.

Following Louw's intervention, it is clear that Sir Vernon Thomson had come to the conclusion that the South African flag could not be kept out of the Conference without cost to the Union-Castle Line.

[22] Ibid.   [23] Ibid., 26 July 1949, min. 8874.
[24] This was in a speech at the first congress of the Cape Chamber of Commerce: P. Meiring, *Tien Politieke Leiers* (Kaapstad en Johannesburg, 1973), 150.
[25] *Cape Times*, 26 Jan. 1950; and Ingpen, 45.
[26] See Berridge, 188, n. 6.

Consequently, consoling himself with the thought that a South African flag ally would be a political asset in future negotiations with the Union government, he immediately offered Louw a choice of Conference concessions: either the Conference—or Union-Castle itself—could register a shipping company in the Union, or SALines could be admitted to the Conference, provided that the Union government would be satisfied with this and would not 'sponsor' any other applications from the South African flag.[27]

Sir Vernon never received a reply to the letter offering these alternatives to the government. Eric Louw chose to respond in a different way. As if the magnates in London had assumed an air of arrogant indifference to his threat, he said in a speech at Vereeniging on 11 October that the Union had been wholly dependent on foreign shipping lines for too long, and that the government would not remain aloof should any attempt be made to 'stifle' South African shipping ventures.[28] Stiffened by this statement, SALines, which had already started sailings to North-West Europe in association with DOAL, kept up its pressure for admission to the Conference. Meanwhile, it was learned in Fenchurch Street that the Fenton Steamship Company of London was entering into an agreement with South African interests for the inauguration of another service in the Europe–South Africa trade. Safmarine, too, was rumoured to have similar plans.[29] Against this ominous background a meeting of the leaders of all of the lines in the Conference was held in London on 2 November 1949, the first 'Joint Meeting' to be called since 1938.

The November meeting authorized Sir Vernon Thomson to go out to South Africa with a free hand to negotiate a settlement on one or other of the lines already suggested to Eric Louw. In the meantime, although SALines was considered to be employing 'underhand methods' to acquire cargo, the Conference would not worsen the atmosphere by starting a freight war. Eight days later, and having appointed a Deputy Chairman—Sir George Christopher—to look after Fenchurch Street during what he thought would be a prolonged absence,[30] Sir Vernon sailed for South Africa, determined to resolve the crisis before the Union Parliament assembled in January and threatened his task with unwanted publicity.

[27] Cayz. H., U-C DM, 26 July 1949, min. 8874.
[28] SA Shipping News, Dec. 1949.
[29] Cayz. H., U-C DM, 25 Oct. 1949, min. 8290.
[30] Ibid., 8 Nov. 1949, min. 8938.

The Union-Castle Chairman arrived in South Africa on 24 November and remained there for seven weeks.[31] In the first of several meetings with Eric Louw, on 2 December, he found the Minister in typically combative mood. Louw said that as far as he was concerned the Conference was 'a cartel formed to protect its members and to keep up rates', that the Lines and their shareholders 'had done well for themselves out of the service to South Africa', and that the Union government could not tolerate a South African company being prevented from trading by a monopoly. He mentioned that the Ocean Freight Agreement did not 'last for ever', and once more flourished the Undue Restraint of Trade Act.

Replying that he did not take kindly to threats, Sir Vernon nevertheless found that he had little room for manœuvre. Louw would emphatically not be satisfied with a South African company established by the Conference itself, while the case against SALines was substantially weakened by the Minister's information that control of this line had passed from Greek to South African hands. This had been secured by none other than Claud Sturrock, Minister of Transport in the Smuts government, father of the South African merchant marine, and now Managing Director of SALines itself. Neither was Louw prepared to see South African participation in the Conference limited to one company, since he was anxious to promote the general expansion of South African shipping. In the circumstances, Sir Vernon saw no alternative but to agree to enter negotiations with SALines and settle for a 'gentleman's understanding' with the Minister that 'the Lines would not be expected to take in others indiscriminately'. Eric Louw had no difficulty in accepting this.

It was obvious by this time that Sir Vernon would do well if he could close the door behind SALines, especially since he now knew that Safmarine was also considering entering the trade, with or without the agreement of the Conference. His information was that, with the support of Anglo-Transvaal, Safmarine intended to carry mineral ores to Europe and return with mining machinery.[32] Though he had contemplated it for some time, it was almost certainly alarm at this possibility which led Sir Vernon to register a South African shipping

[31] The following account of Sir Vernon's negotiations in South Africa is based on Conference transcripts (CAL) and the report which he submitted to the Union-Castle Board on his return to England. The latter is appended to Cayz. H., U-C DM, 31 Jan. 1950.
[32] CAL, Conference paper, 8 Dec. 1949.

company of his own, and on 7 December he registered the Springbok Shipping Company Limited in Pretoria.

The creation of Springbok, however, was to prove a futile gesture, for two weeks later, with the negotiations for the entry of SALines already at an advanced stage, Sir Vernon received the half-expected application from Safmarine as well. The Company's Managing Director, Sir Arthur 'Bomber' Harris, informed Sir Vernon that it had always been the intention of Safmarine to enter the Europe–South Africa trade, that he was confident of government support, and that he would enter the trade either inside or outside the Conference.

Sir Vernon's response to this sort of approach was naturally cool, the more so because he had an extremely low opinion of Sir Arthur Harris's competence in shipping matters. Nevertheless, he felt that Safmarine was financially stronger than SALines and, notwithstanding his view of its Managing Director, 'probably more efficiently managed'. Two days later, on 23 December, and despite the fact that the general terms of an agreement for the admission of SALines had been provisionally negotiated,[33] Sir Vernon put to Eric Louw the idea that Safmarine should be admitted instead of SALines.

Though he did not say so in so many words, it was obvious that Louw had encouraged Safmarine to make an application to Sir Vernon. As for the suggestion that this Company should be preferred to SALines, the Minister reminded Sir Vernon that he was opposed to the restriction of the South African flag to one company, and pointed out that, in any case, SALines 'was the first in the field and had the benefit of Mr Sturrock's shipping experience'. In other words, Sir Vernon should admit *both* lines into the Conference. The Union-Castle Chairman was neatly cornered.

It now fell to Sir Vernon to limit the damage to the interests of the Lines by negotiating Agreements with the two South African companies which restricted their sailing rights and tied them to these restrictions for long periods. In this at least he was successful, though the negotiations with Safmarine proved particularly difficult. On 28 December final agreement was reached with SALines and on 12 January 1950 an Agreement was signed with Safmarine as well. Both became members of the South African Conference as from 1 January. On the day following the signature of the Agreement with Safmarine, a relieved Sir Vernon sailed for home on the *Warwick Castle*.

[33] Ibid.

The Chairman of Union-Castle had been obliged to give away rather more than he had hoped in this first serious test of strength with the new government in South Africa, but he believed that the Conference had been relatively fortunate, and that in any case the new situation had its compensations. As he told the Board on his return to London:

Within recent months there has been a marked growth of nationalistic sentiment in the Union of South Africa (as elsewhere in the world) . . . and in certain maritime countries Government support of Shipping has taken the form of subsidies and even ownership by the State. . . .

I consider . . . that, by this stroke of British policy, not only are South African aspirations met and the prospects of adverse propaganda thereon minimised, thus strengthening the Conference position, but that, instead of a hostile and costly opposition, South African flag allies have been made whose interest it should now be to defend the South African Shipping Conference.

Since it was also believed in the Conference that neither SALines nor Safmarine would turn out in the long run to be major threats because of the lack of interest of South African money in shipping investment, the results of Sir Vernon's negotiations were—by and large—well received at the Joint Meeting which followed his return. Nevertheless, there were rumblings from the Continental Lines that the South Africans had been bought off at the expense of their sector of the trade. This was a portent.

Union-Castle and the National Finance Corporation

Sir Vernon Thomson clearly felt that his admission of two South African flag lines into the Conference, together with the further general cultivation of the government and its Shipping Board which he had also undertaken during this latest visit to the Union, had defused a serious crisis and achieved a *modus vivendi* between the Lines and Pretoria. However, it is also evident that he felt this needed further consolidation. As a result, at its first meeting after the Chairman's return, the Union-Castle Board decided to start depositing much of the Company's earnings in South Africa with the National Finance Corporation (NFC),[34] which had been established by the government the previous year in order to mobilize idle capital in the Union on behalf of 'the national interest',[35] and whose terms in any case

[34] Cayz. H., U-C DM, 31 Jan. 1950, min. 8978.
[35] D. H. Houghton, *The South African Economy*, 3rd edn. (Cape Town, 1973), 193.

compared favourably with the fixed deposit terms of the commercial banks.

It was thus with 'possible political advantages'[36] very much in mind, that between 2 February and 25 May 1950 a total of £1.1m. was invested in the NFC by the Union-Castle Line. This was almost as much as the Company had on deposit with the two commercial banks in South Africa put together (see Appendix III). Furthermore, this investment proceeded despite a Board discussion on 28 February of the possibility of remitting surplus cash to the United Kingdom in view of the heavy shipbuilding commitments during the rest of the year.[37] At its meeting on 23 May, the Board decided that all further surplus cash becoming available in South Africa should be deposited with the NFC until total deposits reached £1.5m.[38]

Dr Norval, Freight Rates and Fruit

Unfortunately for both Union-Castle and the Conference as a whole, not even these substantial deposits with the NFC proved to be sufficient to consolidate the *modus vivendi* with Pretoria which Sir Vernon Thomson thought he had achieved. In June 1950, even while Union-Castle investments in the NFC were approaching new heights, Dr A. J. Norval, the Chairman of the powerful Board of Trade and Industries, was also appointed Chairman of the Shipping Board, even though the Shipping Board Act, 1929, expressly forbade the appointment of public servants to the Board in a voting capacity (see Appendix V). This development, together with the commencement of the Conference's first post-war campaign for a general increase in freight rates, was a guarantee of fresh hostilities between the government and the Lines.

Under Norval, whose long-standing chairmanship of the Board of Trade and Industries already made him one of the most powerful officials in the Department of Commerce, the influence of the Shipping Board grew perceptibly. Unfortunately for relations with the Lines, Norval was both a trained lawyer and an academic economist,[39] probably the two most serious vocational handicaps from which anyone

---

[36] Cayz. H., U-C DM, 31 Jan. 1950, min. 8978.
[37] Ibid., 28 Feb. 1950, min. 8996.
[38] Ibid., 23 May 1950, min. 9071.
[39] He had been Professor of Commerce and Industrial Economics at the University of Pretoria from 1927 until 1937.

required to act in a diplomatic capacity can suffer. He also had a highly abrasive and domineering manner, and was given to sermonizing. Given that one of his favourite sermons was on the pernicious consequences of unregulated shipping conferences, it is not surprising that he very soon came to be cordially loathed by the Lines.

It was to such a high official in the South African government, then, that the Conference was required to make its plea for a general increase in freight rates, knowing that under the OFA either party could propose an increase but neither could prevail except by consent of the other. (In the absence of mutual agreement, the only recourse was termination of the OFA, which required a full eighteen months' notice.) The Conference's case was that shipbuilding and ship-operating costs had risen very considerably since the end of the war, and that, reflecting this, freight rates in other trades were already rising. At the beginning of 1951 it asked the government for a 15 per cent increase from 1 March. The view of the Shipping Board, however, was that the profits of the Conference Lines seemed satisfactory, that costs (especially shipbuilding costs) were likely to fall before long, and that in any case the excessive secrecy of the Lines with regard to their costs and returns made it impossible for the Shipping Board to make an intelligent judgement on their appeal. Before Dr Norval could eventually be persuaded to recommend an increase—only 10 per cent, from 1 July—Union-Castle, representing the Lines as a whole, had to lay before the government an unprecedented degree of information on its financial affairs.[40] Still dissatisfied, however, Norval dug in his heels after this and turned a deaf ear to the appeals for further freight increases which were soon being made by the Lines. The consequences of this impasse for the Conference, and especially for the Union-Castle Line, were alarming, for not only were profits reduced, but the Conference itself threatened to split over its response to the government's attitude.

Union-Castle, acutely conscious of its dependence on the South Africa trade and the Mail Contract (due to expire at the end of 1956), favoured a patient and restrained approach to Pretoria on the issue of freight rates, as it had on previous matters. It was encouraged in this attitude by a private warning issued to Sir Vernon Thomson by Eric Louw in late 1951, that the government would support the development of state shipping unless the Conference made concessions to the

[40] Cayz. H., U-C DM, 27 Feb. 1951, min. 9254, 24 Apr. 1951, min. 9292, and 22 May 1951, min. 9312.

Union point of view.[41] This was not entirely bluster either, since a committee of inquiry into the small state fleet had been taking evidence since the end of the previous year.[42] (A small expansion was subsequently recommended, principally on the argument that private enterprise had failed to provide an adequate national merchant marine.[43]) At a Joint Meeting of the Conference held in January 1952 the (Union-Castle) Conference Chairman, Stanley Barr, repeatedly drew attention to the threat of state shipping in South Africa.[44]

Warnings of this nature, however, carried less weight with other lines in the Conference, especially the Continental Lines; with less at stake in the South Africa trade than Union-Castle, they were more inclined to be hawkish towards Pretoria. Indeed, it was not long before the Continental Lines began to voice the thought that the Ocean Freight Agreement was a millstone around the neck of the Conference and that, failing satisfaction from the government on freight rates, notice of termination should be promptly given. It was even implied, *sotto voce*, that because of Union-Castle's peculiar tie to South Africa Sir Vernon Thomson could not be relied upon to negotiate with Pretoria on behalf of the Conference as a whole. This, of course, was true.

Matters within the Conference came to a head during the unusually lengthy and acrimonious Joint Meeting which was held at the Savoy Hotel in London on 17 January 1952. This was a watershed in the post-war affairs of the South African Conference. In the argument which ensued over the level of increases to be demanded of the Union government and the tactics to be employed in achieving it, Union-Castle found itself unable to command a majority for the moderate position—let alone unanimity. Not having planned to attend this meeting, which had been chaired in the morning by Stanley Barr, Sir Vernon Thomson had to be hastily summoned to retrieve the situation at 3.35 in the afternoon. He readily agreed that policy in the Conference was determined on the basis of unanimity, but insisted that, since he 'spoke for the principal interest in this Conference', in practice the other lines had to fall in with the view from Fenchurch Street if there was to be any policy at all. Stating the Union-Castle position flatly and replying to questions with some acerbity, he declared that large rate demands on the government were out of the

[41] Ibid., 23 Oct. 1951, min. 9401.   [42] *Cape Times*, 25 Oct. 1950.
[43] *SA Shipping News*, May 1952.
[44] Greenwich, Joint Meeting Minutes, 17 Jan. 1952.

question, that there would be no termination of the OFA, and that he would conduct the next round of freight negotiations on his own (as had been the custom) and *not* at the head of a Conference delegation, as had been widely agreed in the morning. In the end, however, such was the feeling against Sir Vernon at the Joint Meeting that he could only secure a continuation of the moderate line towards Pretoria by effectively agreeing to representation from the other lines in future negotiations.[45]

This compromise held the Conference together, but it also registered a small shift in power within it: Union-Castle influence was on the wane. The Conference delegation which met with the Union government the following April consisted of representatives from two of the Continental Lines and Safmarine, as well as representatives from two British lines. The leader of the delegation was the Conference Chairman, Stanley Barr. Sir Vernon Thomson, who had been pressed to take the lead himself, declined to go, clearly bitter at the criticism of his earlier negotiations which was implicit in the new arrangement. He was never to represent the South African Conference in freight negotiations in the Union again, for in a little over a year he was dead.

Despite the infusion of a hawkish element into the delegation which went to South Africa in April 1952, and despite the hurried provision of even more financial information to the government to prevent the negotiations breaking down altogether, the Conference team returned home empty-handed. Eric Louw, still the Minister of Economic Affairs, and Dr Norval were adamant that there would be no general increase in freight rates in the trade with Europe.[46]

The Conference was angry at its treatment in South Africa, but the experience had been an educative one for the Continental Lines. A world trade recession had begun to depress the shipping market, and in the Union there was political turmoil as a result of the impact of apartheid legislation on the 'non-white' population and the fears of the English-speakers provoked by the government's attack on the entrenched voting rights of the Coloureds; in 1953 the National Party (formed in 1951 by a merger between the HNP and Havenga's Afrikaner Party) would have to face a general election.[47] The results of such events in

[45] Ibid.
[46] Cayz, H., Clan Line Directors' Minute Book 10, 1 May 1952; and U-C DM, 27 May 1952.
[47] K. A. Heard, *General Elections in South Africa, 1943–1970* (London, 1974), 48 f.

South Africa had not yet become a foregone conclusion. In these circumstances there was none of the talk of giving notice on the OFA which might otherwise have been expected, and even the idea of seeking arbitration was only half-heartedly canvassed.[48] Instead, the Lines resolved to hold their fire and, in the meantime, make sure that they were in a position to make a better statistical case to the government on the next occasion; pending that, they would press for increases on selected items of cargo. This, the government had hinted, it might consider.[49]

It was during this uneasy stand-off between the Lines and the South African government over the vital question of the general level of freight rates that Sir Vernon Thomson died, on 8 February 1953. This may have removed from the direction of the Conference and the Union-Castle Line a man who, despite his attempts to reach a *modus vivendi* with Afrikaner nationalism, remained the embodiment of the British imperial idea which was so resented by the National Party. But, unfortunately for the Conference and the mail line, his successor, Sir George Christopher, was even less well-equipped than Sir Vernon to reach a lasting accommodation with the National Party government, which, to the acute disappointment of the Lines, was returned in the general election held two months after Sir Vernon's death with an increased majority.

Inexperienced in passenger liners at the time of his appointment to the deputy chairmanship of Union-Castle in 1949, and considering himself too old for the job anyway, Sir George had been pressed into service against his better judgement only as a result of his friendship with Sir Vernon.[50] Worse still, though he lacked the autocratic manner of his predecessor, he was insular in outlook. He also had an incomplete grasp of the fundamental bargain which was at the heart of relations between Union-Castle and Pretoria, exclaiming in exasperation at a Board meeting as late as July 1954 that he 'did not know what had actuated the Company's policy whereby financial losses had been incurred in past years on the carriage of fruit'.[51] Because his wife was an invalid, he was under pressure to spend as little time away from home as possible, and as a result, he never once visited South Africa, which, in view of increasing government irritation at the need of

---

[48] Greenwich, Joint Meeting Minutes, 12 June 1952, and 24 Oct. 1952.
[49] Ibid., 16 Jan. 1953.
[50] Sir G. P. Christopher, *Roots and Branches* (Liverpool and London, n.d.), 54 f.
[51] Cayz. H., U-C DM, 13 July 1954, min. 10264.

Union-Castle officials to refer even relatively minor matters for decision to 'London Principals', was unfortunate, to say the least.

Perhaps there was also an element of pique in Sir George's refusal to visit the Union, for his own offers of hospitality to the government were spurned very soon after his elevation to the chairmanship. Learning that Dr Malan and a party of government Ministers were to travel to England to attend the Royal Coronation, Sir George offered them all complimentary passages from Cape Town to Southampton, together with luncheon with the Directors of Union-Castle during their stay.[52] Both were declined on thin pretexts.[53] In this chilly atmosphere, Union-Castle became embroiled in further difficulties with the South African government, this time over the shipment of fruit.

In November 1953 the PPECB offered Union-Castle first option on the shipment of greatly increased quantities of fruit from the Union. On receiving this information, however, Sir George Christopher was less than ecstatic. Present rates, he thought, were far too low to justify the building of the extra refrigerated tonnage, or the chartering of the additional vessels, which this would require. Nevertheless, he was anxious not to alienate the PPECB with a flat refusal. Union-Castle was already anticipating difficulties in renewing the Mail Contract under the present tense political circumstances, and the PPECB was seen as a possible ally in this matter. Union-Castle shipped out most of South Africa's fruit exports and their fast and reliable despatch was largely dependent on the berthing priority which the mail ships received under the Mail Contract. This gave the PPECB an interest in its continued retention by Union-Castle.[54] Moreover, Jack Gibson, the Secretary for Transport and Chairman of the PPECB, was on excellent terms with the Company's Cape Town Manager and Deputy Manager for South and East Africa, W. R. H. Austin.[55]

It was in this light that the Lines indicated to the PPECB that they could cope with some increases in fruit carryings as things stood, and would also act, free of charge, as agents for PPECB chartering. However, if additional refrigerated capacity was to be built, there would have to be a 50 per cent increase in the rates on perishables, together with assurances concerning the renewal of the Mail Contract

[52] Ibid., 21 Apr. 1953, min. 9833.
[53] Ibid., 28 May 1953, min. 9862.
[54] Ibid., 22 Dec. 1953, min. 10044.
[55] Ibid., 26 Apr. 1955, min. 10522.

on acceptable terms.[56] Though Sir George would have gone as low as 27 per cent on fruit rates,[57] he was to be disappointed again.

In the course of negotiations in the second half of 1954, Dr Norval completely undercut Sir George's position. With Cabinet approval, he took the PPECB in hand (much to the latter's chagrin) and forced it to withdraw its request for extra refrigerated tonnage from the Lines. There was, he maintained, no tonnage crisis: the fruit interests could cope with the increased quantities in the short term by stretching existing shipping capacity and by chartering for the rest,[58] while in the longer term, Safmarine would be encouraged to build fruit ships with the promise of substantial low interest loans from the government and new tax laws favouring South African registered shipping.[59] At their first meeting, in London in August, Norval told Sir George Christopher that he should think of ways to reduce his costs rather than look to pass them on to the South African fruit industry.

By this time, with the further probings into the affairs of the Lines which had also been a feature of these latest talks, Norval had confirmed his position as the *bête noire* of the South African Conference—barely human, merely 'an electronic brain', acting on 'purely political motives', and, cruellest thrust of all, 'an economic theorist'! This was the flavour of the comment at the first Joint Meeting of the Conference after the talks on fruit rates had ended.[60]

It is true that some of Union-Castle's fears had been allayed when it had learned in July that the government had agreed *in principle* to award the Mail Contract to the Company for a further period of ten years, and also to renew the OFA for a similar period.[61] This scotched a rumour which had been circulating since the previous October that the government was thinking of splitting the annual mail subsidy between two contractors, giving each an alternate sailing, as had been the case for a time in the late nineteenth century.[62] For relief from this threat, Union-Castle had in part to thank the exertions of its friends

---

[56] Ibid., 22 Dec. 1953, min. 10044, and 13 July 1954, min. 10264.

[57] His minimum would have been 33⅓% if he was to be persuaded to build an additional mail ship as well as two new refrigerated vessels: ibid., 13 July 1954, min. 10264.

[58] Ibid., 17 Aug. 1954, min. 10298, including Recapitulation of Interview with Dr Norval, 6 Aug. 1954, and Note of Meeting with Fruit Delegation and Dr Norval, 9 Aug. 1954.

[59] Cayz. H., U-C DM, 22 June 1954, min. 10252.

[60] Greenwich, Joint Meeting Minutes, 10 Aug. 1954.

[61] Cayz. H., U-C DM, 27 July 1954, min. 10280.

[62] *Cape Times*, 17 Oct. 1953.

within the South African civil service, for the senior civil servants at Transport, Commerce and Industries, and Posts and Telegraphs had all recommended renewal of the Mail Contract.[63]

Satisfaction at the news that the Mail Contract was to be renewed was soon overtaken by anger, however, when it was learned in October that renegotiation of the two contracts was not to take place until the end of 1955 or even the beginning of 1956, and that the government did not wish to reconsider the question of freight rates until then either. Union-Castle was anxious for early renewal—as in late 1944—so that it could proceed with confidence on its ship replacement programme, and the Lines as a whole were determined to get a general increase in freight rates as soon as possible and certainly well before the formal expiry of the two contracts at the end of 1956. As a result, they had pressed for the negotiations to take place in February or March 1955. Unfortunately for the Lines, their friends among senior government officials, who were themselves unhappy with this timing,[64] had been outflanked by Norval, who was obviously quite happy to see the shipowners sweat. He would have more time to encourage the expansion of the South African fleet and to drum up tonnage from outside the Conference; should he be successful, he would obviously be in a stronger bargaining position by the time the negotiations took place. What he told the Lines by way of explanation for the proposed delay, however, was that 'economic trends would be clearer towards the end of next year'.[65]

The gap between Sir George Christopher and Dr Norval had now become a chasm. While the latter thought that the Conference had been milking South Africa for years, the former was of the opinion that under earlier direction Union-Castle had been if anything too generous to the Union, especially in the matter of Northbound rates. By October 1954 Sir George had become 'profoundly disturbed' at the attitude of the Union government.[66]

It is not surprising, therefore, that Union-Castle set its face firmly against the possibility of transferring further vessels to the South African flag at this juncture,[67] and, at the end of 1954 and to the accompaniment of dire threats of government retaliation from Sir

[63] Cayz. H., U-C DM, 22 June 1954, min. 10252.
[64] Ibid., 21 Dec. 1954, min. 10396.
[65] Ibid., 20 Oct. 1954, min. 10327.   [66] Ibid.
[67] Ibid., 27 July 1954, min. 10281, 21 Dec. 1954, min. 10403, and 25 Jan. 1955, min. 10425.

Arthur Harris, led a Conference rejection of Safmarine's request for additional sailing rights in the trade (under its Agreement it was entitled to a review after five years).[68] Whether by coincidence or not, within days the SA Reserve Bank, which had taken over responsibility for arranging the shipment of gold to Britain from the Bank of England at the beginning of the year,[69] had threatened Union-Castle with exclusive use of air-freighting unless the mail line reduced the freight rate on gold bullion from 3s. per cent to 1s. 8d. per cent.[70] In January 1955 the Company was forced to 'compromise' on 2s. per cent.[71]

With the help of pressure from the PPECB, which was having to pay very high charter rates for the fruit which the Lines could not take,[72] and probably because Dr Norval had been unsuccessful in raising tonnage from other sources, in February the government compromised a little on the timing of the renegotiation of the OFA and the Mail Contract, which would now commence on 1 August 1955 in Pretoria.[73] Clearly, matters would come to a head between the South African Conference and the South African government on this occasion—if not before.

Domestic troubles in Fenchurch Street

The unhappy state of relations between the Conference and the government in early 1955 would have been worrying to Union-Castle at any time, but at this point it was especially disquieting, since the strong financial position which the Company had built up in the late 1940s and early 1950s was being rapidly eroded. This—as Sir George Christopher never tired of explaining—was the result of the effect on profits of escalating operating and shipbuilding costs on the one hand, and restrictions on earnings consequent upon the Union government's attitude towards freight rates (including gold rates) on the other. Inability to increase passenger fares for fear of driving customers into the arms of mounting air competition, port congestion, and periodic import restrictions in the Union had further added to the Company's financial worries.

One of the most significant consequences of Union-Castle's

[68] Ibid., 21 Dec. 1954, min. 10402.
[69] Information supplied to the author by the Bank of England on 19 June 1984.
[70] Cayz. H., U-C DM, 21 Dec. 1954, min. 10406. The gold freight rate had been reduced from 4s. to 3s. per cent in October 1949, following sterling devaluation.
[71] Ibid., 25 Jan. 1955, min. 10429.   [72] Cape Times, 14 May 1955.
[73] Greenwich, Joint Meeting Minutes, 3 Mar. 1955.

dwindling financial strength was its reluctance to invest in major replacements for its ageing fleet. (Another was its disinclination to continue to hold large deposits with the National Finance Corporation, from which the political dividends had in any case been so slender.[74]) To make matters worse, Sir George Christopher also felt that the fleet had been badly maintained, and the mail service received poor publicity in this period as a result of engine failures on the mail ships following the switch from diesel to boiler oil as an economy measure.[75] In consequence, there was considerable tension between Sir George and James Gray, the Engineer Superintendent of the fleet, and in early 1955 the latter left the Board of Directors.[76]

Outside of Fenchurch Street, however, not all of Union-Castle's problems were attributed to technical difficulties and conditions in South Africa or in the trade generally. There was a widespread feeling that some of the blame should be placed on the shoulders of the Company's leaders, who were felt to lack energy and imagination.[77] In his memoirs, Sir George Christopher seems to admit these charges, while seeking to pass the blame to Sir Vernon Thomson for promoting him against his own better judgement.[78] It was in these circumstances— and with these views in the air—that Union-Castle became the victim of rumours of take-over. This brought to the brim Sir George Christopher's cup of bitterness.[79]

Waiting for the right opportunity was the Cayzer family's Clan Line, a British member of the South African Conference with a substantial interest in the trade, which had previously sought control of the mail line in the mid-1930s[80] and again in 1944.[81] Clan had always resented Union-Castle domination of the South Africa run and the insistence of the mail line that Clan should stay out of the passenger business. As recently as 1949 Clan had sought increased sailing rights from South Africa but had been rebuffed in Fenchurch Street.[82] Clearly, there was a fresh edge to Clan's long nourished ambition of acquiring control of Union-Castle.

[74] In May 1952 these deposits had been reduced to zero and, as far as can be told from the Company's records, this remained the case in 1955 (see Appendix III).
[75] G. Young, *Salt In My Blood* (Cape Town, 1975), 147 f.
[76] Cayz. H., U-C DM, 26 Jan. 1954, min. 10075, 23 Feb. 1954, min. 10093 and 26 Apr. 1955, min. 10531.
[77] E.g. Young, 167 f.; and Sturmey, 373 f.   [78] Christopher, 54 f.
[79] See his speech to shareholders at the Union-Castle AGM on 27 May 1954, repr. in *The Times*, 28 May 1954.
[80] Cayz. H., U-C DM, 5 Sept. 1935, min. 5747.
[81] Ibid., 19 June 1944, min. 7766.   [82] Ibid., 26 Apr. 1949, min. 8807.

It was against this background of already exceptionally bad relations with the National Party government and domestic worries that Union-Castle learned, in March 1955, that a new Shipping Board Bill was to be rushed through the South African Parliament. Designed to transform the Shipping Board into a formidable weapon in the hands of Dr Norval, this, as far as Sir George Christopher was concerned, was the last straw.

The Crisis Over the Shipping Board Bill

The new Bill was introduced into Parliament on 1 April by Dr A. J. R. van Rhijn, who had replaced Eric Louw as Minister of Economic Affairs in the Cabinet reshuffle following J. G. Strijdom's assumption of the premiership a few months earlier. Unlike the Shipping Board Act, 1929, under which the Shipping Board currently operated, the new Bill was a much longer and more detailed document, and, while still accepting that shipping conferences were not *necessarily* injurious to trade, its tone in regard to them and also towards foreign shipowners was more hostile.[83] It was scheduled to become law on 1 June.

In addition to the oversight of freight rates, the Shipping Board was now to have the general duty of advising on 'economic measures . . . to encourage the development of the South African merchant fleet', and also the duty of investigating conference practices. To help it with this work it was to be given tougher powers, in particular the right to compel the surrender of conference 'Agreements'. These documents spelled out the terms on which individual lines participated in a trade, or sector of a trade, and hitherto had been denied to the Shipping Board by the Conference.[84] The Minister of Economic Affairs was to be given the right to vet these Agreements, and all those made subsequently were to be submitted to him for approval. Foreign shipowners who refused to co-operate could be fined or have their vessels seized and be made to pay a 'special levy', which was obviously a strong incentive to transfer the registry of their ships to South Africa. For good measure, the Minister was also to be given the right to

---

[83] SOUTH AFRICA. *Parliament. House of Assembly.* Bills: AB 52 series.

[84] In 1939 the Lines had declined a Shipping Board request for a copy of the Agreement under which Blue Star had entered the trade in 1935. The Board did not pursue the matter after that, even though a Regulation had been issued in 1937 under the 1929 Act to strengthen the Board's authority for such requests: CAL, Note, South African Shipping Board, 22 Mar. 1950.

reserve the Union's coastal trade to vessels of the South African flag. To ensure that the intent of the Bill would not be lost in implementation, the constitution of the Shipping Board was to be changed so that government influence on it would be paramount (see Appendix VI).

It can safely be assumed that van Rhijn himself had no strong personal commitment to the new Shipping Board Bill. He had only just been moved to the Ministry of Economic Affairs and still retained the portfolio of Mines, which, in addition to Health, he had held in the Malan government. He was, reported Britain's High Commissioner in South Africa, Sir Percival Liesching, 'imperfectly informed about the Bill and . . . had no wide grasp of shipping matters'.[85] It is perhaps also worth adding that Verwoerd, who had a very low opinion of van Rhijn's ministerial competence, lost little time in getting rid of him to the High Commission in London when he took over as Prime Minister in late 1958. Had van Rhijn not been leader of the National Party in South-West Africa, the pasture to which he was put out would have been less green.[86]

The Shipping Board Bill, then, was clearly Norval's Bill and he wanted it so that he would be able, as he explained to the PPECB, to 'drive a wedge' between Union-Castle and the rest of the Lines and so break the Union-Castle 'monopoly' of the South Africa trade.[87] Therefore, it was the provisions concerning the Conference Agreements which were particularly important to him. Norval would obviously have known of the general discontent on the part of the Continental Lines at Union-Castle's autocratic style; he would also have been aware that a number of lines—the French ones, for example, as well as Safmarine— were very dissatisfied with the limited rights which they possessed under their own current Agreements. Equipped with all these Agreements, Norval would be in a position to document the extent of Union-Castle's dominant position in the trade and play on the jealousies of the disgruntled lines. If, in addition, his Minister was given ultimate *control* over the Agreements, the Shipping Board would become master of market shares in the South Africa trade as well as master of the freight rates which the Lines could charge. In short, the Shipping Board Bill, 1955, represented an attempt on the part of the Union government to wrest control of the South African Conference from the

[85] Cayz. H., U-C DM, 28 June 1955, min. 10578.
[86] B. Schoeman, *My lewe in die politiek* (Johannesburg, 1978), 243 f.
[87] Cayz. H., U-C DM, 26 Apr. 1955, min. 10522.

Union-Castle Line. It was a take-over bid of another sort for Fenchurch Street to contend with.

Sir George Christopher was so appalled at the implications of the new Bill that his first reaction was to wonder if, in the circumstances, Union-Castle should proceed with the construction of the next mail ship (only recently announced), and even whether the Lines as a whole should go ahead with the August negotiations in Pretoria. In the end, though, he decided that such action would be seen as 'a sign of weakness' by Dr Norval and that it would not in any case be likely to have much effect. He decided instead to seek the assistance of the British government in killing the Bill, or at least in postponing it until after the August negotiations.[88]

Fortified by counsel that the new Bill was contrary to international law,[89] and encouraged by Sir Gilmour Jenkins, the Permanent Secretary at the (British) Ministry of Transport,[90] Sir George Christopher was on the point of communicating to van Rhijn his opposition to the Bill 'in its entirety on principle', when he was forestalled by his Chief Agent in South Africa, R. M. Mackenzie, acting without authority.

At the instigation of Dr Norval, an informal meeting was held on 21 April between government officials and local representatives of the Lines in order to discuss the proposed Shipping Board legislation. Having lodged a strong protest against the Bill, Mackenzie suggested that at least it should be delayed so that it could be fully discussed by the Lines and the government during the August negotiations on the OFA; the following morning, he was informed that van Rhijn had decided to postpone its further progress until early in 1956.[91] This might have been thought a limited success for the Lines but, pleased though he was at the postponement of the Bill, Sir George Christopher was not at all happy at the indications from Cape Town that the government had only agreed to it on condition that the Lines would discuss its details during the August negotiations. (Sir George's own reason for supporting postponement as a minimum goal was

---

[88] Ibid., 14 Apr. 1955, min. 10496.

[89] Legal advice to the Lines held that the fines and special levies appeared to be 'imposable by means of droit administrative and in the case of special levies to be discriminatory against non-Union Shipping Companies', and that there also appeared to be 'no right of appeal to any Court of Law against their imposition'; CAL, Memorandum by the Lines' Delegation: South African Shipping Board Bill, 1955, 5 July 1955.

[90] Cayz. H., U-C DM, 21 Apr. 1955, min. 10508.

[91] Ibid., 26 Apr. 1955, min. 10522.

presumably his desire to prevent a reconstituted Shipping Board from facing the Conference delegation in August.) Spoiling for a fight on the principles of the Bill, Sir George proceeded with his own formal protest and instructed the hapless Mackenzie to elicit from van Rhijn's Ministry agreement that postponement of the Bill had been consequent upon the Lines' objections to it rather than upon the understanding that it would be discussed in August.[92] After some understandable foot-dragging, the Chief Agent, in an interview with the Secretary for Commerce and Industries on 2 May, subsequently succeeded in doing this.[93]

Despite Sir George's heroic stance, however, pressure soon mounted in favour of the quid pro quo which Mackenzie had implicitly offered to Norval on 21 April. On 2 May the Secretary for Commerce and Industries had informed Mackenzie that Sir George's attitude was unlikely to prove fruitful,[94] and at a meeting at the Ministry of Transport on 18 May the Union-Castle Chairman learned that Britain's High Commissioner in South Africa thought that the Lines should be prepared to discuss the Shipping Board Bill in August. Furthermore, Sir Percival thought that the Conference would have to surrender its Agreements and also go along with Norval's idea of a 'Liaison Committee' in South Africa if the latter were to be persuaded that the Bill was unnecessary. On the same day, Mackenzie, after further talks with Norval, wrote from Cape Town of his confidence that, 'having thrown his bomb shell into the arena . . . Norval is prepared to compromise and withdraw the objectionable features of the Bill if the suggested Liaison Committee can be evolved'.[95]

Sir George Christopher was naturally disconcerted at the idea of surrendering the Conference Agreements to Dr Norval, and indicated to the British government that this proposal would need 'most serious consideration'.[96] Perhaps because Union-Castle was strongly represented in South Africa, and certainly because even Sir George was aware by now that some offering would have to be made to Norval, Fenchurch Street was more prepared, however, to explore the idea of a 'Liaison Committee'. Indeed, on 18 May Sir George was able to tell the meeting at the Ministry of Transport that the Lines were already 'sympathetically considering the setting up of such a body'.[97]

Influenced by his experience at the Board of Trade and Industries,

[92] Ibid.   [93] Ibid., 24 May 1955, min. 10542.   [94] Ibid.
[95] CAL, Mackenzie to Bevan, 18 May 1955.
[96] Cayz. H., U-C DM, 24 May 1955, min. 10542.   [97] Ibid.

what Norval had in mind was a high-level committee of shipowners' representatives located in the Union which would be constantly at hand for discussions with the Shipping Board. It would have one spokesman for the British Lines, one for the Scandinavian Lines, and another for the remaining 'Continental' Lines. On questions such as individual freight rates and space for low-rated commodities, concerning which Norval maintained that the Shipping Board was receiving a 'stream of complaints', this Liaison Committee would have authority to make decisions without the need for constant reference to 'London Principals'.[98]

Changes of this sort in Conference decision-making would have three clear advantages for Dr Norval. Firstly, they would reduce delay in the taking of decisions. Secondly, they would dilute the influence of Union-Castle within the Conference. Thirdly, they would make the Conference even more amenable to local pressure. Clearly, this would not be a bad substitute for the Shipping Board Bill at all.

The Bill, then, had been quickly postponed, and by the middle of May it was apparent that Norval was prepared to compromise on its details. This was no doubt because the British side had already hinted at concessions, and perhaps also because Pretoria did not wish to appear unreasonable just before F. C. Erasmus, the Minister of Defence, was due to resume talks in London on the return of the Simonstown naval base to Union sovereignty and Pretoria's long-cherished plan for an African Defence Pact.[99] Nevertheless, there had merely been a postponement of the Bill and it remained clear that, one way or another, Norval was resolved to increase still further government influence over the Conference. As a result, Union-Castle and most of its colleague lines, together with the British government and ASSOCOM (at the instigation of the Cape Town Chamber of Commerce), now launched a major campaign to have the Bill killed altogether.

At Union-Castle's Annual General Meeting on 2 June, Sir George Christopher told his shareholders that a spirit of 'unfriendliness towards shipping lines' was behind the Shipping Board Bill, thus drawing public attention for the first time to the rift which had opened between the Conference and the government. At about the same time,

[98] CAL, Mackenzie to Bevan, 18 May 1955.
[99] On the Simonstown negotiations, see J. E. Spence and G. R. Berridge, 'The Road to Simonstown', in J. W. Young (ed.), *The Foreign Policy of Churchill's Peacetime Administration 1951–55* (Leicester, forthcoming).

the High Commissioner delivered the British government's formal protest in the shape of an *aide-mémoire*, and followed this up with a personal visit to van Rhijn.[100] In Cape Town, the Chamber of Commerce—encouraged and assisted by Union-Castle—produced a memorandum which was severely critical of the proposed legislation and urged the Minister to withdraw it. This was subsequently unanimously adopted by the Executive Committee of ASSOCOM and handed to van Rhijn.[101]

While this campaign was in full swing, a Joint Meeting of the Conference was held, on 10 June, in order to determine the Lines' attitude towards the government in the August negotiations. This meeting was presided over by John Bevan, who had been Conference Chairman since the retirement of Stanley Barr in February 1954. (Unlike Sir Vernon Thomson, Sir George Christopher did not even attend Joint Meetings, let alone take the chair.) Bevan, Deputy Managing Director of Union-Castle, was a lifelong servant of the Company and had been extremely close to Sir Vernon Thomson, whom he had served as Personal Assistant at the Ministry of War Transport throughout the war. As a result, he was intimately acquainted with the problems of the South Africa trade. He was quiet and unassuming, hard-working to a fault, tactful, patient, difficult to ruffle, and a man of acknowledged integrity. All of this was just as well, though his qualities were not put to severe test at the Joint Meeting in June.

At this meeting of the Conference, Bevan had little difficulty in securing the Lines' endorsement of the strategy which had been evolved in recent weeks. This rested on the assumption that it was of the utmost importance that the negotiations for the new OFA (and the Mail Contract) should be conducted in an atmosphere of goodwill. And so, before the negotiations proper began, it was proposed that the Conference delegation would offer Norval the following inducements in an attempt to persuade him to drop the Shipping Board Bill: firstly, a Liaison Committee in South Africa (though 'any major question such as rates of freight would have to be referred to Principals'); secondly, description of the Conference's working arrangements; and thirdly, the secret Conference Agreements.

[100] Cayz. H., U-C DM, 28 June 1955, min. 10578.
[101] Ibid. See also Cape Archives, Minutes of Meeting of Group 14 (Shipowners and Ships' Agents), 6 May 1955, CC 3/1/2/1/1/24; and Cape Archives, Cape Town CC Secretary to Transocean Liners Cape Town (Pty.) Ltd., 29 July 1955, CC/3/31/1/18.

The implication of Bevan's remarks on Conference Agreements at the Joint Meeting, and at a meeting at the Ministry of Transport ten days later,[102] was that these would be held back until the last minute and only surrendered if it seemed to the delegation that no other concession would persuade Norval to withdraw the Shipping Board Bill. Bevan's authority to surrender them, though, was ample; indeed, the Joint Meeting positively urged him to lay them before the South Africans. This in itself was a sign of the differences within the Conference between Union-Castle and many of the other lines, and it was as well for the Conference that Bevan laid great stress on the need for unity in the coming months.

Clan Moves on the Union-Castle Line

As if by June 1955 the attitude of the Union government had not already made matters bad enough for Union-Castle, disturbing news was now received from a different quarter: not for the first time, J. A. Billmeir was seeking control of the Company. A tramp owner who had made his fortune gun-running in the Spanish Civil War, Billmeir was the sort of shipping man who made Fenchurch Street recoil in horror. Given that vital negotiations in Pretoria were now only weeks away, Union-Castle felt that this move could not have come at a worse time. If it became public knowledge that the affairs of the Company might pass into other hands in the near future—especially the hands of Billmeir—'Mr Bevan's task at Pretoria would be made immeasurably harder and no doubt in that event', lamented Sir George Christopher, 'the Union Government would seek to drive a much harder bargain, and would in any case feel a lack of confidence in the continuity of the Company, even if they were prepared to negotiate at all'.[103]

Billmeir was rebuffed, but within days the Clan Line, which had been in consultation (some members of the Un on-Castle Board believed 'in collusion') with Billmeir, approached i enchurch Street with an offer of 'amalgamation'. Sir George Christopher, who by this time seems to have become deeply demoralized, found himself unable to reject this offer outright. After digesting the details of the Clan scheme, and after discussing them further with Sir Nicholas Cayzer, Vice-Chairman of the Clan line, it became clear that Clan itself was more interested in a take-over than in a merger. On 28 June, after a

---

[102] Cayz. H., U-C DM, 28 June 1955, min. 10578.
[103] Ibid., 17 June 1955, min. 10560.

lengthy Board meeting which saw some sympathy for pursuing negotiations with Clan in spite of this, Union-Castle finally agreed to inform the Cayzers that it could not recommend their offer to the Company's shareholders.[104]

Sir George Christopher's faction on the Union-Castle Board nevertheless remained attracted to the idea of a genuine amalgamation with Clan, as Sir George explained informally to Sir Nicholas Cayzer on 7 July.[105] This prompted Clan to make its proposal more palatable to Fenchurch Street by explaining that it would not destroy the 'separate identity' of Union-Castle in any scheme to achieve 'closer collaboration'.[106] Following these assurances from Clan, negotiations picked up again and moved quickly towards the idea of achieving the amalgamation by the device of a holding company. This plan emanated from Fenchurch Street, where it was seen as the only way in which amalgamation could be prevented from being—in effect—a take-over by the stronger Clan Line. For this reason the Cayzers, who held 66 per cent of Clan's shares,[107] were initially suspicious of the idea, but they came round to it when they were sure that they had the financial strength to dominate any holding company as well.

At the end of July Union-Castle decided to strive for a merger with the Clan Line as a matter of urgency. Billmeir had acquired powerful backers in the City and made an even more serious bid for control. Against this background, the two lines began to discuss their respective shares in the proposed holding company. However, all of this was kept a closely guarded secret.

On the eve of the August negotiations between the Conference and the Union government, the National Party had been in power in South Africa for just over seven years. During that period Union-Castle had been forced to make concession after concession to the new government. First there had been small financial concessions in order to secure the orderly termination of the Special Immigrant Service, and then not one but two South African flag lines had had to be accepted into a trade which was already regarded as over-tonnaged. Subsequently, large sums had been deposited by the Company in the NFC, and the humiliation of answering more and more detailed questions about its affairs had been borne.

All that Union-Castle had to show for this was the government's promise, *in principle*, that the Mail Contract and the Ocean Freight

[104] Ibid., 28 June 1955, min. 10566.   [105] Ibid., 13 July 1955, min. 10594.
[106] Ibid.   [107] Ibid., 26 July 1955, min. 10599.

Agreement would be renewed. Against this, Conference policy under Union-Castle direction had failed to secure any general increase in freight rates since 1951, and had not even managed to raise perishable rates (despite some sympathy from the fruit interests themselves). It had failed to persuade the government to agree to an *early* renewal of the two main contracts, and currently it was being threatened with legislation which would give the government control over market shares—as well as prices—in the Europe–South Africa trade.

Clearly, Union-Castle, especially under Sir George Christopher, had not been prepared to do enough to appease Afrikaner nationalism. Sir George seemed to have grasped that Union-Castle needed South Africa more than South Africa needed Union-Castle, but he had failed to understand the full extent of the discrepancy. In short, he had overestimated his power. Partly as a result of all these difficulties, Union-Castle's fortunes had begun to decline, and its leadership of the South African Conference had been called into question. With negotiations for renewal of the Mail Contract and the OFA now imminent, and with negotiations for a 'merger' with the Clan Line continuing, August and the remaining months of 1955 were clearly going to represent a watershed in the affairs of Union-Castle, and, indeed, in those of the South African Conference as a whole.

3

THE PRETORIA FORMULA
1955–1964

FORTUNATELY for the South African Conference, the omens were good for the negotiations to be held in Pretoria in August 1955. Defence negotiations with Britain in June had been successfully concluded,[1] and, as a result, relations between South Africa and Britain were probably warmer than at any point since 1948. Furthermore, the bargaining position of the Conference had been improved by a strengthening of the shipping market. Reflecting this, most liner conferences increased their tariff rates by between 10 and 15 per cent in 1955.[2]

The Pretoria Settlement, August 1955

The Pretoria negotiations began, as agreed, on 1 August 1955.[3] The Conference delegation (Sir Nicholas Cayzer, Vice-Chairman of the Clan Line; Sj. Mook, Managing Director of the Holland-Afrika Lijn; Per Carlsson, Manager of Transatlantic; and J. G. Finlay, Managing Director of Safmarine) was headed by the Conference Chairman, John Bevan, while the government side was led during the detailed discussions by Dr Norval. There were three items on the formal agenda: firstly, an urgent application from the Lines for a general increase in freight rates under the existing Ocean Freight Agreement; secondly, revision of the OFA; and thirdly, revision of the Mail Contract. (The first two matters concerned the Conference as a whole,

---

[1] See G. Berridge, *Economic Power in Anglo-South African Diplomacy: Simonstown, Sharpeville and After* (London, 1981), chap. 4.
[2] Organization for European Economic Co-operation, *Maritime Transport 1956* (Paris, 1956), 43 f.
[3] Unless otherwise stated, this account of the Pretoria negotiations is based on CAL, Conference between the Union Government, the PPECB, and the South African Conference Lines relative to the Negotiation of a new Freight Agreement and the Revision of Freight Rates: Record of Proceedings (Pretoria, Aug. 1955).

while the last was exclusively a matter for Union-Castle.) There was also an informal agenda devoted to the Shipping Board Bill.

It will be recalled that Conference strategy was to offer the government certain concessions straight away in return for dropping the Shipping Board Bill, and so clear the air before the main negotiations began. The signs for the success of this particular strategy, however, were mixed. While the indications from van Rhijn were encouraging, Norval had been irritated by the High Commissioner's *aide-mémoire* and Sir George Christopher's speech at the Union-Castle AGM, and had let it be known that he was not prepared to discuss the Bill in Pretoria and certainly not as 'a prerequisite to talks about the Freight Agreement'.[4] The belief that the Chairman of the Shipping Board was in an 'uncompromising mood'[5] was further reinforced when, shortly after its arrival in the Union, the Conference delegation found itself on the receiving end of one of his lectures on the decadence of the British Empire.[6]

The opening remarks at the negotiations of D. De Waal Meyer, the Secretary for Commerce and Industries who led for the government during the plenary sessions, contained clear evidence of the deep ill will which had crept into the relations between the Conference and the Union: the suggestion of sarcasm in his reference to the unfortunate absence of Sir George Christopher; the firm statement of his Minister's intention to press ahead with the Shipping Board Bill together with his refusal to countenance formal representations against it; and, above all, the astonishingly disingenuous suggestion, made by Norval but at once endorsed by De Waal Meyer, that the government team would be happy to acknowledge the well-known distaste of the Lines for public discussion of their internal affairs by conducting the negotiations on freight rates with each of the delegates separately! For his part, John Bevan emphasized the feeling of 'acute anxiety and uncertainty' caused by the Shipping Board Bill, and clearly implied— albeit in guarded fashion—that pursuit of this Bill by the government, and failure on its part to meet the minimum demands of the Lines on freight rates and the OFA, would force them to take drastic action.

De Waal Meyer may have indicated that he would not consider *formal* discussion of the Shipping Board Bill during the following negotiations, but he also plainly implied that his Department would accept informal representations concerning it from the delegation,

[4] Cayz. H., U-C DM, 28 June 1955, min. 10578.
[5] Ibid.   [6] Information supplied to the author by Lord Cayzer.

thus suggesting that in practice Norval had reverted to his original position. On the available evidence, it seems reasonable to suppose that this invitation was quickly seized by Bevan, and that informal discussions with De Waal Meyer and Dr Norval followed on the same day.[7] In the course of these, Bevan offered the government a description of the Conference's working arrangements and a 'Liaison Committee' in the Union—but *not* the Conference's Agreements[8]—if the Shipping Board Bill were shelved. This was accepted, and, at a dinner given that evening for the Minister by the Conference delegation, van Rhijn indicated that the Bill in its present form would be dropped altogether.[9] Thereafter the atmosphere improved. The Lines seem to have achieved their initial objective without having had to play their trump card.

As the Conference hoped, the new atmosphere helped it to win increased freight rates, though the significance of this lay less in their size than in the basis on which they were granted. Exactly what the Lines asked for to begin with is not entirely clear, but it was at least an immediate increase of 50 per cent on perishables, 10 per cent on Southbound general cargo, and 15 per cent on Northbound general cargo—and probably more.[10] These figures were justified by the Lines on the grounds that such increases were necessary to generate a 7½ per cent return on capital, together with an allowance for depreciation at 5 per cent (both to be calculated on replacement value, since shipbuilding costs were increasing), which they thought fair. The basis of the claim advanced naturally provoked discussion.

After some sparring, Norval conceded that both return on capital and depreciation should be calculated on replacement rather than historic cost. However, basing his position on the argument that the average life of the Lines' ships was well over twenty years, he forced the delegation to accept depreciation at 4 per cent (average life twenty-five years) rather than 5 per cent. Furthermore, maintaining that there was hardly any risk at all in the South Africa trade, and that the average return on risk capital in the United Kingdom itself was under 5 per cent, he successfully insisted on a 5 per cent return on capital instead of 7½ per cent, claiming that this was liberal.

On the face of it, agreement on this *formula*—the so-called 'Pretoria

[7] CAL, Bevan to Lines, 31 Aug. 1955.
[8] Information supplied to the author by Lord Cayzer.
[9] Cayz. H., U-C DM, 23 Aug. 1955, min. 10619.
[10] Ibid., 26 July 1955, min. 10615.

Formula'—was a breakthrough as far as relations between the Lines and the South African government were concerned, and to some extent it certainly was. From now on, the level of freight rates was not to be determined by a contest of nerve and power, but by the rational application of a formula—at least for as long as agreement on the Pretoria Formula itself endured. Here, of course, lay the rub, for as these negotiations themselves revealed, there was plenty of scope for disagreement on such matters as what constituted a proper rate of return, and whether replacement or historic cost should be employed. Changing economic circumstances would also lead to different attitudes on these questions. In effect, therefore, the contest between the Lines and the government had in principle merely been transferred from the level of freight rates to the terms of the Formula itself.

Nevertheless, for the moment a formula had been agreed and having applied it to Union-Castle's accounts for 1954—'which were taken as fully representative and as the pattern of the trade'[11]—Norval was obliged to admit to a shortfall in earnings. Consequently, he eventually offered the Lines an increase of 10 per cent from 1 September 1955 on both Southbound and Northbound rates, except that the increase was to be limited to 5 per cent in the case of railway materials, and extended to 25 per cent and 40 per cent respectively in the case of perishables and most kinds of baled produce. Bevan accepted this offer on two important conditions: firstly, that freight rates would be subject from now on to a 'Triennial Review' and could be reviewed in the interim in specific cases and, 'in exceptional circumstances', in general as well;[12] and secondly, that on the basis of the meagre increases granted by the government under this formula the Lines would not be expected to enlarge their fleets but merely to replace ageing vessels.

Following this agreement on the contentious issue of current freight rates and on a formula for the calculation of future ones, revision of the OFA itself was completed with surprising speed, the announcement of the news to the press being delayed from 8 until 12 August only by the absence from Pretoria of Eric Louw—now Minister of Finance—whose formal assent was required to the financial provisions of the various agreements. (Gerhardt Jooste, South Africa's High Commissioner in London, thought that Louw's absence from Pretoria was probably one

[11] CAL, Bevan to Lines, 31 Aug. 1955.
[12] This agreement for a Triennial Review, together with its qualifications, was subsequently written into the OFA as cll. 23(a) and 23(b).

of the reasons for the success of the negotiations.[13]) Nevertheless, a number of significant changes to the OFA were adopted.

First of all, the new OFA provided for an increase in the quantity of perishables to be shipped to Europe. This had been sought by the PPECB for some time, and was a concession by the Lines. Secondly, a sizeable new structure of consultative machinery was established. In addition to the Triennial Review of freight rates (which Norval said could take place alternately in Europe and South Africa), an 'Annual Conference' was to be held in the Union at which all those interested in the trade could discuss the problems affecting it; this would be presided over by the Chairman of the Shipping Board. 'Allocation Committees' were also to be established by the Lines in both Britain and South Africa in order to ensure that cargo bearing relatively low rates of freight was not discriminated against by the Conference. Finally, a seven-member 'Liaison Committee' was to be appointed by the Lines; designed to obviate the constant need for reference to 'London Principals', this was conceived by Norval as tantamount to a resident Conference delegation in the Union. These were all further concessions by the Lines.

Of the remaining changes in the OFA, probably the most significant were the modification of the 'break clause'—or 'escape clause' as it was now known—and the ending of the preferential rates for government cargo. Reducing the period of notice to be given in the event of termination of the Agreement from eighteen to twelve months, the new escape clause reflected the determination of the Conference to have a weaker legal commitment to freight rates which—formula or no—might once again prove unremunerative, and also to be less firmly tied to a government which might introduce legislation hostile to foreign shipping.[14] However, this was probably not regarded by the government as a serious concession. As for the ending of preferential rates on government cargo, van Rhijn subsequently explained that this was a quid pro quo in exchange for the Lines' agreement to lower increases in the general level of tariffs.[15]

On 8 August the negotiations on the OFA were formally wound up in an atmosphere of mutual congratulation, with much talk of a new spirit of understanding and co-operation. Norval himself expressed a 'sincere wish that the formula arrived at and the machinery created

[13] Cayz. H., U-C DM, 27 Sept. 1955, min. 10644.
[14] CAL, Bevan to Lines, 31 Aug. 1955.
[15] *Senate Debates*, c. 4565 (11-14 June 1956).

would be found adequate to meet the future needs of the Union and the Conference in regard to shipping and trade', while van Rhijn, when revealing the success of the negotiations to the press on 12 August, announced that, in view of the special consultative machinery created in the new OFA to deal with the situations envisaged in the Shipping Board Bill, he was prepared to modify that Bill very considerably, and even to consider withdrawing it altogether.[16] For Union-Castle itself, all that remained was to secure renewal of the Mail Contract on satisfactory terms.

In the months preceding the August negotiations, Sir George Christopher had naturally thought about the changes he would like to see in the Mail Contract. Smarting under the threat of the Shipping Board Bill, he felt that for a start the mail line could no longer afford to be a party to a long-term contract from which there was no possibility of legitimate withdrawal. Living with the fear that the Nationalist government would go ahead and introduce its discriminatory legislation, Sir George was of the opinion that the watertight ten-year contract which for Sir Vernon Thomson had been an indispensable guarantee of long-term security, was now an insupportable hostage to fortune. There would have to be a similar means of escape to that which was already provided in the OFA.[17] In addition, Sir George wanted the annual subsidy increased from the present level of £300,000 to £400,000 or even £500,000, 'especially as it was understood that the Union Government was presently making a profit by paying the Company less than the amount which they collected for Mail conveyance'.[18] Finally, he resolved to resist the expected attempt on the part of the Minister of Posts and Telegraphs to have the mail service accelerated (which Sir George regarded as too costly in terms of fuel and wear on the engines), and therefore to seek to eliminate from the existing Contract the reference to the ability of new mail ships to perform the voyage between Cape Town and Southampton in 12½ days.[19]

In the event, John Bevan successfully concluded negotiations for the new Mail Contract on behalf of Union-Castle as expeditiously as he had concluded the earlier negotiations on freight rates and the OFA on behalf of the Conference as a whole. When its details were made public, it became clear that the minimum goals of the Company had

[16] *The Times*, 13 Aug. 1955.
[17] Cayz. H., U-C DM, 24 May 1955, min. 10544.
[18] Ibid.   [19] Ibid., and 13 July 1955, min. 10595.

been achieved. The annual subsidy was increased by a third, as in 1945, to £400,000, and the service was not to be accelerated. The 'special undertakings' made in the Contract by Union-Castle in response to nationalist sentiment in 1945—and which might have been expected to be of particular interest to the National Party government—were still included, but were in no way strengthened. (In so far as these covered the employment of South Africans in Union-Castle ships, this was without doubt because white South Africans had shown no great interest in the work.[20]) Most significantly, an escape clause was included in the Contract which in all important respects was the same as that which had just been inserted in the OFA. Either Union-Cstle *or the government* could now terminate the ten-year Mail Contract at twelve months' notice. Whether this made sense to Union-Castle now that the Shipping Board Bill had been dropped, and now that relations between the Lines and the South African government had been placed on a relatively firmer foundation, was another matter. To overthrow in these circumstances what Sir Vernon Thomson had regarded as the cardinal point of the Mail Contract was a remarkable act, and was eloquent testimony to Sir George Christopher's refusal to believe that a new spirit really had entered into the relationship between the Conference and the Union government or, at any rate, into relations between *Union-Castle* and the government.

There was, nevertheless, considerable relief in London at the outcome of the August negotiations. In Fenchurch Street, Sir George Christopher grumbled about Bevan's concessions in the OFA on the depreciation allowance, and was reluctant to accept that the Lines could afford to replace existing tonnage as a result of the meagre advance in freight rates, let alone build additional vessels. However, it was generally accepted by the Union-Castle Board that Bevan had done as well as could have been expected.[21] As for the renewal of the Mail Contract, this was regarded as 'eminently satisfactory', especially since 'it was clear that the Union Government was also pleased'.[22] The Conference Principals, for their part, did not dispute Bevan's opinion that 'a fair advance had been made',[23] while the Permanent Secretary at the Ministry of Transport expressed the hope that 'the arrangements

[20] Union of South Africa, Dept. of Commerce and Industries, 'The South African Shipping Board—Report for the Year ended 31st May, 1955', *Commerce & Industry*, Feb. 1956.

[21] Cayz. H., U-C DM, 27 Sept. 1955, min. 10644.

[22] Ibid., min. 10645.

[23] Greenwich, Joint Meeting Minutes, 7 Oct. 1955.

made by the delegation would prove as satisfactory from the commercial point of view as they seemed to be on the Governmental plane'.[24]

In South Africa there was equal satisfaction with the results of the August negotiations, although Parliament had to wait for almost a year in order to voice it. In June 1956 both the new Mail Contract and the new OFA were passed unopposed. Indeed, while there were one or two general complaints in the House of Assembly about the treatment of passengers on the mail ships—one member thinking it worthwhile to object to being served roast beef and Yorkshire pudding on the Equator—the terms of the agreements themselves caused barely a ripple.[25] This stood in stark contrast to the ratification debates of 1945.

The success of the August negotiations was the result of many things. The Lines had gone to Pretoria knowing that they would have to make concessions to Dr Norval to secure the shelving of the Shipping Board Bill; this had been accomplished, and the atmosphere had improved as a result. Norval himself had not been able to oppose increases in freight rates, since the logic of the formula to which he had agreed pointed in this direction; besides, in the absence of such increases, the Lines' reluctance to carry perishables would have deepened and Norval had been unable to find alternative shipping. As for the Mail Contract negotiations, these had evidently been eased by the government's recognition that greatly improved air services—which already carried all express letter traffic as well as hurrying travellers—had made less important the faster sea voyage against which Sir George Christopher had so firmly set his face.[26] Last but not least, the old bargain at the heart of the relationship between the South African government and the still Union-Castle-dominated South African Conference had held good: concessions to the government in the OFA had been granted as part-payment for the renewal of the Mail Contract. As Bevan, on his return to London, had occasion to remind Sir George Christopher when the latter complained to him about these concessions: 'the Board would appreciate that, unless a satisfactory 10 years Freight Agreement had been concluded, it was doubtful if a new long-term Mail Contract would have been secured'.[27] The 'linkage' of

---

[24] Cayz. H., U-C DM, 25 Oct. 1955, min. 10678.

[25] *House of Assembly Debates*, c. 7549-79 (11-14 June 1956); and *Senate Debates*, c. 4445-79 (11-14 June 1956).

[26] G. Young repeatedly drew attention to this in the *Cape Times*; e.g. 18 Jan. 1954, and 2 July 1954.

[27] Cayz. H., U-C DM, 27 Sept. 1955, min. 10644.

the OFA and the Mail Contract—assisted by the diplomatic skill of John Bevan—had worked its traditional magic.

As a result of the negotiations in Pretoria in August 1955 Dr Norval failed to acquire the control over market shares in the South Africa trade which had been promised to him in the Shipping Board Bill. Nevertheless, he had been presented with a vast architecture of consultative committees and conferences expressly designed to make the Conference even more responsive to the interests of the Union than it was already. It remained to be seen whether the practical working of this new machinery would see the Lines drawn even further under the government net.

The Formation of 'British & Commonwealth'

In the aftermath of the Pretoria settlement, however, what was of more immediate concern to Union-Castle than its relations with Pretoria was the question of control of the Company in Britain. The Pretoria negotiations had certainly brought it some net additional revenue (£1.6m. in a full year[28]), but it seemed clear that this had come too late to save it from a take-over by the Clan Line, which was also better off in consequence of the August negotiations.[29] Discussions between the two companies had proceeded while the Conference delegation had been in South Africa, and by the middle of August Union-Castle had resigned itself to the probability of having to accept a 60 : 40 ratio of control in favour of the Clan Line in the new holding company.[30] Before long the capital structure of the proposed company had also been determined, and Union-Castle had persuaded itself—rightly—that the Union government would have no serious objection to the merger plan.[31] As a result, the scheme was unanimously approved by the Board in late September, and on 3 October, having been approved by the Clan Board as well, it was announced to the press.

Following assurances from South Africa House in London that this would cause no offence in Pretoria, the new holding company was christened 'The British and Commonwealth Shipping Corporation Limited' (B & C).[32] Under this new control Union-Castle was not to lose its separate identity, but it was clearly to be subject to different

[28] Ibid., 23 Aug. 1955, min. 10620.
[29] Cayz. H., Clan Line Directors' Minute Book 10, 19 Oct. 1955.
[30] Cayz. H., U-C DM, 23 Aug. 1955, min. 10621.
[31] Ibid., 27 Sept. 1955, min. 10643.   [32] Ibid., 3 Oct. 1955, min. 10663.

direction. It had been privately agreed that Lord Rotherwick, Chairman of the Clan Line, would become the first Chairman of B & C, while Sir George Christopher would become Deputy Chairman. Furthermore, while three Clan directors were to be added to the Union-Castle Board, only two Union-Castle directors (Sir George and John Bevan) were to be given seats on the Clan Board.[33] Such is the nature of 'mergers'.

However, it was one thing for the Boards of the two companies to agree on a scheme of this kind; it was quite another for the Board of the weaker company to persuade its shareholders to accept it. The announcement, in fact, evoked strenuous protest from one section of the mail line's shareholders, which formed a committee and gave its Board a very hard time for several months. In the end, with its hand strengthened both by the seriousness of the protest against the scheme, and by the discovery of greater earnings in 1955 than in 1954 (the division of interest in the holding company having been worked out on the basis of the respective earnings of the two companies, rather than on the basis of their assets), the Union-Castle Board managed to extract agreement from the Cayzers to a modification in the holding company division of interest from 60 : 40 to 53 : 47.[34] With this the protest was defused, and by January 1956 the 'merger' had been accepted by the shareholders. British & Commonwealth was a reality.

Despite Union-Castle's increased stake in B & C, it remained in a minority. In February 1956 one of its senior directors resigned, and in May Sir George Christopher himself surrendered both his chairmanship of Union-Castle and his deputy chairmanship of B & C. Lord Rotherwick took the vacant Union-Castle chair, and at the same time four additional Clan directors (including Sir Nicholas Cayzer) were appointed to the Union-Castle Board. John Bevan was elevated to the managing directorship but, nevertheless, the Cayzer family take-over was now complete. From now on, the Cayzers would run the Union-Castle Line and, *ipso facto*, constitute the single most powerful voice in the South African Conference.

Cayzer 'Flexibility'

The great dependence of Union-Castle on the South Africa trade had always made its earnings somewhat vulnerable, particularly in view of

---

[33] Ibid.   [34] *The Times*, 4 Jan. 1956.

the government veto on increases in rates in this trade. It was the Company's misfortune that its direction passed into weaker hands just when the Union government's shipping policy fell under the influence of Dr Norval, a man resolved to humble the Union-Castle Line and to tighten further the regulation of the shipping conference over which it presided. In view of Norval's policy, it is not surprising that the news of Union-Castle's demise was received with studied equanimity in Pretoria. As Bevan had predicted, and as the South African High Commissioner confirmed on 9 January 1956,[35] there was also no government anxiety about the implications of the merger for competition in the trade. The explanation of this complacency is not hard to find.

In the first place, after the August negotiations both Union-Castle and Clan had gone out of their way to keep the Union government informed of developments, and to reassure it that the merger would not adversely affect South African interests: the South African High Commissioner was assured that the two companies would continue to operate as separate entities in their respective spheres.[36] Secondly, it must have been difficult for Dr Norval and his colleagues to separate their feelings about the humbling of Sir George Christopher from their feelings about the way this had been brought about: quiet satisfaction at the one no doubt spilled over into benevolence towards the other. Finally, and perhaps most importantly, the Cayzers had shown themselves more inclined than Fenchurch Street to come to terms with shipping nationalism in the Union. Thus, even if the degree of monopoly in the South Africa trade had been increased by the merger, it was unlikely that this would be employed to stifle the growth of the South African merchant marine.

The central fact about the Cayzers—in contrast to the *ancien régime* at Fenchurch Street—was that they were single-minded about the pursuit of profit. They were not romantic about ships, nor were they haunted by the ghosts of the British Empire. 'Flexibility' was their motto.[37] In the light of this, and since Sir Nicholas Cayzer was also on excellent personal terms with Sir Arthur Harris, it is not surprising that Clan should have helped to keep Safmarine afloat with a capital injection when South African investors themselves had cooled towards

[35] Cayz. H., U-C DM, 24 Jan. 1956, min. 10754.
[36] Ibid.
[37] G. Turner is good on the Cayzer philosophy in his *Business in Britain*, rev. edn. (Harmondsworth, 1971), chap. 11.

shipping speculation at the beginning of the 1950s.[38] By the middle of the decade, Clan probably held about a quarter of Safmarine's shares.[39] It is true that Clan, along with Union-Castle, had opposed Safmarine's demand for an increase in sailing rights at the end of 1954,[40] but it had simultaneously taken the lead—albeit unsuccessfully—in trying to persuade Sir George Christopher to take a more sympathetic attitude towards the transfer of Conference vessels to the South African flag.[41] The Cayzers, unlike Sir George, were also aware of the great political importance of personal diplomacy in post-war conditions,[42] and had paid regular visits to the Union.

The Formation of the Union-Castle Local Board

The first task as the Cayzers saw it was to consolidate the improvement in relations with South Africa which the Pretoria settlement had brought about. This was the more urgent since Safmarine remained disgruntled with its existing sailings and both the Conference and Dr Norval began to be disenchanted with the way in which the Pretoria settlement was working. Further diplomacy was also considered to be essential since the second half of the 1950s promised no diminution in either the determination or the ability of the National Party government to establish the general supremacy of Afrikanerdom in South African life.

In May 1956, the same month that Lord Rotherwick took over the Union-Castle chairmanship, the mail line decided to give active consideration to the establishment of a Local Board in the Union. In addition, it felt that it should consider developing 'the South African aspect of the Company's business' through a locally registered company such as Springbok[43] (which, it will be recalled, had been created by Sir Vernon Thomson in an unsuccessful bid to close the door on further South African participation in the Conference after he had been obliged to concede entry to SALines at the end of 1949, and had remained dormant ever since). Lord Rotherwick also decided to

[38] B. D. Ingpen, *South African Merchant Ships* (Cape Town, 1979), 47. Lord Cayzer disclaims any special foresight in this move, though in an interview with the author he described it as 'the best investment we ever made . . . I'm not really sure that we thought it through. Arthur Harris offered the shares to me and I was friendly with him'.

[39] F. H. Y. Bamford, 'The South African Merchant Marine', *SA Shipping News*, May 1964.

[40] Information supplied to the author by Lord Cayzer.

[41] Cayz. H., U-C DM, 25 Jan. 1955, min. 10425.

[42] Cayz. H., Cayzer, Irvine Directors' Meetings' Minutes, 13 Jan. 1949.

[43] Cayz. H., U-C DM, 29 May 1956, min. 10895.

make a goodwill visit to the Union in January 1957. This would coincide with the first Annual Conference between the Lines and the government, as provided for in the Pretoria settlement, and would give added emphasis to the break with the regime of Sir George Christopher. Although no serious steps were taken to develop Springbok until 1958, the Cayzers pushed ahead quickly with the plan to create a Local Board in South Africa. During the rest of 1956 the idea was discussed repeatedly with leading members of the Union government, whose advice was sought on nominees for the Board as well as on what functions it should perform. As a result, Lord Rotherwick was able to announce both the formation and the composition of the Board during his visit to the Union in early 1957.[44]

The Local Board met for the first time in March 1957 and for the last time in December 1962. It was not original in conception (as early as 1891, a Local Board had been formed in South Africa by the British & Colonial Steam Navigation Company[45]), it is not remembered today as an institution of any practical significance, and its records have been destroyed. Nevertheless, it was the right political move at the right time. It showed a proper deference to Nationalist sentiment, it was probably a useful instrument for the gathering of 'general intelligence' (this, at any rate, was one of its avowed purposes[46]), and it served as a respectable additional means for Union-Castle to give financial rewards to influential South Africans. Initially, the Chairman of the Local Board was paid an annual fee of £1,000, the Deputy Chairman £750, and each other member £500, plus expenses.[47] Van Rhijn accepted membership in January 1961.[48]

New Tonnage for the Trade

Under Cayzer ledership, Union-Castle also demonstrated a much greater readiness to provide new tonnage for the South Africa trade. In the middle of 1956 the Company acceded to a request from the PPECB to build two new fruit ships,[49] and, even more significantly, decided to build bigger and faster vessels for the mail service in order

---

[44] Ibid., 27 Mar. 1957, min. 11090.
[45] V. E. Solomon, *The South African Shipping Question, 1886–1914* (Cape Town, 1982), 10.
[46] Cayz. H., U-C DM, 19 Dec. 1956, min. 11037.
[47] Ibid., 27 Feb. 1957, min. 11075.
[48] Ibid., 22 Feb. 1961, min. 11878.   [49] Ibid., 26 June 1956, min. 10923.

to operate it with seven vessels rather than eight, and reduce the voyage time from 13½ to only 11½ days. The specifications for the *Pendennis Castle*, already being built in Belfast when the Cayzers secured control of Union-Castle, were modified accordingly,[50] and before long announcements were made of plans to build the *Windsor Castle* and the *Transvaal Castle* in line with the new thinking.[51]

The Pretoria Settlement Runs into Difficulties

Even as the Cayzers were making these moves on various fronts to propitiate South African opinion and restore the prestige of the mail service, the Pretoria settlement was running into difficulties. The Liaison Committee sought by Dr Norval to shift the locus of Conference decision-making from London to the Union had been appointed in October 1955. However, with the exception of the Chairman of Safmarine, it was inevitably composed exclusively of the senior local representatives of the Lines and headed by Union-Castle's Chief Agent, R. M. Mackenzie. In effect, therefore, there had merely been a change in the form, rather than in the substance, of Conference representation in the Union: the new Liaison Committee was no more in a position to negotiate with the government on major questions independently of reference to 'London Principals' than its individual members had been prior to the Pretoria settlement. The different attitudes of the Lines and Dr Norval on this matter had only been reconciled in August 1955 by fudging the description of the new Committee's functions in the OFA, where it was charged with maintaining 'close liaison' between the two sides and, to this end, 'empowered to *consult* with the appropriate Union authorities'.[52]

Though the vague formulation of the Liaison Committee's functions had served an important diplomatic purpose in 1955, it naturally led to difficulties at its first meeting with the Shipping Board, which took place at the end of January 1956. Confronted by Dr Norval with what the Conference Chairman regarded as 'very far reaching' proposals for the reclassification of certain items in the Northbound tariff, the Liaison Committee had no alternative but to shuffle its feet and confess that it could not take an immediate decision. Though he could hardly have been surprised, Norval was by no means happy about

[50] G. Young, *Salt In My Blood* (Cape Town, 1975), 169.
[51] *The Times*, 15 Aug. 1956.
[52] OFA, 19 Aug. 1955, cl. 26, my emphasis.

this,[53] and the small increases in discretion subsequently granted to the Liaison Committee by Bevan did nothing to remove the low opinion formed of it by the Chairman of the Shipping Board.[54]

If Norval was disenchanted with the Liaison Committee, the Lines were alarmed when, in the run-up to the first Triennial Review of freight rates, scheduled for October 1958, they found themselves faced with a request for information on their financial affairs which was far in excess of anything which they had provided before. This led to suspicions within the Conference that Norval—who believed that he had been too generous to the Lines in 1955—was planning to renounce the Pretoria Formula itself.[55] In the event, after a firm stand had been taken by the Lines on the extent of financial disclosures, Norval backed down; he also reaffirmed his commitment to the Pretoria Formula.[56]

This, however, was not the end of the Lines' worries. By exploiting the vagueness of the Pretoria Formula—especially with regard to its time-scale—the Conference thought that Dr Norval was denying it the promised returns. Though trade had been brisk since 1955, the freight rate increases which he had granted had been meagre,[57] and the Lines had suffered a shortfall in terms of the Formula.[58] If they were forced to accept this even in good times, then the arrangement was never going to work, for they could hardly recoup a deficit during a recession, when competition from tramps and charters would make it impossible for the Lines to implement a general increase and would be more likely to force them to make reductions in order to retain business.

By 1958 the feared recession in world trade had set in and South Africa's exports were hit badly.[59] Against this unpromising background, John Bevan launched a campaign to persuade the Nationalist government—by now virtually impregnable following the further increase in its majority at the general election in April—to accept a revolutionary change which would enable the Pretoria Formula to

[53] Greenwich, Joint Meeting Minutes, 17 Feb. 1956.
[54] CAL, Norval to Bevan, 11 Sept. 1956.
[55] Greenwich, Joint Meeting Minutes, 28 June 1957.
[56] Ibid., 18 Oct. 1957.
[57] An interim increase of 5% (plus a 2½% fuel oil supplement) had been granted at the Annual Conference in January 1957.
[58] CAL, Bevan to Norval, 3 July 1958.
[59] D. H. Houghton, *The South African Economy*, 3rd edn. (Cape Town, 1973), 178 f., and 182 f.

deliver in practice what it had promised in theory. Thus he urged Norval to allow the Lines 'some measure of flexibility in fixing freight rates'. By this he meant that in good times the Conference should be allowed to increase rates sufficiently to make a surplus in terms of the Formula, which could then be used to offset a deficit when times were bad. Implicit in this proposal was the notion that the time period by the end of which the Lines should have received the return promised in the Pretoria Formula should be represented by the *trade cycle*.[60] To secure this new arrangement—'free tariff rates', as it came to be called—was a major objective of the Conference at the Triennial Review in October 1958. Success on this point would mean breaking the major chain of its captivity.

As the Lines were preparing to send their delegation to South Africa for the Triennial Review, the thoughts of the Cayzers were turning to the possibility of making good a promise of their own. This was the indication given to Dr Norval in 1956 that they might transfer certain cargo vessels to South African registry, probably by placing them under the control of the still dormant Springbok Shipping Company. The resuscitation of Springbok in this manner would help to generate a good atmosphere for the Triennial Review. It might also undermine the renewed agitation of Safmarine for an increase in sailing rights,[61] since with more Conference vessels flying the South African flag, it would be possible to claim that Safmarine no longer had a national—as opposed to a commercial—case for any advance in its position. Treasury consent to transfers to Springbok was obtained, and the decision to breathe life into the Company was announced publicly on 16 October by Sir Nicholas Cayzer (Chairman of B & C since the death of his uncle, Lord Rotherwick, in March), following his arrival in the Union for the Triennial Review.[62]

The Triennial Review itself, which was marked by a particularly bad tantrum from Dr Norval, produced mixed results as far as the Conference was concerned. With the trade in recession, its delegation did not travel to Pretoria with any intention of pushing for a major general increase in freight rates,[63] and it was not surprised to find Norval less than anxious to press one on it. Certain selective increases

[60] CAL, Bevan to Norval, 3 July 1958.
[61] CAL, Bevan to Sir Nicholas Cayzer, 15 Aug. 1958, and Cayzer to Bevan, 16 Aug. 1958.
[62] Cayz. H., B & C, Board Meetings, 24 Sept. 1958, min. 10; and U-C DM, 19 Nov. 1958, min. 11441.
[63] CAL, Joint Meeting Minutes, 26 Sept. 1958.

were granted which, in the circumstances, Sir Nicholas thought reasonable;[64] at least they covered the shortfall in the Lines' earnings in terms of the Pretoria Formula.[65]

The Triennial Review also witnessed a tense discussion between Sir Nicholas Cayzer and Dr Norval on the mail service, the latter claiming that the new building programme was extravagant and—since Union-Castle results were the basis of the Pretoria Formula—was placing an unwarranted burden on freight rates. Temperamentally incapable of resisting the temptation to add insult to injury, he added to this an expression of his doubts as to 'whether the *Windsor Castle* is in conformity with the modern spirit and in particular with the spirit of this country'.[66] This attack was bitterly resisted by Sir Nicholas, who insisted on completing the cycle of faster vessels which Lord Rotherwick had commenced, and for which the government itself had previously pressed. However, he was only able to persuade Norval to retain the mail ships in the Pretoria Formula (and this was qualified) by agreeing to give the government a say in the general design of the two ships still to be built.[67] This marked a futher advance in Union-Castle subservience to the government, if not in that of the Conference as a whole. During repeated discussions with the government over the following four years, Sir Nicholas stuck to his view that the faster mail service was desirable, but eventually accepted that the last two mail ships should be 'modest', to the point of carrying no passengers at all.[68]

The vital proposal for a 'free tariff' regime which would enable the Lines to earn the returns promised in the Pretoria Formula over each trade cycle, also fell victim to Norval's bile, and the delegation returned home with no tangible advance on this score. However, partly as a result of what seems to have been a meeting of minds between the leading financial experts on the two sides,[69] the possibility of the government's eventual agreement to this was perceptibly increased. The subject was to be placed on the agenda of the next Annual

[64] Ibid., 20 Feb. 1959.
[65] CACT, Notes on Meeting of Conference Lines held in the Culemborg Hotel, Pretoria, at 3.30 p.m. on Thur, 23 Oct. 1958.
[66] CACT, Unheaded transcript of discussions between the Conference delegation and Dr Norval (with Dr Meijer), appended to Summary of Main Decisions Reached at Pretoria Negotiations—22-24 Oct. 1958.
[67] CAL, De Waal Meyer to Bevan, 10 Nov. 1958.
[68] Cayz. H., B & C, Board Meetings, 5 Oct. 1960, min. 7; and U-C DM, 27 June 1962, min. 12140.
[69] J. A. Thomson of B & C and Dr Meijer, Norval's Chief Cost Accountant: CAL, Joint Meeting Minutes, 20 Feb. 1959.

Conference and there were to be consultations on it in the intervening period. The Pretoria Formula itself, which had not been written into the OFA or expressed as a 'back letter', was also formally endorsed by the government for the first time (see Appendix VI).

Free Tariff Rates and the 'Revised Pretoria Formula'

As agreed at the Triennial Review in 1958, the Conference was allowed to pursue the matter of free tariff rates with the government in the run-up to the Annual Conference in June 1960. Indeed, in May 1959 Bevan succeeded in persuading H. R. P. A. Kotzenberg (who had succeeded De Waal Meyer as Secretary for Commerce) to accept the Conference point of view,[70] and in September Norval himself gave a clear indication that he also was coming round.[71] By October, following discussions in Pretoria between the financial experts, it was clear that agreement to the Conference proposal was very close.[72] After further exchanges in the first half of 1960, which culminated in a discussion of the remaining difficulties on Norval's arrival in London for the Annual Conference in June, the Lines were finally granted a substantial proportion of the freedom in fixing freight rates which they considered essential if they were to have any chance of earning the returns promised under the Pretoria Formula.

The 'Revised Pretoria Formula' tightened up the 1955 Formula and also increased the allowance for depreciation from 4 to 5 per cent. However, the essence of the new Formula (which is reproduced in full in Appendix VII) was the statement contained in its preamble, 'That the South African Conference Lines shall have the right to adjust freight rates, without prior approval, so as to yield up to 10 per cent during the upward swing of the trade cycle in order to realise *five* percent on replacement value over the complete cycle or cycles'.

Of course, the Lines' new liberty was by no means as absolute as the preamble to the Revised Formula suggested. Indeed, it was subject to two important provisos: firstly, that government approval was still required for freight rate increases on Southbound shipments of 'essential plant and raw material' (on the understanding that these would not 'on an average, exceed 20% of the total southbound

[70] Ibid., 22 May 1959.   [71] Ibid., 16 Oct. 1959.
[72] Ibid., 12 Feb. 1960; and CAL, Proposed Amendment and Implementation of Pretoria Freight Rate Formula—Summary of position resulting from interview between Mr J. A. Thomson and Dr A. J. Norval at Pretoria, Mon. 26 Oct. 1959.

freight'[73]); and secondly, that government approval remained necessary for increases in the rates on South African exports which were not subject to tramp competition, that is to say, most of them. The new freedom, then, was really only a freedom to adjust rates in the *Southbound* direction (though this was the most profitable). Furthermore, in view of the fact that he had made it easier for the Lines to earn their agreed return, Norval insisted that this was now their exclusive responsibility; in other words, the government could no longer be expected to make up any shortfall which remained at the end of a trade cycle.[74]

Nevertheless, even with these important provisos, and despite the new Formula's vagueness at one or two vital points, the Revised Pretoria Formula seemed to be an advance for the Lines and was accepted as such at the Joint Meeting on 22 June. When this meeting was joined by Dr Norval and his Chief Cost Accountant (who had both been pressed to attend by Bevan to answer any remaining doubts about the new arrangement),[75] there was mutual congratulation and much talk of 'partnership' and a 'new chapter' in the relations between the Conference and the government. Shortly afterwards, Norval wrote of the 'well-run international shipping lines' linking South Africa to the northern hemisphere, of the 'extremely fortunate' position in which South African industrialists found themselves as a result of 'the very unique arrangement which exists between the Government of the Republic and the Conference Lines', and of 'the very excellent understanding' which obtained between them.[76] The government and the Lines certainly had come a long way since 1955.

In view of this remarkable improvement in relations, it is necessary to stand back for a moment and sum up the reasons for it. Certainly, Norval had been encouraged to grant the Conference more freedom by the logic of the Pretoria Formula of 1955, but there is little doubt that he was led in the same direction by other considerations as well. One of these was the Cayzer policy of accommodation with Afrikaner nationalism, an interesting instance of which was Sir Nicholas Cayzer's successful insistence in October 1957—over the dogged

[73] When Norval supplied the Lines with a list of items deemed to be 'essential plant and raw material' later in the year, these were calculated at 18% of the aggregate Southbound freight: CAL, Joint Meeting Minutes, 14 Oct. 1960.

[74] CAL, Norval to Bevan (telegram), 24 May 1960.

[75] CAL, Bevan to Norval, 17 Mar. 1960, and Norval to Bevan, 3 Mar. 1960.

[76] A. J. Norval, *A Quarter of a Century of Industrial Progress in South Africa* (Cape Town, 1962), 62 f.

resistance of another British line—that the Conference should grant Norval's request for a reduction in the rate on Karakul skins, even though it was known that this was not being sought on commercial grounds but in order to assist the National Party with the influential Karakul interests prior to the general election in 1958.[77] This was 'the long view' at work.

Circumstances also played their part in the improvement in relations in 1960. Amongst these was the growth in Conference unity which had taken place since the mid-1950s, which reduced the temptation to Dr Norval to play off one line against another. This growth in unity was partly a result of the less autocratic style of the Cayzers, and partly a consequence of the changing balance of power between the British Lines and the Continental Lines. Significantly, in June 1957 the tradition of holding all Joint Meetings in London, which went back to the origins of the Conference in the nineteenth century, was broken when the Lines met in Amsterdam as guests of the Holland-Afrika Lijn. Thereafter, one meeting a year was usually held on 'the Continent' and even, occasionally, in South Africa itself.

South Africa's deteriorating international position also played its part in changing the atmosphere of government–Conference relations. Mounting racial unrest at home, together with the rapidly growing influence of the new states in the Commonwealth and the UN General Assembly, had placed South Africa in a position of unprecedented diplomatic isolation. In such circumstances the government was obviously more disposed to listen to the reasonable requests of those friends it retained.

B & C and Safmarine Form an Alliance

For the reasons outlined above, then, relations between the Conference and the South African government were much improved by the middle of 1960. However, one irritant still remained: the anger of Safmarine at the Conference refusal to grant it the increase in sailing rights to which it believed it was entitled. As a result, peace with Safmarine now became a major priority of the Conference Chairman, the B & C Board, and—albeit with somewhat less enthusiasm—the Conference as a whole.

It will be recalled that on the eve of the Triennial Review in 1958 Sir

[77] CAL, Joint Meeting Minutes, 18 Oct. 1958.

Nicholas Cayzer had announced the decision to resuscitate Springbok, partly to improve the atmosphere for the Review and partly to weaken the 'national' case of Safmarine for more sailings. Unfortunately for Sir Nicholas, it had not been obvious from Dr Norval's demeanour at the Triennial Review that his Springbok strategy had paid any significant diplomatic dividends; and, while it may have strengthened his hand in current discussions with Safmarine, it had done nothing to reconcile the national line to the very modest increase in rights which at that time had been on offer. Arguing, apropos of Springbok, that when *ownership* as well as the registration of vessels was taken into account it (Safmarine) was the only 'true' South African shipping line in the Conference, Safmarine had rejected this offer and negotiations had collapsed.[78] In these circumstances, B & C decided to press ahead at once with Springbok, and in early 1959 a small line in the group, Bullard, King, and Company, had been transferred (together with its sailing rights in the Conference[79]) to the hitherto dormant company, which had then been made a wholly owned subsidiary of the Clan Line.[80] An Afrikaner, D. G. Malan, previously General Manager of the Deciduous Fruit Board and before that Shipping Manager of the SAR&H, had been appointed as Springbok's Chairman and Managing Director.

It is no exaggeration to say that the Safmarine Chairman, F. H. Y. Bamford, had been incensed by this Cayzer action. As a result, he had made great difficulties over the transfer of Bullard, King's sailing rights to Springbok,[81] and, at the Joint Meeting held in London in February 1960, insisted on unburdening himself at length, even though it was not customary for the position of individual lines to be discussed at these gatherings. Fortified by a knowledge of government favour but virtuously claiming, nevertheless, that Safmarine had never sought special government assistance, and—ironically enough—invoking the plea for sympathy with the growth of national consciousness in Africa made by Harold Macmillan in his famous 'Wind of Change' speech in Cape Town only nine days earlier, Bamford had read out a prepared statement in which he attacked the 'nominal South African character' of Springbok, demanded 'additional sailing rights free from trading restrictions of any kind', and insisted on an end to the 'covert

[78] Cayz. H., B & C, Board Meetings, 28 Jan. 1959, min. 4.
[79] Ibid., 25 Feb. 1959, min. 5.
[80] Cayz. H., U-C DM, 30 Sept. 1959, min. 11610.
[81] CAL, Bevan to Rood, 9 Feb. 1960.

understandings' within the Conference which he believed were an important obstacle to the fulfilment of Safmarine's aspirations.

Safmarine, its Chairman had claimed, was entitled to a larger share of the trade with Europe because it was 'still the only true South African shipping company, in the full meaning of the phrase'. There had also been a great increase in South Africa's external trade since his Company had joined the Conference in 1950, and a sizeable merchant marine was of great importance to the South African state. If these arguments were not recognized, and if the Lines continued to discriminate against Safmarine by means of covert understandings, the Conference, Bamford had warned, could not prosper.[82]

As might have been expected, this substantively and procedurally radical outburst elicited little more than formal acknowledgement from John Bevan, and was received in virtual silence by the assembled shipping magnates. Nevertheless, B & C had clearly been unsettled by the strength of feeling demonstrated by Safmarine and was anxious about the degree of support which the Company might raise in Pretoria. This is understandable, since Safmarine, which had suffered badly during the shipping recession in the late 1950s and had received what could have been a mortal blow when States Marine was forced to sell its 54 per cent shareholding in order to qualify for federal assistance, had been taken under the wing of the semi-state Industrial Development Corporation (IDC) in May 1959.[83] The IDC had a brief 'to bring about a substantial and profitable increase in [Safmarine's] size and the scope of its activities'.[84] The major national line had fallen to *volkskapitalisme*. In March 1960, therefore, John Bevan had taken the opportunity of a visit to the Union designed primarily for negotiations on the Revised Pretoria Formula to sound out the government's attitude towards Safmarine.

In South Africa, Bevan had been informed by Dr N. Diederichs (who had taken over from van Rhijn as Minister of Economic Affairs) that it was his policy to protect local shipping and that Safmarine was first in his esteem, followed by Springbok and SALines—in that order.[85] In the light of this information, it had been considered expedient to make a more generous offer to Safmarine, and in May

[82] CAL, Statement by Safmarine Embodying Proposals in respect of the Conduct of the European/South & South-East Africa Conference, Appendix 'B', Joint Meeting Minutes, 12 Feb. 1960.
[83] Ingpen, 60 f.; and Bamford, 'The South African Merchant Marine'.
[84] *SA Shipping News*, July 1961.
[85] Cayz. H., U-C DM, 30 Mar. 1960, min. 11698.

1960 it had been agreed that its rights in the trade with Europe should be increased from twelve to eighteen Southbound sailings, to be reviewed after the relatively brief period of three years.[86]

Safmarine, however, had not accepted this increase with a particularly good grace, and, in view of the importance which the government was now attaching to its success, it was apparent to B & C that something further would need to be done if this matter was not to undermine the relations between the Conference and Pretoria, which were now otherwise on a much better footing. (In late January 1961 Sir Nicholas Cayzer was so alarmed at the success of Safmarine in the propaganda war which it was waging in South Africa against Springbok that he even contemplated asking Dr Norval to join the Board of the latter![87]) The problem was how to satisfy Safmarine (and the government) without conceding too much in commercial terms and without causing unmanageable resentment within the Conference. The essence of the plan that B & C came up with was that the Springbok fleet—augmented as necessary—would be sold to Safmarine in return for sufficient shares to take B & C's holding in the government's 'chosen instrument' in shipping from 28 to 47½ per cent. By doing this Safmarine's fleet would be doubled and it would add to its existing sailing rights those of Springbok as well. This could hardly fail to please the South Africans and thus 'should enable us', Sir Nicholas told the B & C Board, 'to look forward to a period of tranquillity'.[88] For his part, Sir Nicholas would acquire a sizeable investment which would be likely to flourish under the protection of the government.

Not surprisingly, the IDC soon fell in with the B & C plan, and in June 1961 not only was Springbok absorbed by Safmarine in the manner envisaged (with the IDC taking overall control),[89] but a new, long-term Agreement on increased Safmarine rights was concluded. In return for a promise that from 1 July 1963, when the new Agreement was to take effect, it would not ask for any further increase in sailings for ten years, Safmarine was granted an increase from eighteen to twenty-four Southbound sailings, and from twelve to twenty-four Northbound sailings.[90] B & C also undertook to provide

[86] CAL, Bevan–Bamford correspondence, Apr.–May 1960.
[87] CAL, Cayzer to Bevan (coded cable), 24 Jan. 1961.
[88] Cayz. H., B & C, Board Meetings, 26 Apr. 1961, min. 5.
[89] The negotiations were concluded in June but the transfer did not take effect until July: ibid., 28 June 1961, min. 4; and Ingpen, 63 f.
[90] CAL, Bevan–Bamford correspondence, 26–7 June 1961.

Safmarine with a 'guiding hand' in technical and other matters.[91] Not only, therefore, had peace between the Cayzers and Safmarine been restored but an alliance had been forged. This was to be of considerable significance in the subsequent history of relations between the South African Conference and the government.

Loading the Southbound Rates

In between Dr Norval's attendance at the Joint Meeting in June 1960 and the settlement with Safmarine twelve months later, the Lines had begun to take advantage of the new liberty in fixing freight rates provided under the Revised Pretoria Formula. On 1 November 1960 Southbound rates were increased by 7½ per cent, and by the end of the year Diederichs had accepted Norval's recommendation that this should apply to all 'essential plant and raw material' as well.[92] After the inevitable display of reluctance, the government also allowed the Lines to go up to 5 per cent (they had asked for 7½) when increasing Northbound rates the following February.[93] This evidence of government attitudes—particularly its recognition of 'the principle that each sector of the trade should bear its share of the burden'[94]—encouraged the Conference to believe that at last it had an understanding with Pretoria which was actually working. Furthermore, in March 1961 the Minister of Posts and Telegraphs, Dr Albert Hertzog, who subsequently founded the extreme right-wing Herstigte Nasionale Party, assured Sir Nicholas Cayzer that Union-Castle would be awarded a further ten-year contract for the mail service after the expiry of the current Contract at the end of 1966.[95] During 1961, therefore, it seemed that the relations between the Conference and the government were better than at any time since the days of General Smuts and Sir Vernon Thomson. External events, however, were soon to plunge them back into acrimony.

The political crisis in South Africa which had erupted with the Sharpeville shootings in March 1960 and resulted in the withdrawal of Dr Verwoerd's new Republic from the Commonwealth a year later, had caused a massive loss of confidence in the South African economy. As a result, foreign capital fled, and by May 1961 South Africa faced a

[91] *SA Shipping News*, July 1961.
[92] CAL, Norval to Bevan, 2 Dec. 1960, and Bevan to Norval, 14 Dec. 1960.
[93] CAL, Joint Meeting Minutes, 10 Feb. 1961.   [94] Ibid.
[95] Cayz. H., U-C DM, 29 Mar. 1961, min. 11896, and 23 May 1961, min. 11931.

balance of payments crisis 'more severe than any experienced since 1932'.[96] Among other measures which the government took to restore the position was the positive *encouragement* of the South African Conference to *increase* Southbound rates, together with an obdurate refusal to countenance any further general increments in Northbound rates. By insisting on an even greater discrepancy in rates between the two sectors than had traditionally prevailed, the government obviously hoped to discourage imports and encourage exports, and so help to compensate on current trading account for the haemorrhage on capital account; in addition, the protection afforded to domestic manufacturing by high Southbound rates would be increased. The result was that by April 1964, when new rates were introduced following a settlement in the previous January of the crisis in Conference–government relations to which this policy had led, Northbound rates had been increased by less than half of the amount imposed on the Southbound trade since 1960 (see Table 1 and Appendices VIII and IX). European shippers contributed to this extent to the resolution of South Africa's post-Sharpville economic crisis.

TABLE 1. *Northbound and Southbound Freight Rates, 1960–1964: An Index Based on Rates in 1959*

	Northbound	Southbound
Base year, 1959	100.0	100.0
1 Nov. 1960	100.0	107.5
1 Jan. 1961–13 Feb. 1961	105.0	107.5
1 Jan. 1962	105.0	115.6
1 Apr. 1964	112.9	127.2

In itself the freeze introduced on Northbound tariff rates was not quite as worrying for the Lines (as distinct from European shippers) as it might have been, since a third of the Northbound traffic was by this time being carried under annual contracts negotiated directly with the shippers in South Africa (see Appendix X); these remained immune. What was really alarming, however, was that general increases confined to the Southbound trade would be likely to provoke such resentment in Europe that the extent to which the Lines would be able to get away with it would be limited. In short, the Conference feared that a brake on Northbound increases would soon be tantamount to a

[96] Houghton, 184.

brake on Southbound ones and, indeed, on increases on the East Africa and Rhodesia/Nyasaland traffic as well. Patriotic considerations no doubt also counted for something with some members of the Conference: Britain, too, had become anxious about its exports, not least to South Africa.[97]

Oddly enough—in view of the ability of their leaders, the considerable experience they had of their opposite numbers in South Africa, and the contacts in the government cultivated by their agents in the Republic—the Lines seem to have been slow to grasp the nature of the government's strategy; or perhaps they saw it, but were reluctant to acknowledge it because of its implications for the good relations so recently and laboriously established.

It has already been noted that Dr Norval had agreed, in late 1960, that the 7½ per cent Southbound increases introduced by the Lines could be extended to *all* 'essential plant and raw material'. Since at the same time the Chairman of the Shipping Board also stated plainly that the Lines ought to be thinking of larger Southbound increases, one might be forgiven for thinking that the Lines should have smelled a rat.[98] That they did not, however, is suggested by their feeling at the Joint Meeting in June 1961 that they should forgo a further Southbound increase of 5 per cent in the autumn (which Bevan thought justified by recent increases in operating costs) 'so as not to embarrass the government' in the present payments crisis.[99] When Dr Norval reacted to this at once by stating that he had no objection to an increase even of 7½ per cent in Southbound rates, *including* all 'essential plant and raw materials', the rat had jumped on to the table and was staring the Lines in the face.[100] Averting their eyes even now, Norval's suggestion was gratefully adopted, and at the Joint Meeting in October it was unanimously agreed to increase Southbound rates by 7½ per cent from the beginning of 1962.[101] Only at the second Triennial Review, which was held in Cape Town on 7 February, were the Lines finally forced to face up to the government's strategy. By this time, however, the rat was at their throats.

The main objective of the Conference at the Triennial Review, not surprisingly, was to secure a general increase in Northbound rates, and

[97] See Berridge, 32–4, and 37–9.
[98] CAL, Norval to Bevan, 2 Dec. 1960.
[99] CAL, Joint Meeting Minutes, 22 June 1961.
[100] CAL, Norval to Bevan, 7 July 1961, and 3 Oct. 1961.
[101] CAL, Joint Meeting Minutes, 20 Oct. 1961.

7½ per cent was also thought appropriate here. The Conference argued that this was a modest increase which the trade could bear, that it was justified in terms of the Revised Pretoria Formula by the shortfall demonstrated in the figures presented to Dr Norval, and that without it the Lines would not find it politic to increase even further the Southbound rates.

The formal proceedings of the Triennial Review were all over in three hours, its conclusion having been foreshadowed by Norval's contention at the Annual Conference held on the previous day that the Lines were at the point in the trade cycle at which freight rates should be decreased rather than increased.[102] Embellishing his response at the Review, Norval said that the Scandinavian and Continental Lines were doing quite well, and that Union-Castle was only doing badly because it was 'hopelessly inefficient'. Although the mail line took most of the abuse during this acrimonious session, not even DOAL escaped: 'you cannot hold us responsible for building up your fleet—you started the war'! Having thus contested the Lines' claim that there was a shortfall in their earnings in terms of the Revised Pretoria Formula, and indicated that even if there were there should not have been, Norval reminded the representatives of the four so-called 'Questionnaire Lines' (DOAL, Transatlantic, Holland-Afrika, and Union-Castle) that under the new arrangement the government was no longer responsible for a shortfall anyway. In any case, he was not prepared to grant a general increase in Northbound rates in view of the 'exigencies of the country's economy'.[103]

Assembling a few hours later in Joint Meeting, the Lines were in rebellious mood. There was no general certainty that Dr Norval was in breach of the terms of the Revised Pretoria Formula—on which point even Bevan was unable to give a clear lead—but no doubt that he had not honoured its spirit.[104] A tête-à-tête between Norval and the Conference Chairman immediately afterwards merely produced a promise that selective Northbound increases would be considered,[105] and a subsequent appeal to the Minister of Economic Affairs over

[102] CACT, Minutes of the Third Annual Shipping Conference between the Government of the Republic of South Africa and the South African Conference Lines held in Cape Town on 6 Feb. 1962, 10.
[103] CACT, Notes covering Second Triennial Review of Freight Rates between the Government of the Republic of South Africa and the South African Conference Lines held in Cape Town at 9.30 a.m. on Wed., 7 Feb. 1962.
[104] CAL, Joint Meeting Minutes, 7 Feb. 1962.
[105] CAL, Bevan to London Conference Secretary (telex), 8 Feb. 1962.

Norval's head secured no further advance. Indeed, stiffened in his attitude by a fear of the effects on South Africa's exports of the likely entry of Britain into the Common Market, Diederichs was, if anything, more obdurate than Norval in his refusal to bow to Conference pressure for a general increase in Northbound rates.[106] On 26 April, Austin cabled to London that Norval was now prepared to 'make some gesture' to the Lines, but Diederichs would not approve it.[107]

Despite the outrage of the Lines, they were on weak ground: weak in principle and weak in fact. There was no doubt that the government was entitled to refuse a Northbound increase under the Revised Pretoria Formula and—Conference bluster notwithstanding—it was perfectly obvious that there could be no other ground for this than the 'exigencies of the country's economy'. Furthermore, the vagueness of the time period over which the Lines were promised their 5 per cent—'over the complete [trade] cycle or cycles'[108]—made it child's play for Norval to maintain that the absence of a Northbound increase at this juncture did not necessarily jeopardize the eventual earning of the agreed level of return on capital.

Thus weak in principle, the Lines were also weak in fact because of the world surplus of shipping which had existed since the end of the 1950s. This meant that Dr Norval could threaten the Lines with resort to outside tonnage for the fruit trade more plausibly than he had been able to do in 1954–5—and he did. 'Dr Norval', complained Sir Nicholas Cayzer to the PPECB, 'had even said that the Lines could take it that the present contractual ships would not be needed any more. This', he said, employing a metaphor to savour, 'left the Lines in the air.'[109]

At the subsequent Joint Meeting in May, Bevan had to report that the Conference was 'faced with a serious situation and an apparent deadlock'.[110] Nor did further lobbying in the following month produce anything to render this description less apposite. Though the Conference Chairman found Kotzenberg, the Secretary for Commerce, more sympathetic, Diederichs would not shift[111] and Norval remained 'unyieldingly obstinate'.[112]

---

[106] CACT, Diederichs to Bevan, 21 Feb., and 3 May 1962.   [107] CACT.

[108] My emphasis; see Appendix VII.

[109] CACT, Notes on Meeting between PPECB and Representatives of Union-Castle, Clan, and Transatlantic Lines held in Cape Town at 11.50 a.m. on Fri. 9 Feb. 1962.

[110] CAL, Joint Meeting Minutes, 25 May 1962.

[111] CAL, Brief Notes of Conference Chairman's Interviews: Dr Diederichs (London, 19 June 1962).   [112] Ibid.: Dr Norval (Pretoria, 22 June 1962).

Recording his interview with Dr Norval in Pretoria on 22 June, Bevan said that the Chairman of the Shipping Board was 'obsessed', *inter alia*, 'with the consequences of E.C.M. [the EEC] on South African exports, with the inflation and Communism which continually press for wage increases in Britain . . . and with the necessity for costs generally to come down. I tried', lamented Bevan,

to get him down to earth by stating that ships were not even earning their depreciation today and he re-iterated that ships would not need to earn depreciation as some of them would not be replaced . . . He re-iterated that we should put up individual items for consideration but he rejected everyone I casually mentioned . . . Whilst he agrees . . . that in two or three months conditions of Britain's entry into E.C.M. will be known, he thinks it will take a year or two to see how it will work out for South Africa, and he could hold out no hope of a general increase of Freight Rates before then.

'I am sorry to say', concluded Bevan, 'that objective discussion with Dr Norval is now practically impossible, even tête-à-tête.'[113]

As if relations between the Conference and the Shipping Board were not already bad enough, by October 1962 the confrontation had broadened as a result of something which had not been seen in the South Africa trade since the late 1940s: the intrusion of 'outsiders', that is to say, liner companies operating in opposition to the Conference. The addition of outsiders to the existing competition from tramps and charters (already at a worrying level because of the world surplus of ships which, against the long-term trend, had shot up sharply in late 1962[114]) was of particular concern to the Lines for two reasons. In the first place, the lines concerned—Polish Ocean Lines (POL) of Warsaw and Deutsche Seereederei (DSR) of Rostock in East Germany—originated from the Soviet bloc and were thus thought to be relatively immune to merely *commercial* retaliation. In the second place, the South African Conference had comparatively few means of commercial retaliation in its armoury anyway. It had (except in Southern Mozambique) no deferred rebates, and in the Southbound trade it did not even have a contract system ('dual rating'). Moreover, despite the 'flexibility' in fixing freight rates apparently granted in the Revised Pretoria Formula, the Conference delegation to the Annual Conference in February had been forced to accept Norval's demand that the Lines could not even introduce 'fighting rates' in the

---

[113] Ibid.
[114] Committee of Inquiry into Shipping, Cmnd. 4337, May 1970 ('The Rochdale Report'), para. 76.

Southbound trade without first seeking the Shipping Board's permission *in each individual case*;[115] in practice, freedom to 'adjust' Southbound rates only meant freedom to *increase* them. As a result, in early October the Conference Chairman led a small deputation to Dr Norval in an attempt to enlist his support against the outside lines.

Norval, however, turned a deaf ear, minimizing the size of the problem and rejecting each of the proposals put forward by the Conference deputation to counter the opposition. Dual rating, import permits stipulating exclusive support for the Conference, advance notice of the issue of import permits for large cargoes, *carte blanche* in the use of fighting rates, all were turned down. The most that he would concede was that if shipments by outsiders became substantial the Lines could come back to him. 'Our opinion', reported Bevan on this tense interview, 'is that Dr Norval is not interested in our problem and will not help us unless he must.'[116] Clearly, Norval was not at all unhappy to see competition to the Conference in the South Africa trade: this further weakened its position in demanding an increase in Northbound rates.

Faced with this attitude in Pretoria, the Lines had no alternative but to combat the outsiders with fighting rates, and hope that their introduction on individual items of cargo would receive the 'immediate and sympathetic attention' of the Shipping Board which Norval subsequently saw fit to promise them by way of consolation.[117] To implement these rates as speedily as possible it was decided that an 'Action Committee' would be created.[118]

It occurred to the Conference that, notwithstanding Norval's attitude, the political hostility between South Africa and the Soviet bloc might be exploited in order to encourage the government to adopt a tougher view towards the intrusion of POL and DSR. Accordingly, Bevan wrote to Diederichs in December and suggested that the Republic might consider taking 'political' as well as commercial action to meet this 'Communist economic penetration'.[119] Though Kotzenberg expressed sympathy informally,[120] no official response to this request was ever received, and in February 1963 the Conference Chairman

---

[115] CACT, Minutes of the Third Annual Shipping Conference, 6 Feb. 1962, 7 f.
[116] CAL, Note by Conference Chairman: Competition, 12 Oct. 1962.
[117] CAL, Norval to Bevan, 23 Oct. 1962.
[118] CAL, Joint Meeting Minutes, 19 Oct. 1962.
[119] CAL, South & East African Conference Lines, Joint Meeting Minutes, 15 Feb. 1963.
[120] Ibid.

had to report to a Joint Meeting of both the South and East African Lines that while 'both opposition lines were having difficulty in getting a foothold in the trades Southbound, there was some evidence that they were having some success in the Northbound direction'.[121] In the circumstances, the Lines decided to intensify the activities of the Action Committee, while at the same time keeping open the possibility of some sort of restrictive arrangement with POL, which, of the two Soviet bloc lines, had shown itself to be 'conference-minded'.[122]

As to what the Lines should do next in pursuit of their aim of a general increase in Northbound rates, there was some feeling at the Joint Meeting in October 1962 that they should press for the removal of Dr Norval, upon whom anathemas were generously heaped. Opposition to this proposal was led by Sir Nicholas Cayzer, however, who feared that such a demand might cause the government to close ranks behind the Shipping Board Chairman. This might lead to a breach in relations with the government which, in turn, he thought, would be 'the Lines' undoing'. In the light of this advice, and conscious of the influence on their bargaining position of the weak shipping market, the Lines decided instead to continue 'to press their case diplomatically'. To keep the pressure up, they also resolved to apply for immediate increases of 10 per cent on certain *selected* commodities in the Northbound trade,[123] and on 1 November they were allowed to introduce a 7½ per cent increase on citrus and deciduous fruit. Shortly afterwards, when it was learned that Britain's application to the Common Market had been blocked by General de Gaulle, and that in consequence this particular threat to South Africa's exports had been removed, the Lines raised their application for a *general* increase in the Northbound rates to 10 per cent.[124]

By the beginning of 1963 Sir Nicholas Cayzer could justifiably claim to have done a great deal for South Africa but not to have received much in return. He had doubled the size of South Africa's merchant marine, spent millions on new tonnage for the trade, and successfully contained the periodic calls within the Conference for a more aggressive line towards the government. To show for this he had a promise that the Mail Contract would be renewed and—after much

[121] Ibid.
[122] POL had in fact written to the Conference on 6 July 1962 requesting such an arrangement. For political reasons, it did not wish to become a full member of the Conference: CAL, South & East African Conferences, Notes of Special Meeting, 1 Aug. 1962.
[123] CAL, Joint Meeting Minutes, 19 Oct. 1962.   [124] Ibid., 15 Feb. 1963.

toing and froing—an assurance that the two fast cargo-liners which
were to be built for the mail service to please the South Africans would
receive the same priority in the Republic's harbours as the passenger-
carrying mail ships.[125] Freedom for the Lines in the fixing of
Southbound freight rates had also eventually been wrenched from the
government, but this had turned sour following Norval's exploitation
of the new arrangement to make the structure of freight rates an even
more useful tool of South African economic policy. It was perhaps
partly because they realized that they were in danger of alienating him,
that at this juncture the South Africans decided to do something
further for Sir Nicholas Cayzer.

The Renewal of the Mail Contract

Ever since 1956 the South African government had refused to see the
need for an accelerated mail service, to the great chagrin of Sir
Nicholas, whose uncle, Lord Rotherwick, had more or less committed
Union-Castle to a faster service by injecting a vast capital sum into the
building of bigger and faster ships. In February 1963, however,
Union-Castle announced that the mail service would shortly operate
on an 11½-rather than a 13½-day schedule, using seven vessels
rather than eight.[126] Clearly the government—perhaps impressed by
the Company's argument that speed was of increasing economic
importance since the savings in crew costs were now greater than the
cost of increased fuel consumption—had given way. It was at this
point, too, that the need to make a decision on ordering the proposed
cargo-liners led Union-Castle to press for the start of negotiations on
the new Mail Contract.[127] The government acceded to this and a new
Contract was signed on 16 May.

The amicability of the Mail Contract negotiations was reminiscent
of the days of Smuts and Sir Vernon Thomson, partly no doubt
because Norval played no direct role in them. The two main issues
were the size of the subsidy and the registration in South Africa of
further Union-Castle vessels. Sir Nicholas Cayzer asked for a
'reasonable increase' in the annual subsidy in the light of his great

---

[125] A request for priority for these vessels was initially denied by Schoeman, the
Minister of Transport: Cayz. H., U-C DM, 6 Mar. 1962, min. 12070, and 1 Nov. 1962,
min. 12196.
[126] *Fairplay*, 28 Feb. 1963.
[127] Cayz. H., U-C DM, 27 Mar. 1963, min. 12255.

expenditure on new tonnage, though the government thought that a reduction was more in order since mail carryings were declining; this facilitated a compromise on the status quo, £400,000 a year. (In April 1971 the subsidy—by then being reckoned at R800,000—was increased to R1,162,000 on condition that no further increase would be sought during the period of the contract.[128]) To the government's request that his Company should register further vessels in South Africa, Sir Nicholas replied that the Republic's departure from the Commonwealth in 1961 had made this legally impossible. Nevertheless, he undertook to consider accomplishing it through a South African subsidiary. The new Mail Contract also provided, as already agreed, that the voyage time between Southampton and Table Bay would be reduced from 13½ to 11½ days. In other respects the new Contract remained essentially the same as its predecessor; in particular, the escape clause, which had been insisted upon by Sir George Christopher and which completely undermined the legal security of the mail line, was retained.[129] Nevertheless, Sir Nicholas was 'very pleased at the way things had gone',[130] and parliamentary ratification was a mere formality. Having lopped a year off the existing Contract, the new Mail Contract would start on 1 January 1966 and run until the end of 1976, that is to say, for eleven years.

Perhaps Sir Nicholas's pleasure at the conclusion of the Mail Contract negotiations was influenced by another consideration. By securing the Contract *before* negotiations for a new OFA (the current one was due to expire at the end of 1966), he had weakened the traditional 'linkage' between the two contracts, that is to say, the ability of the government to extract better terms in the OFA by providing a quid pro quo (to Union-Castle) through the Mail Contract. Sir Nicholas had not destroyed this linkage altogether, of course, because the escape clause in the Mail Contract meant that, *in extremis*, the government could use the threat of termination on twelve months' notice during any future OFA negotiations.

The Settlement of the Northbound Freight Rates Crisis

Sir Nicholas may have been pleased that Union-Castle had retained its hold on the Mail Contract, but neither he nor any other Principal in

[128] CACT, Postmaster General to U-C Cape Town Manager, 15 Apr. 1971.
[129] Cayz. H., U-C DM, 30 May 1963, min. 12285.
[130] Ibid., 27 Mar. 1963, min. 12255.

the Conference was happy at the South African government's continuing refusal to grant an increase in Northbound freight rates. Relentless pressure from the Conference had succeeded in doing nothing more than transforming a routine stalling operation into a virtuoso procrastination.

In June 1963, by which time it was eighteen months since the Conference application was first made (at the Triennial Review), the Lines learned that Diederichs was sympathetic to an 'interim' offer of 5 per cent. There would be certain unspecified exceptions to this, and the increase would embrace Southbound as well as Northbound rates (note the use of obtuseness in procrastination: under the Revised Pretoria Formula the Conference did not need government approval to make increases in *Southbound* rates). The offer would also require Cabinet approval.[131]

In the absence of anything better, the Lines agreed to accept the 'interim' offer, only to be informed in July that not only was this conditional on Cabinet approval, but also upon the provision of fresh information, since the cost data on which the original application was based was now out of date![132] This information was reluctantly provided, and at the Joint Meeting in October—while the government reaction was still awaited—consideration was given to the Lines' tactics in the event of an unfavourable decision. John Bevan was in favour of the despatch of 'a high-level delegation', and there was serious discussion of whether or not the issue should be taken to arbitration under the terms of the OFA.[133]

By the end of 1963, however, circumstances had changed, and it did not prove necessary for the Lines to take drastic action. For one thing, the bargaining position of the Conference had been greatly improved. The freight market had strengthened generally, and the Lines were able to claim that they were on the upswing of the trade cycle and thus entitled to increases of up to 10 per cent under the Revised Pretoria Formula. It was difficult for Diederichs to resist this, since he was recently on record as stating that 'the upward phase of the trade cycle which had been in evidence during the past two years was continuing strongly and had recently shown signs of growing strength'.[134] Furthermore, both POL and DSR—responding indirectly to UN

---

[131] CAL, Joint Meeting Minutes, 7 June 1963.
[132] Ibid., 25 Oct. 1963.
[133] Ibid.
[134] *Business Bulletin* (South African), Nov. 1963.

pressure for an economic boycott of South Africa—had withdrawn from the trade in the final months of the year.[135] If by the end of 1963 the Conference was in a stronger position to push for an increase in Northbound rates, the government had less reason to oppose it. South Africa's balance of payments crisis was now well behind it and, as a result, the government was less anxious to preserve the discrepancy between Northbound and Southbound rates.[136] In these new circumstances, therefore, the Lines eventually won their Northbound increase; but not without further difficulty. Indeed, Norval declined to recommend acceptance of their case on the basis of the new cost data, and Diederichs backed him up. Nevertheless, the Minister of Economic Affairs indicated that he was prepared to receive a Conference delegation on 20 January 1964.

After four gruelling sessions, which lasted until late in the night of 21 January and 'witnessed a particularly antagonistic and histrionic . . . performance by Dr Norval', Diederichs was persuaded to change his mind. The Conference delegation returned to London with a general Northbound increase of 7½ per cent from 1 April (though there were four important exceptions), which also enabled 'the brake to be released on the announcement of a Southbound increase in rates, and on increases in other spheres which were of greater value to the Lines'.[137] Shortly afterwards an announcement was made that Southbound rates were to be increased by 10 per cent.[138] The Lines, said John Bevan, had taken 'a step in the right direction . . . without impairment of their good relations with the South African Government'.[139] So ended the most serious threat to those relations since Dr Norval had brandished the Shipping Board Bill at the Conference in 1955.

[135] CAL, Joint Meeting Minutes, 25 Oct. 1963; and *Fairplay*, 21 Nov. 1963.
[136] Houghton, 179.
[137] CAL, Joint Meeting Minutes, 21 Feb. 1964.
[138] According to Bevan, this would generate an extra £700,000 a year for the B & C Group, compared to a mere £200,000 a year extra from the (slightly smaller) Northbound increase: Cayz. H., U-C DM, 29 Jan. 1964, min. 12384.
[139] CAL, Joint Meeting Minutes, 21 Feb. 1964.

4

SANCTIONS AND SOVEREIGNTY
1964–1966

As if the existing agenda for discussions between the Lines and the South African government was not already full enough, further items were added to it by the government in the mid-1960s which amounted to a bid for control over the Conference's internal affairs every bit as serious as that contained in the aborted Shipping Board Bill a decade earlier. This new threat to the internal sovereignty of the Lines was prompted partly by the government's fear of the growing campaign for economic sanctions to force South Africa to abandon apartheid, and partly by commercial considerations encouraged by developments in the international world of shipping.

African calls for the economic boycott of South Africa had started shortly before the Sharpeville shootings in 1960, and had become louder with each passing year.[1] In early 1964 they were intensified by a threat from the Organization of African Unity (OAU) of an all-Africa ban on aircraft and ships trading with the Republic.[2] Fearing political and economic reprisals, the attentiveness of the world to Africa's demands increased. In 1962 the UN General Assembly had asked its members 'to break off diplomatic relations with South Africa, close their ports to South African shipping and their airports to South African aircraft, prevent their own ships from calling at South African ports, boycott all South African products and suspend exports to South Africa'. In August 1963 the Security Council, while rejecting the call for a total economic boycott of the Republic, had nevertheless called for a total—if non-mandatory—arms embargo against it, which was supported by the United States and given qualified support by the United Kingdom as well. In the following June the Security Council appointed a committee to investigate the feasibility of applying economic sanctions against South Africa, while later in 1964 the newly

[1] J. Barber, *South Africa's Foreign Policy, 1945–1970* (London, 1973), 144.
[2] *The Times*, 2 Mar. 1964.

elected Labour government in Britain followed the example of the Americans by introducing a total arms embargo.

It is true that by 1965 the failure of the campaign to persuade South Africa's major trading partners to apply economic sanctions against the Republic, coupled, *inter alia*, with the remarkable growth which its economy was now enjoying, had done much to restore South African confidence. However, the judgement of the International Court of Justice on South Africa's administration of South-West Africa was now imminent and was not expected to favour the Republic. Furthermore, economic sanctions were introduced against Rhodesia following UDI on 11 November, thus bringing the spotlight back to racial oppression in Southern Africa, creating a precedent for sanctions, and causing many to feel that the downfall of Ian Smith—let alone the ending of apartheid and South African control of South-West Africa—required the extension of sanctions to South Africa, by far his most important supporter.[3] In short, by late 1965 the threat of economic sanctions against South Africa had to be taken seriously once more.

Developments which would have a significant bearing on relations between the South African Conference and Pretoria were also occurring in the international shipping world. Believing—like the South Africans—that high freight rates in the liner trades were impeding their exports, and anxious to remove obstacles to the development of national merchant marines, the underdeveloped countries were currently in the process of launching a major campaign for the reform of the liner conference system. Following UNCTAD I in 1964, a permanent UNCTAD Committee on Shipping was established and held its first meeting in November 1965.[4] Since the early 1960s there had also been a reawakening of anti-conference sentiment in the United States.[5] In short, the first half of this decade witnessed the appearance of a double challenge to the liberal international shipping regime which, under West European dominance, had prevailed since the end of the Second World War.[6] Government interference in shipping—whether designed to destroy closed conferences altogether,

[3] Barber, *South Africa's Foreign Policy*, 175–80.
[4] L. Juda, *The UNCTAD Liner Code: United States Maritime Policy at the Crossroads* (Boulder, Colo., 1983), 4.
[5] A. W. Cafruny, 'The Political Economy of International Shipping: Europe versus America', *International Organization*, 39.1, Winter 1985.
[6] The best general account of this double challenge is provided in the excellent article by Cafruny, ibid.

as the Americans wished, or to make them suit protectionist ends, as the UNCTAD countries were to prefer—was on the increase.

Neither the Council of European National Shipowners' Associations (CENSA) nor their governments, it is true, adopted a supine attitude in the face of these threats. Believing that if government regulation of the liner trades was to be forestalled, or at least kept to a minimum, their *self-regulation* would have to be demonstrably improved, the shipowners had cultivated the national shippers' councils which had been springing up in Western Europe since the mid-1950s with a view to achieving agreement on formal procedures for consultation and the settlement of disputes which would serve as a model for the world as a whole. In March 1963 a Note of Understanding governing the relations between CENSA and the European National Shippers' Councils (ESC) was endorsed by the governments of the ten Western European maritime powers.[7] Nevertheless, this was clearly a rearguard action and did little to counter the encouragement which South Africa drew from UNCTAD thinking on shipping, which was almost identical to its own.

The threat of economic sanctions against South Africa and the growing challenge from UNCTAD to the CENSA/ESC approach to the regulation of the liner trades, thus provided the international backdrop to negotiations between the Conference and the South African government over the next few years. Having said this, there was little alarm in the Conference itself at the threat of an all-Africa ban on ships trading to South Africa made by the OAU Foreign Ministers in early 1964, because the Lines were convinced that their own governments would prevent it from materializing—as it turned out, with good reason.[8] Nor do they seem to have been worried that a general economic boycott of South Africa would ever be supported by the Western powers. Member lines were left to lobby their own governments as they saw fit, and the general issue was never discussed in a Joint Meeting. What was exercising the Conference instead in 1964 was whether or not it was in the interests of the Lines to negotiate a new OFA, and, if so, what shape a new one should assume. Here, developments in the high politics of international shipping began to have an impact. Before this question is investigated, however, it is necessary to consider the evolution of the alliance between B & C

[7] The Rochdale Report (Comittee of Inquiry into Shipping: Report, Cmnd. 4337, May 1970), paras. 394–7.
[8] CAL, Joint Meeting Minutes, 25 June 1964.

and Safmarine which had been launched following the merger of the national line with Springbok in 1961.

The Strengthening of the B & C–Safmarine Alliance

Following the merger with Springbok, Sir Nicholas Cayzer had agreed that Safmarine should enter the fruit trade. Safmarine seems to have thought that he had also agreed to any expansion in this trade being catered for by extra Safmarine ships, thus providing a 'natural method' by which the national line might grow. When, in the course of 1964, it emerged that B & C was building four new ships for the reefer trade, Safmarine was therefore annoyed, particularly since Sir Nicholas had omitted to consult it on the matter. This hiccup in B & C–Safmarine relations was the subject of an important conference between the two companies at Cayzer House on 10 November 1964.[9]

The Cayzer House conference was amicable and productive. In effect Sir Nicholas Cayzer conceded the future of the fruit trade to Safmarine, and also expressed sympathy with its perennial complaint about the allocation of sailing rights in the trade.[10] In return, Safmarine promised to use its influence with the government and the IDC to secure more protection for the Conference against outsiders, to join forces with B & C in the preparation of the Conference case to be presented at the negotiations which had since been scheduled for revision of the OFA, to hold annual discussions with B & C to discuss matters of common interest at both management and technical levels, and—not least—to support another B & C man, A. E. Lemon (Deputy Conference Chairman since October 1963), as next Conference Chairman upon the imminent retirement of John Bevan. Safmarine, said its Managing Director, 'had a common interest with B & C in the South African trade and . . . [would] . . . work in the closest harmony and in co-operation with B & C in furthering the interest of the . . . trade'.

The readiness with which Sir Nicholas Cayzer conceded the future of the fruit trade to Safmarine was conclusive evidence of his gradual withdrawal from *direct* involvement in South African shipping. This policy had been adopted not only because of the government-backed

[9] The following account is based on CAL, Notes of meeting held in the Board Room of Cayzer House—Tue., 10 Nov. 1964.

[10] This had surfaced again because of recent negotiations between the Holland-Afrika Lijn, DOAL, and SALines which had been based—to the disgust of Safmarine—on the historically acquired 'unlimited rights' of the Holland-Afrika Lijn.

determination of Safmarine to obtain a major share of the trade in general, but also because the recent appearance of new techniques in shipping ('the container revolution') had led him to believe that major investment in new *conventional* tonnage was unwise.[11] In 1965, following a threat of competition in the passenger traffic from the newly formed company South African Passenger Shipping, which advertised its intention to run the first passenger-line to Europe under the South African flag and was supported by the Afrikaner insurance combine SANLAM,[12] even more startling evidence both of B & C's withdrawal from direct involvement in South African shipping and the further strengthening of its alliance with Safmarine was provided: Safmarine was to take over three-sevenths of the accelerated mail service. The *Transvaal Castle* and the *Pretoria Castle* were to be sold to Safmarine at the end of 1965, while the national line would be responsible for replacing both the *Pretoria Castle* and the *Edinburgh Castle* at about the end of 1972. Safmarine would be allowed to pay for the two mail ships already in service by instalments over a ten-year period and, in the meantime, 'bareboat' them back to Union-Castle, which would continue to manage them as before. As part of the agreement, Union-Castle also undertook to train Safmarine personnel against the day when the South Africans would run the vessels entirely on their own.[13]

Under this latest agreement between B & C and Safmarine, the *Transvaal Castle* was subsequently renamed the *SA Vaal* and the *Pretoria Castle* the *SA Oranje*. On 1 June 1966 Castlemarine (Pty) Ltd., created by Union-Castle and Safmarine to take over all passenger booking for mail ships and other passenger vessels owned by Union-Castle, came into operation.[14] Safmarine was now well and truly part of the mail service, and Sir Nicholas Cayzer had more shares in the favoured national line.[15]

---

[11] Information supplied to the author (indirectly) by A. E. Lemon.
[12] *The Times*, 14 May 1965.
[13] Cayz. H., U-C DM, 24 Nov. 1965, min. 12664.
[14] Ibid., 13 Apr. 1966, min. 12731.
[15] B & C took up its entitlement of £1,539,000 in the new rights issue of shares made by Safmarine to fund its recent expansion, thus retaining its 48% holding. Shortly afterwards, however, B & C was required to reduce this to 38.5% as the result of the flotation of 20% of Safmarine stock to the South African public: ibid., 24 Nov. 1965, min. 12664.

Drawing the Battle-lines for the OFA Negotiations

While Sir Nicholas Cayzer had been busy strengthening his alliance with Safmarine, the battle-lines were being drawn for a major set-piece negotiation on the revision of the current Ocean Freight Agreement. Shortly after the negotiations in January 1964 which had ended the Northbound freight rates crisis, Bevan had learned from Diederichs and Kotzenberg that the government itself had overcome any doubts it may have had about the need for a new OFA (in an aberrant moment in 1962 Kotzenberg had asked Bevan why the OFA was needed).[16] The South Africans had also suggested that it should be negotiated at the same time as the next Triennial Review of freight rates, in October 1965.[17]

As it happened, at the beginning of 1964 some thought had also been given in the Conference Chairman's office to the question of the need for a new OFA. In a brief written for Bevan, probably by A. E. Lemon, it was maintained that while the restrictions imposed on the Lines by the OFA remained as onerous as ever, the advantages had diminished. In particular, since imports of government cargo had dwindled to no more than a trickle, the monopoly on its conveyance was no longer worth having, while the Pretoria Formula—child of the rate restrictions in the OFA if not itself part of the OFA—had 'proved unworkable through ex parte interpretation on the Government side'. If, as the Lines would prefer, negotiations on perishables were taken out of the OFA and conducted exclusively with the PPECB[18] (which had 'always' been found 'more reasonable than the Shipping Board'), there would be little left for the Lines in the Agreement. On the other hand, if the Conference declined to enter into the new OFA, the government would be likely to preserve and possibly extend its control over freight rates through 'a more stringent Shipping Board Bill', and the door would also be opened to further flag discrimination by the government. (Discrimination in favour of South African flag vessels by the government was not explicitly prohibited under the OFA, but the Lines held that such prohibition was implicit, and this had been accepted by the government. However, in the 1961–2 period the semi-

---

[16] CAL, Brief Notes of Conference Chairman's Interviews: Mr Kotzenberg (Pretoria, 21 June 1962).

[17] CAL, Joint Meeting Minutes, 25 June 1964.

[18] Under the existing arrangement the Lines only negotiated with the PPECB about quantities of fruit in excess of OFA specifications. For the rest, it had to negotiate with the Shipping Board.

state corporations ISCOR, Vecor, IDC, and Escom had instituted a policy of flag discrimination, and Norval had given the most evasive replies when challenged on this by the Conference.[19]) An aggressive government reaction on freight rates and flag discrimination would be more likely in view of the existing world trend towards greater government intervention in the affairs of shipping conferences. Consequently, Bevan was advised, the Lines should seek a new OFA 'on the principle that the Devil one knows is better than the Devil one does not', but press in particular for a better method of adjusting freight rates in the future.[20]

This conclusion was sound, and when the question of a new OFA was put to the Conference in June 1964 Bevan had no difficulty in securing its adoption, despite the fact that the government wanted further information on the confidential domestic arrangements of the Conference and financial data on a more representative group of lines.[21] The Lines consoled themselves with the thought that Dr Norval was on his way out (a development which was perhaps not entirely unconnected with the fact that Sir Nicholas Cayzer had informed Diederichs that he would never negotiate with him again[22]), and that a good relationship had now been established with Diederichs and with Kotzenberg, the Minister's senior civil servant.[23]

On 29 March 1965 exploratory discussions on the OFA were held in Cape Town between Bevan, who was accompanied by A. E. Lemon, and Kotzenberg, who was supported by his own deputy, G. J. J. F. Steyn. (Norval had duly retired and had been replaced as Chairman of the Shipping Board by the Deputy Secretary of Finance, J. J. Kitshoff; the latter, however, was not yet in post.) Following this meeting, both sides set out their maximum demands.

The position of the Lines was stated in a Memorandum from Bevan to Kotzenberg despatched on 27 April.[24] This emphasized the necessity for Northbound rates to carry their fair share of the burden, and asked for all remaining restrictions on the Lines' ability to adjust

[19] CACT, Minutes of the Third Annual Shipping Conference, 12 f.
[20] CAL, Confidential Brief for J. S. Bevan, Esq., for Freight Rate Negotiations Capetown, 20–22 Jan. 1964.
[21] CAL, Joint Meeting Minutes, 21 Feb. 1964.
[22] CAL, Notes of Meeting Held in Office of Secretary for Commerce & Industries, Marks Buildings, Parliament Street, Cape Town, at 10.00 a.m. on 7 Feb. 1966. The view of A. E. Lemon (indirectly communicated to the author) is that Sir Nicholas Cayzer was in fact responsible for having Norval 'removed'.
[23] CAL, Joint Meeting Minutes, 25 June 1964.   [24] CAL.

Southbound rates to be removed. It asked for freedom to deal directly with shippers of all Northbound traffic (especially the fruit interests), and also for 'security of tenure to create the conditions under which they can perform their part of the Contract'. It indicated a willingness to continue with a 'Formula system' for fixing freight rates, but made it clear that the present one would have to be changed considerably: instead of basing this on the figures of selected individual lines (which had allowed Norval to play one line off against another, that is to say, Union-Castle against the rest), the Lines wanted to 'submit their figures in an agglomerated form through the medium of independent Chartered Accountants'; instead of 5 per cent on replacement costs the Lines wanted a 10 per cent return on their capital, based (since ships were no longer so costly to replace) on written-down *historic* cost; and instead of freight rate increases being acts of grace granted with prior regard to the South African economy rather than to the Pretoria Formula, the Lines demanded that they should be introduced 'automatically', so as to generate the returns stipulated in the Formula.

In May the thoughts of the South Africans on the new OFA were received in the shape of a letter from the Secretary for Commerce.[25] This made it clear that, far from being induced by a bout of post-Norval guilt to fall in with the Lines' request for more freedom, the government intended to secure the captivity of the South African Conference even more firmly. What was also evident was that there was now a strong *political*, as well as economic, motive behind the government's attitude. Indeed, faced with the threat of an international economic boycott and even interruptions to traditional shipping services, the government was obviously anxious to ensure that arrangements with the Conference should not place any obstacles in the way of the precautionary measures it was now taking in the shipping and commercial spheres; these included expansion of the national fleet and diversification of the country's overseas trade. Equally apparent was the government's desire to ensure that future arrangements with the Conference would increase its ability to employ economic power in high diplomacy.

It was against this background, then, that Kotzenberg stated that 'any new Ocean Freight Agreement should provide adequate scope for increased South African participation', and further indicated Diederichs's particular wish 'to see more flexible arrangements introduced with

[25] CAL, Kotzenberg to Bevan, 7 May 1965.

regard to the respective shares in this trade of the individual non-South African Lines, the idea being that the government should be able in exceptional circumstances to arrange with the Lines that the share of a particular Line be adjusted in order to meet new situations which may arise'. Consequently, he also wanted full knowledge of the Lines' Agreements (withheld in 1955), and information on how new members were admitted to the Conference. For good measure, he indicated that the government wanted to reassume total control over freight rates (including Northbound contract rates), and thus retrieve from the Lines the limited freedom which they had won under the Revised Pretoria Formula. As to the other issues raised by the Lines in the April Memorandum, Kotzenberg was vague, guarded, or openly opposed. Altogether, this amounted to a take-over bid for the Conference which was every bit as comprehensive as that made in the Shipping Board Bill of 1955.

The Conference Chairman, John Bevan, was naturally alarmed by the government's attitude, and had no illusions about the political impulse behind its demand for control over market shares in the trade. In his notes he wrote that 'the Government may wish to be able to bring pressure to bear upon individual foreign Governments by discriminating against Lines operated by their respective nationals'.[26] This suspicion was widely held in the Conference, not least by Safmarine. In a B & C/Safmarine conference on 19 May, a Safmarine representative stated that the government was 'probably thinking of closer connections with the Portuguese, French and possibly the Italians',[27] while at a Conference meeting at the end of the month the Safmarine Chairman said that the government was trying to find out if it could exploit the Conference in order to 'stimulate' the friendship of countries such as France and Italy which were inclined to be scornful of the UN arms embargo. Interestingly enough, he stated firmly that this should be opposed.[28] Encouraged by the Safmarine attitude, the Lines determined to resist any attempt on the part of the government to use the Conference as an instrument of its foreign policy: it was wrong in principle and clearly threatened the position of the existing lines in the trade.

---

[26] CAL, Notes by the Conference Chairman on Mr Kotzenberg's letter of 7 May 1965.
[27] CAL, Note of Private discussion held in the Board Room, 4 St Mary Axe, London EC3, at 10.00 a.m. on Wed. 19 May 1965.
[28] CAL, Notes of a Special Meeting of a Principal of each Line, 28 May 1965.

Even more threatening to the security of tenure of the Lines was the government proposal for increased South African flag participation in the trade, the eventual target for which was known to be 50 per cent of total sailings, even though Kotzenberg had conceded that it would take between twenty-five and fifty years to achieve.[29] Conference feeling on this was that while a gradual increase in South African participation could not be resisted, safeguards should be sought against non-South African lines seeking to use the South African flag as a way of breaking into the trade. Once more, encouragement was drawn from the attitude of Safmarine and SALines, both of which expressed the view that increased South African participation should only occur in proportion to growth in the size of the trade; in other words, the existing interests of non-South African lines should not be impaired.[30]

On the remaining matters the Lines decided to stand firm and, pending the start of formal negotiations, to seek elucidation of Kotzenberg's views in a further tête-à-tête. Consequently, Bevan and Lemon flew out to the Republic again and interviewed Kotzenberg in Cape Town on 8 June.

Kotzenberg confirmed the government's anxiety over the possibility of an economic boycott and indicated its intention to pursue greater trade diversification. As the Lines suspected, it wanted control of the Conference so that it could retaliate against the shipping of those countries which boycotted South Africa (the Transatlantic Lines of Sweden, for example),[31] and reward the lines of friendly countries with additional sailing rights. Kotzenberg also restated his determination to have the figures of individual lines and not to be satisfied with 'agglomerated' ones. Nevertheless, Bevan was relieved to find that the Secretary for Commerce was prepared to back down from his demand for a reassertion of full government control over Southbound freight rates, and Northbound contract rates as well. Since useful clarification on other matters had also been achieved and the whole interview had taken place in a 'very friendly and pleasant' atmosphere,[32] the Conference Chairman felt that the incipient crisis portended by Kotzenberg's letter of 7 May had been averted. The formal

---

[29] CAL, Private notes by the Conference Chairman: OCEAN FREIGHT AGREEMENT, Kotzenberg's letter of 7 May 1965 (24 May 1965).

[30] CAL, Notes of a Special Meeting of a Principal of each Line, 28 May 1965.

[31] CAL, Bevan to Sir Nicholas Cayzer, 8 June 1965; and Conference note, 10 June 1965.

[32] CAL, Report of Discussion between Mr Kotzenberg and Messrs Bevan, Lemon, and Austin in Cape Town on 8 June 1965.

negotiations would still be difficult and probably protracted—especially on the new Formula for freight rate changes and what Bevan called 'the boycott question'—but there was a fair prospect of eventual success. The negotiations would start in November and it was his hope that 'the broad terms' of the new OFA would be agreed by the end of the year.[33]

The OFA Negotiations: Thirty-three Meetings

In the event the negotiations for revision of the OFA turned out to be even more protracted than Bevan had envisaged, extending to three separate series and encompassing in all thirty-three minuted meetings. This was partly because the South Africans had things on their minds which they had not yet brought to the surface, and partly because some of the differences which Bevan thought had been smoothed over at the meeting on 8 June re-emerged. Thus the government insisted that provision should be made in the new Agreement for the shipment of armaments in national flag vessels, and the similar shipment of general cargo in the event of balance of payments difficulties, though the Lines, of course, were vehemently opposed to flag discrimination. The government also requested the regular provision of information on space utilization in Conference vessels, in order to put pressure on the Lines to deal with the over-tonnaging of the berth which was privately admitted in London. In this period of heightened hostility to black Africa, the government also needed to be convinced, for the first time, that the freight rates which it sanctioned did not include a hidden element designed to cover inefficiencies suffered by Conference vessels (especially in East Africa) *en route* to and from the Republic. And finally, the government resurrected its ambition of earlier in the year of being included in the negotiation of contract rates in the Northbound trade. Covering about 30 per cent of Northbound cargo (see Appendix X), contracts were regarded with suspicion by the government since any significant extension of their use (for which the Conference was pushing) could undermine its control of the cost of South Africa's exports.

The first series of negotiations on the new OFA involved ten meetings in Pretoria, starting on 8 November 1965 (three days before Rhodesia's UDI) and finishing on 18 November. The second, which

---

[33] CAL, Memorandum from the Conference Chairman, London, 14 June 1965.

took place in Cape Town between 31 January and 10 February 1966, stretched to an awesome sixteen sessions. The third and concluding series consisted of a mere seven sessions, for which the negotiators returned to Pretoria, where from 2 until 5 May the Conference team was again ensconced between meetings in its 'enclave' at the Boulevard Hotel. Altogether (including meetings with the PPECB), there were about seventy-six hours of formal negotiations, and a great many unofficial encounters between individual members of the two sides.

In view of the length and difficulty of the negotiations it is not surprising that there were occasions when both the Conference and government negotiators seemed pessimistic about ever reaching a final settlement, or, at least on the government side, contrived to give this impression for the sake of tactics. Bevan, of course, led for the Conference, while Kotzenberg—cunning and domineering, but also humorous and even a little flamboyant—was the dominant voice on the government side, even though he was dogged by ill health. Despite Lemon's attempts to stiffen him, Bevan was really no match for Kotzenberg.

The Conference had never seriously believed that it would win South African agreement to its main objective in these negotiations—an average 10 per cent return on capital—especially since the request for this was accompanied by a refusal to continue to supply the figures of individual lines upon which the government set such store. Such a target was unrealistic, since shipping had for some years been a notoriously poor investment, and Sir Nicholas Cayzer had informed the Conference that he would be happy with $7\frac{1}{2}$ per cent.[34] Nevertheless, for tactical reasons the Lines started out by demanding 10 per cent, complaining that, in the light of the risks involved, shipping's poor rate of return was unfair, and urging the government to give a lead to the world. This was naturally received with incomprehension by the government, but, realizing that it was the vital point for the Conference, Kotzenberg refused to be drawn definitively on the government attitude until the very end of the negotiations, thereby keeping Conference hopes alive and transforming the issue into an anvil upon which to beat out concession after concession from the Lines. This tactic was facilitated by Kotzenberg's assertion of control over the *order* in which agenda items should be taken.[35]

[34] CAL, Notes of a Special Meeting of a Principal of each Line, 26 Apr. 1965.
[35] CAL, Notes on Meeting at Forum Building, Pretoria, on Mon. 8 Nov. 1965, between Delegation from South African Conference Lines and Representatives of

By the end of the second series of negotiations, in mid-February 1966, it was fairly certain that a new OFA would be achieved, though it had taken some fast talking from Bevan and Sir Nicholas Cayzer to carry along the Continental Lines, who, in late November, had thought that South Africa's demands were so outrageous that the Lines should either break off negotiations or call in the assistance of CENSA.[36]

In the event, the Government had made concessions. It had accepted a fairly harmless document on the origins, composition, and operation of the Conference in place of the full details of the Lines' Agreements which it had originally demanded. While still insisting that the Conference should think again about a return of 10 per cent, the government had raised no serious objection to the substitution of written-down historic cost for replacement cost as the basis on which the return should be calculated. It had also promised to shorten the list of 'essential plant and raw material' in the Southbound trade for which the Lines needed government approval for freight rate increases. Above all, the government had shown an unprecedented willingness to support the conference *system* in the South Africa trade, giving earnest if rather vague assurances of co-operation against outsiders, and agreeing to exhort—if not compel—the statutory corporations to use the Conference exclusively. In the same connection, Kotzenberg had not objected to a suggestion from the Lines that dual rating (now miraculously considered defensible in terms of the Post Office Act, 1911)[37] should be introduced into the Southbound trade, and he had dropped his opposition to the contracts which already helped to tie shippers to the Conference in the Northbound trade. The spirit of the 1911 Post Office Act was by now entirely dead.

Encouraged by the government's attitudes on these questions— especially with regard to the defence of the Conference's general position astride the South Africa trade—and anticipating that the government would be more generous on the rate of return than had been thought originally, Bevan's team had also shown a willingness to compromise. In the face of implacable resistance by the government, the Lines had dropped their insistence that the agglomerated figures of all the Lines rather than the individual figures of selected lines should

South African Government, Commencing 10.00 a.m. (hereafter, '1st Meeting, 1st Series', etc.)

[36] CAL, Notes of Special Meeting of leading members of British and Continental Lines, 23 Nov. 1965.

[37] CAL, Kotzenberg to Bevan, 10 Feb. 1966.

be the sole basis of Formula calculations, and had agreed in future to supply *both* sets of statistics.[38] They would also supply figures on unused space in their vessels, even though they knew that this evidence would be used against them in future freight rate reviews.[39] The Lines would swallow flag discrimination not only for South African arms shipments and other goods of 'strategic' significance, but also if the government was faced with 'serious balance of payments difficulties'.[40] They would allow the government a veto on applications for membership of the Conference.[41] They would look favourably on applications for increased participation in the trade from 'bona fide'[42] South African shipping lines which were sponsored by the government. Having secured the government's agreement to 'the aim' of spreading the burden of future freight rate increases equally between the Northbound and Southbound trades, the Lines nevertheless conceded the government's right to urge differential treatment if it was felt that this was a requirement of the national economy.[43] Finally, faced with an apparent shortage of suitable independent accountants in the Republic, the Conference negotiators had dropped their insistence on the employment of such persons in the application of any new Formula.[44] At the Triennial Review of freight rates conducted at the end of this round of negotiations, the Lines also settled for a 'disappointing' increase in Northbound rates of only 5 per cent on general cargo and 7½ per cent on perishables, and—strikingly—fell in with a government suggestion that Southbound increases should also be limited to 5 per cent. (Though in view of these small increases

[38] CAL, Kotzenberg to Bevan, 22 Aug. 1966, Supporting Letters to be read in conjunction with OFA, 22 Aug. 1966.

[39] Ibid., Bevan to Kotzenberg.

[40] OFA, 22 Aug. 1966, Section D, cl. 1(b).   [41] Ibid., Section A.

[42] 'In considering whether or not a South African Shipping Line is a bona fide South African Shipping Line, the Government will be guided by, inter alia, the following factors: (*a*) to what extent the equity in the Shipping Line is beneficially owned in the Republic; (*b*) to what extent freights are paid in the Republic and profits are retained in the Republic; (*c*) whether or not the Headquarters are in the Republic; (*d*) to what extent the ships in use are registered in the Republic; (*e*) to what extent the ships registered in the Republic are manned by local citizens, if available; (*f*) to what extent the purchases of stores and supplies are made in the Republic; and (*g*) to what extent ship repairs and maintenance are entrusted to local concerns': CAL, Kotzenberg to Bevan, 22 Aug. 1966, Supporting Letters to be read in conjunction with OFA, 22 Aug. 1966.

[43] Ibid.

[44] The 'Schedule of Agreed Accounting Procedures for Operating Formula Arrangements' eventually spoke of the government and the Conference each having 'the *right* to appoint independent accountants', (my emphasis), which is, of course, hardly the same as having an obligation: ibid.

they had secured a promise of a further Freight Review in the first year of the new OFA.[45])

Despite all these concessions from the Lines, their delegation still had to return from South Africa in February 1966 without the government's agreement to a 10 per cent return on capital. Continuing government reluctance to accept this had been underlined by Dr Diederichs himself at the last meeting in the January–February talks, the only one which he attended. Certain difficulties also remained to be resolved with the PPECB, and although common ground had finally been achieved on the government's demand for a formal say in the allocation of sailing rights to non-South African lines, a suitable clause remained to be drafted.[46]

In early May the Conference delegation returned to South Africa for what proved to be the final round of negotiations for the new OFA. This time the discussions were not protracted. Still determined to keep the Lines in an accommodating mood by refusing to be drawn on the rate of return until the last moment, and given that some agreement had been reached on the allocation of sailing rights to non-South African lines at the end of the last series of talks, the South Africans used their control of the agenda to press first of all for a rapid conclusion to the latter issue.

The government had realized that its insistence on dictating *all* sailing rights in the South Africa trade had been demanding too much.[47] Since control of entry and allocation of market shares between member lines was the most important function of the Conference, the demand for authority over the rights of *non*-South African lines, in addition to the veto on new entrants and increased participation for 'bona fide' South African lines which the government had already been granted, was tantamount to a take-over bid. At his first appearance in the negotiations, near the end of the second series, Sir Nicholas Cayzer had accused the government of threatening the 'sovereignty' of the Lines, and had made it clear that he would not allow it.[48] At the first meeting in May, therefore, the South Africans reaffirmed their readiness to compromise on this point. They still wanted *influence* over the sailing rights of non-South African lines, and they wanted this to

---

[45] CAL, Joint Meeting Minutes, 18 Mar. 1966.
[46] 11th Meeting, 2nd Series (7 Feb. 1966).
[47] The extreme demand was made in the 6th Meeting, 1st Series (12 Nov. 1965), while the retreat was made at the 11th Meeting, 2nd Series (7 Feb. 1966).
[48] 11th Meeting, 2nd Series (7 Feb. 1966).

be formally recognized in the new OFA, but by this time they were prepared to forgo the insertion of a clause which would have transformed the Conference into nothing more than an administrative arm of their political and economic foreign policies. Having been assured that the government would not use this influence to introduce new lines into the Conference too quickly, Bevan dropped his opposition.[49]

So, satisfied on the question of what had come to be known as 'flexibility', the government negotiators at last revealed their hand on the central question of the Lines' rate of return. Following a rehearsal of positions on both sides—the Conference insisting that a target of 10 per cent was objectively necessary in order to keep capital in shipping, and the South Africans maintaining that this was well above the market price for shipping generally—the government eventually revealed that it was prepared to offer the Lines 7½ per cent. After a counter-proposal from Bevan of 9 per cent, further argument, and a recess for rumination, agreement was finally reached on 8 per cent.

The pressure was now on the PPECB to resolve its own differences with the Conference and thus remove the final obstacle to the achievement of a new OFA. Nevertheless, the Board remained firm in its refusal to grant the Lines the *complete* monopoly of the perishables trade which Bevan had sought, and the Conference delegation was forced to capitulate. The existing arrangement whereby the Lines were guaranteed the great bulk of the trade and first option on any excess was to be continued, although from now on the fruit industry would pay a premium rate for vessels which had to be ballasted out to South Africa for a quick turn-around at the peak of the season.[50]

The South African Conference had emerged from these seminal negotiations in 1965–6 with government agreement to a regime of freight rates designed to provide it with an annual average rate of return of 8 per cent *over the ten years of the OFA* (rather than over the trade cycle 'or cycles'). This was not bad at all, and was privately acknowledged as such within the Conference.[51] Freight Reviews under

[49] The agreed clause read as follows: 'In the event of the Government considering the Republic's foreign trade and trade relations with any individual country served by the South African Conference to be adversely affected by the South African Conference arrangements for sailings to such country, the Contractors undertake to afford the Government full opportunity for consultation. Both parties also undertake to give due consideration to any representations which either party may make to the other in such connection': OFA, 22 Aug. 1966, Section F, cl. 3.
[50] Ibid., Section E.   [51] CAL, Joint Meeting Minutes, 25 May 1966.

the new Formula were to be biennial rather than triennial. The Lines had also surfaced with the conference system in the trade under firmer government protection than at any time in its long history. However, the government had not given a cast-iron guarantee that the Lines would earn 8 per cent, and it had only warmed to the conference system because it had now won a position from which it could manipulate the Conference to serve the ends of national policy—political as well as economic. In short, just as Union-Castle had 'saved' itself at the end of 1955 by 'merging' with the Clan Line, so the South African Conference saved itself ten years later by co-opting the South African government. It was, of course, partly because the Conference did not wish to advertise the full extent of the compromises which it had been forced to make (especially on South African flag participation and the supply of figures on space utilization), and partly because the government was apprehensive of the domestic reaction to its own promises of support for the Conference, that the agreements bearing on these matters were largely excluded from the OFA (a public document) and confided instead to confidential 'Supporting Letters'.

The new Ocean Freight Agreement was formally signed on 2 August 1966, and in October, apart from some predictable special pleading, it passed through the House of Assembly with barely a murmur.[52] Many of the member lines of the Conference remained sceptical about the new Formula and about the government's promises of support for the Conference. Bevan placed his faith in its increased clarity and in the greater probity and pro-Conference views of the individuals with whom the Lines were now dealing in South Africa—Kotzenberg, Steyn (Kotzenberg's deputy), and Kitshoff, the new Chairman of the Shipping Board.[53] It remained to be seen whether this faith was well placed.

---

[52] *House of Assembly Debates*, c. 4669–74 (18 Oct. 1966).
[53] CAL, Joint Meeting Minutes, 18 Mar. 1966.

5

THE TESTING OF THE NEW ALLIANCE
1966–1968

THE period immediately following the renegotiation of the OFA in
1965–6 was inaugurated by clear evidence of the further strengthening
of white unity behind the National Party in the general election in
March 1966, the dismissal (albeit on a technicality) of the case against
South Africa's occupation of South-West Africa at the International
Court of Justice, and the replacement of Dr Verwoerd by John Vorster
following the former's assassination in September. Thereafter, the
South Africans continued to rebuild the confidence which had been so
badly shaken by the political and economic crises of the early 1960s.
Internal security remained firmly under control, the economy—assisted
by a major return of foreign capital—continued to grow at an enviable
rate, and the rapid increase in the Republic's military strength,
together with the patent ineffectiveness of the OAU, revealed South
Africa as the unambiguous 'great power' of the southern half of the
African continent. Exploiting these developments to the full, South
Africa's increasingly sophisticated propaganda machine stiffened the
West's reluctance to add to the anti-apartheid measures which it had
already adopted, and the possibility of economic sanctions—Rhodesia
notwithstanding—grew steadily more remote; certain Western states,
notably France, even ignored the UN arms embargo. As Barber has
said, 'The Years of Confidence' had come to displace 'The Years of
Crisis and Doubt'.[1]

However, while serious internal threats largely disappeared in the
second half of the 1960s, external ones, though certainly muted, did
not retreat to the same extent. The OAU maintained its hostility
towards South Africa, and in Rhodesia black nationalist guerrillas took
up arms against the Smith regime; in Portugal's colonies in Southern
Africa nationalist guerrillas stepped up efforts which dated back to the
beginning of the decade. It was in these circumstances that Pretoria

[1] J. Barber, *South Africa's Foreign Policy, 1945–1970* (London, 1973), titles to parts 4
and 3 respectively.

attempted to seize the initiative in Africa and extend its influence over the black states to the north. By dint of diplomacy supported by economic aid and technical assistance, as well as by the threat of force and the patent, if discreet, emergence of a military *entente* with Rhodesia and Portugal, South Africa's so-called 'outward-looking policy' sought above all to encourage a relationship between South Africa and the OAU which was based on *realpolitik* rather than *idealpolitik* and which was, therefore, given the discrepancy in their power, deferential to Pretoria. In the ex-High Commission Territories of Botswana, Lesotho, and Swaziland, in Malawi and, to a limited extent in Zambia, this policy met with some success.[2]

It was against this more propitious political and economic background that the South African Conference and the South African government approached the new undertakings of the OFA signed in 1966. Whether these undertakings would be honoured depended to some extent on the men who would play the leading roles in negotiations, and at the beginning of this period there were changes on both sides. On 1 September 1966, A. E. ('Ted') Lemon took over from John Bevan as Chairman of both the South and East African Conferences, while at the beginning of 1968 G. J. J. F. ('Gaby' or 'Joep') Steyn became Secretary for Commerce in place of Kotzenberg. Both remained in these offices until 1977, when they retired within six months of each other, and their personal relationship was to be of the greatest importance to harmony between the Conference and the government.

Lemon had joined the Clan Line in 1929 and worked in management for the Cayzers all of his life. At the time of his appointment to the Conference chairmanship he was Managing Director of both Clan and Union-Castle. He had a considerable grasp of the complexities of shipping, was single-minded of purpose, possessed exceptional energy, and was determined to adopt a tougher attitude than John Bevan in future negotiations with Pretoria. Unfortunately, he also subscribed to the still common view that conferences should conduct their affairs in intense secrecy, sometimes gave the impression that shippers should be seen but not heard, and was inclined to use rather old-fashioned language to describe non-conference shipping lines: at best these were 'outsiders', at worst 'pirates'. He also favoured that shippers' nightmare, the 'conference of

---

[2] Ibid., chaps. 11, 15, and 16; and K. W. Grundy, *Confrontation and Accommodation in Southern Africa: The Limits of Independence* (Berkeley, 1973), chaps. 2 and 7.

conferences'! In the changing climate of international shipping these latter dispositions were to lead the Conference into unnecessary difficulties.

Lemon's interlocutor, Steyn, was—despite a tendency detected by some to over-react in crises—a highly respected lifelong civil servant. He was, like Lemon, extremely hard-working, and he was a forceful speaker in English as well as Afrikaans. He had been Deputy Secretary for Commerce before he became Secretary in 1968, and in that capacity he had played a full role in the OFA negotiations in 1965–6. He was steeped in the thinking which had gone into the new OFA and frequently commented to Lemon on his personal determination to honour the government's part of the bargain and make the Agreement work; this came to be fully recognized by the Lines. Since the Conference–government relationship was extremely complex, and since Steyn lasted much longer than the Ministers who came and went over the next eleven years, his advice on matters relating to the OFA was normally decisive. However, though Steyn, like his immediate predecessor, Kotzenberg, was more approachable and far better disposed towards the Conference than Norval had been, he was certainly no push-over for Lemon. Moreover, as both South Africa's Price Controller and the bearer of 'particular responsibilities' for the assistance which South Africa was giving Rhodesia following UDI,[3] Steyn was sensitive both to inflationary pressures and to international politics. As a result, he was usually well briefed to take issue with Lemon if the Conference Chairman's proposals appeared indifferent to their effect on prices in the Republic, or if they seemed insufficiently attuned to South Africa's political needs.

Steyn and Lemon, who before long were on first-name terms, met on countless occasions before they both retired in 1977. They met formally and informally, in set-piece negotiations and tête-à-tête, normally in Pretoria or Cape Town but sometimes in London (including London Airport, if the need was urgent and Steyn happened to be changing planes there in the course of another mission), and at least once in Lisbon. When they saw eye to eye it was almost always possible for Lemon to carry their decision through the Joint Meeting and for Steyn to persuade his Minister and the Cabinet Committee on Economic Affairs to their point of view. It is not surprising, therefore, given the secrecy surrounding their discussions,

[3] D. Geldenhuys, *The Diplomacy of Isolation: South African Foreign Policy Making* (Johannesburg, 1984), 28.

and the fact that the balance of power between the Conference and the government was now even more clearly loaded in the government's favour, that within the trade Steyn should have come to be known as 'the high priest' and Lemon as 'his assistant', though this obviously did not do justice to the tenacity of the latter.[4]

Safmarine: Sailing Rights and 'Reappraisal'

The first of the parties to the new alliance now holding sway over the Europe–South Africa trade to have its undertakings in the OFA put to the test was the Conference. On 11 May 1966, only days after the conclusion of the final series of OFA negotiations, the Chairman of Safmarine wrote to Sir Nicholas Cayzer to solicit his support for both the doubling of Safmarine's rights in the trade and a reform of the system under which those rights were apportioned. It is not surprising that Safmarine should have linked these two issues, since its Agreement with the Conference had only been revised in 1963 and was of ten years' duration. Since this Agreement contained no 'break clause', in the absence of reform—and in spite of the provisions of the new OFA on increased 'participation' for bona fide South African shipping lines—Safmarine would remain committed to its existing rights until 1973.

What Bamford, the Safmarine Chairman, proposed to Sir Nicholas, therefore, was that there should be an end to the secrecy between lines about each other's rights, open discussion of the division of the trade in Joint Meetings, and a new set of ten-year Agreements for *all* lines; these would commence on 1 January 1967 and thus run concurrently with the new OFA.[5] Bamford made his formal application at the end of June, a month when, according to the *South African Shipping News*, the British seamen's strike was demonstrating 'more effectively than any previous development the value to the Republic of her own merchant marine'.[6] In it he asked for an increase in West Coast UK rights from eighteen Southbound and twelve Northbound to thirty in each direction (twenty-two after rationalization). Such an increase would give Safmarine a quarter of the West Coast trade instead of its existing share of 17 per cent, and also—in the estimation of its Chairman—make

---

[4] Quoted in 'A Survey on Shipping', Supplement to *Financial Mail*, 17 July 1981.
[5] CAL, Bamford to Cayzer, 11 May 1966.
[6] June 1966.

its application for an allocated berth in West Coast ports, which it had long coveted, difficult to resist.[7]

It seems clear that there was qualified sympathy in B & C and the Conference Chairman's office for the general thrust of the Safmarine application, and that this was not merely a reflection of the Cayzers' great financial interest in, and increasingly intimate relationship with the national line. Stability in the trade was regarded as of great—even prime—importance, and linking a new Safmarine Agreement on sailings to the ten-year period of the new OFA was a way of making it particularly difficult for the national line to demand premature revision again. In addition, there was a feeling that the Conference's system of allocating sailing rights was indeed anachronistic, and that the Safmarine application might provide an occasion for the complete reform which Bamford had been canvassing for some time. It was also feared that a flat 'no' to Safmarine might invite intervention from the South African government, and that in any case the famous 1904 Agreement itself provided a precedent for the alteration of a Conference Agreement before its full term had expired—albeit by mutual consent.[8]

However, these views about the Safmarine application were not shared by other leading lines in the Conference. Much feeling was expressed about the importance of the 'sanctity of agreements', particularly by those lines whose interests were intimately touched by Safmarine's demands. (Indeed, this seems to have contributed to a certain ambivalence in Sir Nicholas Cayzer's attitude, since his own Clan Line would be the one required to make the most sacrifices.[9]) Secondly, although the Safmarine fleet was now expanding rapidly,[10] it had recently been operating more chartered than owned vessels in order to implement its existing sailing rights, and it was felt that this was hardly consistent with the claim that even more rights were necessary for the expansion of the *national* fleet.[11] Thirdly, Safmarine had forfeited a certain amount of sympathy in the Conference as a result of its reputation for concentrating on the more lucrative Southbound trade and leaving the burden of carrying its own country's

---

[7] CAL, Bamford to Bevan, 30 June 1966.

[8] CAL, John Bevan, *Aide-mémoire* for Sir Nicholas Cayzer, Bt., Safmarine, 7 June 1966; and anon. memorandum headed 'This application will require most adroit handling', *c.* June 1966, and probably written by Bevan.

[9] Ibid. (*Aide-mémoire* . . .)

[10] *Fairplay*, 6 Jan. 1966; see also Appendix II.

[11] CAL, Bevan, *Aide-mémoire* for Sir Nicholas Cayzer, Bt., Safmarine, 7 June 1966.

exports to Europe to lines of other nationalities.[12] Last but not least, Safmarine was demanding a more or less immediate increase in its sailing rights, while the Conference had been very guarded about the time-scale of increased South African 'participation' in the recent negotiations.

In the light of this broader Conference hostility and also of the enormous complexity of the questions involved, it is not surprising that the national line's application was met with prevarication.[13] Disinclined, on the whole, to grant Safmarine's request, but afraid of the political consequences of saying so, the Lines had little alternative. Fortunately, plausible reasons for postponement were to hand.

The first excuse grasped at by the Conference for putting off Safmarine was the situation in Rhodesia following UDI in 1965. When the West Coast UK Lines met Safmarine to discuss the latter's application at Cayzer House in October 1966 (only weeks after the Deputy Chairman of the national line had publicized South Africa's determination to carry 50 per cent of the Republic's trade in its own ships),[14] the South Africans were prevailed upon to defer their application until the 'uncertain situation in Rhodesia' had cleared up. In return, however, the Lines felt it expedient to promise that 'when the political situation had improved' they would 'give favourable consideration to Safmarine's application'; they also agreed that 'any increase . . . would be implemented with effect from 1st July 1968'.[15]

The West Coast Lines no doubt regarded the wording of the promise given to Safmarine at the October meeting as suitably ambiguous, but the fact is that the national line took it to mean that within two years it would be granted substantial additional sailing rights in the trade with Europe. This satisfied it in the interim, but it was clear that if the Conference were not more forthcoming in 1968 then a better reason than the Rhodesian situation would be needed if Safmarine's demands were to be moderated without causing a serious deterioration in relations. In a bitter twist of irony, this reason was provided by the Conference decision in 1967—for which Safmarine itself had pressed—to investigate the question of internal reform, The catalyst in this decision was the Biennial Review held in April 1967.

[12] CAL, Ellerman & Bucknall to Lemon, 22 Sept. 1969.
[13] CAL, Notes of Meeting with '1904 Lines' Principals, 3.30 p.m. Thur., 14 July 1966 at Cayzer House.
[14] *SA Shipping News*, Sept. 1966.
[15] CAL, Note of Informal Meeting of West Coast Lines and Safmarine at Cayzer House, 11.00 a.m. Tue., 4 Oct. 1966.

The Conference had been disappointed with the increases which it had been granted at the last review of freight rates, in early 1966, and had, as a result, obtained a promise from the government that the next one would be conducted as early as April 1967. This—the first of the Biennial Reviews under the new OFA—duly took place between 17 April and 3 May, and involved nine meetings in all.[16] In the event, though, the Lines did not do too badly. On a strict interpretation of the new Formula they were entitled to an overall increase in revenue of 5.8 per cent (which the government offered to round up to 6 per cent), but they asked for 10 per cent in both directions in anticipation of cost increases before the next Biennial Review. While the government would not agree to this, it conceded 6 per cent Northbound (see Appendix VIII), and encouraged the Lines—as before—to make up the difference by loading the Southbound rates. This the Lines reluctantly accepted, subsequently announcing a Southbound general increase of 7½ per cent, and disguising the further discrimination in favour of South Africa's exports by defining the Northbound increase of 6 per cent as one of 7 per cent 'with some exceptions' (see Appendix VIII).

At the Biennial Review in April the government had, therefore, clearly honoured its commitment to the Formula, which was designed to allow the Lines to earn an average of 8 per cent over the ten years of the new OFA. However, it had also insisted that cost inflation ought to be contained, and that there were considerable savings to be made by the Lines through the 'rationalization' of their sailings. Lemon was clearly impressed by the strength of government sentiment on this point, and it was both in the light of this and the increasing scrutiny to which the conference system as a whole was being subjected (the Rochdale Committee was appointed to investigate British shipping in July), that in June 1967 the Conference decided on a complete overhaul of its domestic arrangements.[17]

Although the immediate objective of the Conference in this 'reappraisal'—as it came to be known—of its arrangements was the further rationalization (i.e. reduction) of sailings, it had been believed by Bevan and was also believed by Lemon that this would be extremely difficult to achieve unless all of the Lines—and especially Safmarine—felt that they were receiving a fair deal. The agenda of reappraisal thus

[16] CAL, Notes covering Discussions held in Marks Building, Parliament Street, Cape Town.

[17] CAL, Joint Meeting Minutes, 2 June 1967.

contained two further items: firstly, the pooling of earnings in order to reduce inter-line friction over the differential profitability of routes and cargoes; and, secondly, the reallocation of sailing rights on the basis of the circumstances and merits of each line, sweeping away the *ad hoc* historical system which had developed on the basis of secret negotiations between individual lines and the Conference Chairman's office and which had greatly favoured the old-established members.[18]

Despite the fond hope of A. E. Lemon that reappraisal could be completed by the beginning of 1968, it was soon evident that the process would take much longer. This was largely because of the intrinsic complexities of the task, together with the natural inertia and mutual jealousies of the Lines. The sluggishness of the exercise also became more pronounced when it was realized in early 1968 that for the year ended 30 September 1967 the Conference had actually generated a *surplus* on the Formula of 3.3 per cent.[19] Since the Lines remained in surplus in 1968 they decided not to ask the government for the interim Freight Review which they had earlier contemplated,[20] and thus the immediate incentive for rationalization was removed. However, if this element of reappraisal was no longer so urgently required in order to impress the South African government, the attitude of Safmarine, which was as irritated by the direction which reappraisal was taking in the other areas which fell under this heading as it was by its sluggishness, meant that no one in the Conference could afford to be complacent about the rut into which it had fallen.

Encouraged by the new receptiveness of the Conference to reform, and anticipating—or pretending to anticipate—an increase in its sailings in 1968 following the promise made by the West Coast Lines in 1966, Safmarine had been quiet for the greater part of 1967. However, those involved in the reappraisal were more concerned with the possibilities of pooling than with the reallocation of sailings, and by late 1967 the national line was voicing its suspicion that pooling would freeze its sailings at their existing level.[21] Furthermore, Sir Nicholas Cayzer reminded Bamford that the Lines had not definitely committed themselves to increasing Safmarine rights by 1 July 1968.[22] Safmarine's

[18] CAL, John Bevan, *Aide-mémoire* for Sir Nicholas Cayzer, Bt., Safmarine, 7 June 1966; and memorandum of 19 Sept. 1967 (probably by A. E. Lemon) entitled 'Trade between United Kingdom and South and South East Africa'.
[19] CAL, Joint Meeting Minutes, 2 Apr. 1968.   [20] Ibid., 2 June 1967.
[21] CAL, Notes on Discussion between Sir Nicholas Cayzer, Bt., and Mr F. Bamford—Mon. 30 Oct. 1967.
[22] Ibid.

patience thus ran out, and it refused to supply performance figures for the reappraisal exercise as a protest against the drift of opinion towards pooling. In March 1968 it stepped up the pressure on the Conference by announcing its intention to start a fortnightly service between South Africa and the Mediterranean in September.[23] This was a shrewd move: although the Lines regarded this route as already well covered and did not by any means anticipate sufficient growth in the trade to justify an additional twenty-six sailings a year in each direction, the South African flag was as yet unrepresented in the Mediterranean trade and Safmarine was in any case entitled to enter it on the basis of previously unexercised Springbok rights.[24]

Having established the formal support of the Conference for his position and propitiated Safmarine in some measure by securing the agreement of the April Joint Meeting to full disclosure to members—for the first time—of all inter-line Conference Agreements,[25] Lemon replied to Safmarine's Mediterranean announcement. Safmarine should bear in mind, he said, that a full reappraisal of the Conference's arrangements was already under way and that this might well produce a different procedure for serving the trade between South Africa and the Mediterranean. In that event, he continued, 'recognition in a tangible form' would be made of 'the aspirations of South African Shipping Lines in the Conference', and in the meantime, the national line should suspend its plans for a Mediterranean service. It would also be best, Lemon implied, for Safmarine to defer its ambitions in the West Coast UK trade until reappraisal had been completed.[26] Clearly, reappraisal had replaced Rhodesia as the basis of Conference prevarication on Safmarine's demands.

However, the national line was not to be easily put off. Replying that its Mediterranean plans were too well advanced for postponement, Safmarine adroitly maintained its pressure on the Conference by indicating that it would concede a reduction from a fortnightly to a monthly service, but would maintain this 'until further notice, on the understanding that the position in this regard *as well as our position in the Trade as a whole*, will be subject to further consideration after the reappraisal study has been concluded'.[27]

---

[23] CAL, D. G. Malan (Managing Director, Safmarine) to Lemon, 22 Mar. 1968.
[24] CAL, Lemon to Lines, 5 Apr. 1968.
[25] CAL, Joint Meeting Minutes, 23 Apr. 1968.
[26] CAL, Lemon to Safmarine, 30 Apr. 1968.
[27] CAL, Malan to Lemon, 3 May 1968 (my emphasis).

Under this threat, sensitive to Safmarine's interpretation of the promise made by the West Coast Lines in October 1966, and aware that—in line with the thinking behind the 'outward-looking policy'—Safmarine also had demands on the table for entry into adjacent trades in what it called 'the Southern African economic group' (see Chapter 6), the Conference now felt it expedient to make a small concession. In September 1968—the same month that Safmarine introduced its new Mediterranean service—the South Africans were informed that the Conference had agreed to increase their sailings in the Southbound trade from the West Coast UK from fourteen to eighteen from 1 January 1969. This was in effect a restoration of Safmarine's 1961 West Coast rights, which had been reduced to fourteen in a rationalization agreement of 1963. In communicating this, however, Lemon did not remind Safmarine that, under its current Agreement, it had an overall *ceiling* of twenty-four sailings from Northern Europe (including the United Kingdom) as a whole. This meant that whereas at this juncture Safmarine was making this up with fourteen sailings from the West Coast UK and ten from the North Continent, it would need to *reduce* the latter to six if it were to take up its new entitlement of eighteen West Coast sailings in full! In short, Safmarine had been offered no net increase in its sailings at all but merely the opportunity to redistribute them. Naturally, this was not what Safmarine had had in mind; nor, apparently, did it immediately grasp what had happened. When it did, much trouble ensued.

The Opening of the Hellenic War

If the Conference's first problem in its new alliance with the government was Safmarine's demand for increased rights, the government's was the announcement by the Greek company, Hellenic Lines, at the end of 1966, that it intended to enter the trade. A Conference refusal to Hellenic and a resulting freight war would put to the test the government's promise in the new OFA—much valued by the Lines—to give active support to the Conference monopoly of the trade.

Hellenic Lines was a long-established and important Greek shipping company: in the liner trades it was the standard bearer of its national flag.[28] In 1967 it owned thirty-six cargo vessels and three years

----

[28] *Fairplay*, 15 May 1980.

later it owned thirty-eight, with a further twelve being built.[29] With these ships, Hellenic operated over twenty services throughout the world and was, so its energetic President, Pericles Callimanopulos, claimed, distinctly 'conference-minded'.[30] Though the headquarters were in New York, all of Hellenic's vessels flew the Greek flag.

As is well known, the Greek merchant marine expanded at an extraordinary rate after the Second World War and, plying the cross-trades, made Greece one of the world's leading maritime states.[31] Not surprisingly, shipowners wielded considerable political influence within Greece, and all post-war governments in Athens had lavished support on their enterprises.[32] In this regard, the military junta which seized power in Greece in April 1967, and in which Colonel George Papadopoulos soon emerged as the strongest figure, went further than most.[33] 'Indeed', writes Richard Clogg, 'so grateful were Greece's shipowners for the concessions they were granted, in an effort to persuade them to register their ships under the Greek flag rather than under flags of convenience, that in March 1972 they elected Papadopoulos president for life of the Association of Greek Shipowners.'[34]

In view of Hellenic's size, its existing commitment to the Greek flag, and the exceptional support given to Greek shipping by the Colonels' regime, it was obvious that in any tussle with the South African Conference Hellenic would receive the strong backing of Athens. However, that this would incline the South African government—either for political or economic reasons, or both—to support its entry into the trade (which under the new OFA it was in a strong position to do), must have seemed unlikely to the Conference at the end of 1966, and even in the months after the coup the following April which installed the right-wing Colonels. Greece, though a member of NATO, was not an important member and, apart from its intimate American connection, had no serious foreign policy concerns outside Europe, the Balkans, Cyprus, and Turkey; until 1971 it had no African policy at all.[35]

---

[29] CAL, Lemon to Lines, 23 Dec. 1970.   [30] *Fairplay*, 23 Nov. 1967.

[31] See M. Serafetinidis, G. Serafetinidis, M. Lambrinides, and Z. Demathas, 'The development of Greek shipping capital and its implications for the political economy of Greece', *Cambridge Journal of Economics*, 5, 1981, 289–96.

[32] Ibid., 294 f.

[33] Ibid., 293 f.; J. Pesmazoglu, 'The Greek Economy since 1967', in R. Clogg and G. Yannopoulos (eds.), *Greece under Military Rule* (London, 1972), 89; and N. Fraser, P. Jacobson, M. Ottaway, and L. Chester, *Aristotle Onassis* (London, 1977), chap. 18.

[34] R. Clogg, *A Short History of Modern Greece* (Cambridge, 1979), 195.

[35] A. G. Xydis, 'The Military Regime's Foreign Policy', in Clogg and Yannopoulos (eds.), 200.

Though there was a substantial Greek community in South Africa, Greece was not a favoured source of fresh white immigration, and it was in 1967, in fact, that Pretoria began to scale down the level of immigration from there, along with that from Portugal and Italy.[36] Moreover, in view of the unpopularity which the junta swiftly acquired, and the fact that South Africa's 'outward-looking policy' both sought and required international respectability, it is unlikely that Pretoria was any more anxious for close identification with Athens than it was with the Smith regime in Salisbury. Finally, general trade between Greece and South Africa was not significant (in 1966 South African exports to Greece were worth only R2.23m. and imports from Greece just R0.09m.),[37] though it is true that the Republic had recently shown an interest in increasing its exports to Greece. Expanding the small Greek market for South African goods was the only point which at this stage argued for South African indulgence towards Hellenic Lines.

It was against this background that Hellenic indicated its desire to run a monthly service between Greece (plus the Eastern Mediterranean) and South and East Africa, calling at Adriatic ports (especially Trieste) in order to make the service viable, and to this end it made a formal application for membership to the South African (as well as to the East African) Conference. However, Hellenic appended to its application the information that it intended to start the service in February 1967, whether the Conference liked this or not; and, if necessary, it would quote rates which were 10 per cent lower than Conference rates.[38] Although no one in the Conference liked this sort of approach, and although the Harrison Line and Lloyd Triestino opposed Hellenic's entry into the East African Conference, and Chargeurs Réunis and Safmarine opposed its entry into the South African sphere, a great majority in both Conferences were in favour of making a deal with the Greek line. Operating as an outsider, it was feared that Hellenic would receive support from ISCOR, which, despite pressure from the government, was still refusing to contract with the Conference, and there was also apprehension that a freight war in the Adriatic would attract cargo to Adriatic ports which would normally move via the North Continent. In addition, it was felt that, on national grounds, the

[36] R. First, J. Steele, and C. Gurney, *The South African Connection: Western Investment in Apartheid* (London, 1972), 251.
[37] UN, *Yearbook of International Trade Statistics 1967* (New York, 1969).
[38] CAL, S. and E. African Conferences, Special Joint Meeting Minutes, 24 Jan. 1967.

Conference could hardly stop Hellenic trading to and from Greece itself.[39]

In subsequent negotiations with Hellenic, however, it was soon found that the ambitions of Pericles Callimanopulos could not be scaled down to an acceptable level. As a result, in early 1967 a freight war began,[40] and the Lines called on the South African government, under the terms of the OFA, to help them either to drive the outsider from the trade or to force it to make peace on terms favourable to the Conference. The response of the government was ambivalent: while it was conscious of its obligations to the Lines under the OFA, it believed that South African exports to Greece would benefit from Hellenic's entry into the trade, firstly because of the good impression this would create in Greece, and secondly because the shipping service between the Republic and Greece would be improved. The government decided, therefore, that it would not oppose Hellenic's entry, *provided* the Greeks did not disrupt the trade by undercutting the Conference tariff. When Hellenic did in fact introduce lower rates to win cargo from the Lines, the government made vague threats against it and promptly endorsed the individual 'fighting rates' with which the Conference sought permission to retaliate, but refused to go beyond this.[41]

Despite difficulties in securing cargo, by the middle of 1967 Hellenic had not only announced its intention to step up its sailings from one a month to one every three weeks, but also to bring Spain into the orbit of its operations.[42] Adding to Conference concern was the fact that plans to introduce dual rating in the Southbound trade in order to encourage shipper loyalty and to show the government that the Lines were prepared to help themselves—plans for which the Conference had received government approval in principle during the recent OFA negotiations—had run into difficulties with shippers in Europe and were shelved indefinitely. In these circumstances the Conference had little choice but to put pressure on the government to give it further assistance against Hellenic by the introduction of such measures as freight-dumping duties.

At this point the government began to show irritation. The Conference was reading too much into the OFA, Steyn informed

---

[39] Ibid.   [40] *SA Shipping News*, Mar. 1967.
[41] CAL, Joint Meeting Minutes, 17 Feb. 1967, and 2 June 1967; Lemon to Kotzenberg, 20 June 1967, and Kotzenberg to Lemon, 11 July 1967.
[42] CAL, Joint Meeting Minutes, 20 Oct. 1967.

Lemon by letter in September and during the course of a visit to London in October. The government had agreed, he said, that the Lines should get as much cargo as possible, but it had *not* guaranteed them a complete monopoly of the trade. Besides, he thought that in view of the diminutive size of the Hellenic operation the Conference was making a mountain out of a mole-hill, and that, on national grounds, Callimanopulos could not be denied the right to trade to and from Greece, or with Eastern Mediterranean ports, and perhaps also Yugoslavia. The imposition of freight-dumping duties was out of the question; they were 'quite impracticable'.[43]

By February 1968 Hellenic had been active in the South Africa trade for a year and a solution was as far away as ever. Meanwhile, the Lines were not only losing revenue as a result of the freight war (which might, or might not, be made up by the government), but were suffering from adverse publicity as a result of Hellenic's loud complaints about their 'monopolistic' practices. The Greeks had suggested that the dispute should be taken to the conciliation machinery of CENSA, but the Conference had resisted this, not least because it would let the South African government off the hook. The Lines decided to continue putting pressure on the government for more assistance; for example, by allowing them a *free hand* in the use of fighting rates rather than requiring them to seek Shipping Board approval for each one (which inevitably delayed the Lines' ability to match Hellenic's quotations), by thinking again about freight-dumping duties, or, best of all, by stipulating in all import licences that cargo should be moved by Conference vessels alone.[44]

Increasingly worried at the future effect on freight rates (via the agreed Formula) of the losses incurred by the Lines during the current freight war, Steyn's response to this renewed Conference pressure was more sympathetic. He remained unable, he told Lemon in March 1968, to give the Lines *carte blanche* in the use of fighting rates, because he feared that this would erode the protection which high Southbound rates afforded to local manufacturing industry. He also maintained his view—based on the opinion of the Board of Trade and Industries—that the large-scale introduction of freight-dumping duties would be a bureaucratic nightmare. However, he was able to report to Lemon on certain other actions which had already been taken and another which was in prospect. Namely, he had written twice to Callimanopulos; in

43 Ibid.   44 Ibid., 16 Feb. 1968.

response to direct representations from the Greek government he had also asked the South African Department of Foreign Affairs to appeal to the Greek Foreign Ministry to try and stop Callimanopulos; and he had gone so far as to threaten two South African importers who had patronized the Hellenic service with 'the cessation of import facilities'. Moreover, while he jibbed at imposing the obvious and comprehensive government control on private trade into South Africa which agreeing to the Conference proposal for endorsed import licences would have meant, Steyn indicated that he was prepared to move substantially in this direction, as indeed his action against the two importers had already suggested. What he would do—with ministerial approval—was 'to approach each individual Importer using, or proposing to use, Hellenic requesting him to desist from doing so or otherwise risk perhaps some restriction of his Import facilities'. With this Lemon had to rest content.[45]

Following the discussion at Cabinet level of the whole problem of Hellenic's opposition to the Conference, Steyn received the approval which he had sought for his approach to importers. In October 1968 he sent a letter to 150 of them in which, having explained the reasons for the government's attitude, he said: 'I would like to receive an early written assurance from your company that it will refrain from importing goods from British and Continental suppliers in vessels owned or operated by "Hellenic Lines" or any other non-member of the South African Conference at freight rates below those of the Conference', upon pain, he concluded, of 'the withholding of further import permits'.[46] As well as this, the government reminded provincial administrations in the Republic of their obligation to support the Conference.[47]

From the first the Conference had not been particularly sanguine about the efficacy of Steyn's letter, and even while it was being distributed was planning to take further action itself by informing its agents and stevedores that work for the opposition would be inconsistent with a continuation of their contracts with the Lines.[48] They also kept up the pressure on the Secretary for Commerce for *carte blanche* in the use of fighting rates. All of this was just as well, for

[45] CAL, Notes covering Discussion held in Marks Building, Parliament Street, Cape Town, at 2.30 p.m. on Wed. 6 Mar. 1968.
[46] CAL, Steyn to Importers, 9 Oct. 1968.
[47] CAL, Safcon (Southbound), Minute Book 74, 13 Aug. 1968.
[48] CAL, Joint Meeting Minutes, 11 Oct. 1968.

Steyn's letter created a furore, both among South African importers and within GATT (whose rules entitled members to resort to measures of import control only on grounds of balance of payments difficulties),[49] and in November Steyn confessed to Lemon that he had 'overplayed his hand' and had now 'gone as far as he possibly could'.[50] By the end of 1968, therefore, Steyn had not merely brought his advance against Hellenic on behalf of the Conference to a halt, but had—privately at least—gone into retreat.

The Secretary for Commerce was now deeply regretting the government's commitment to help preserve the Conference monopoly, however vaguely this had been expressed in the new OFA. Effective assistance seemed to meet with insuperable political problems, and the Conference's fighting rates placed an irksome burden on his office (which was required to vet them) and led to a shortfall in revenue, the bill for which would be placed before the government. As a result, Steyn returned to his initial position in the Hellenic affair: since its service was not a major one, Hellenic should either be treated as a tolerated outsider or brought into the Conference. If the former were to apply, then the Lines should introduce dual rating in order to provide a disincentive to shippers to support the Greeks, though this should be confined to the Southbound trade—South Africa's own exporters should not be penalized![51]

Steyn's retreat lent support to the small number of voices—now including that of Safmarine—which was beginning to be heard within the Conference arguing for an accommodation with Hellenic. However, the majority, led by the Conference Chairman and Sir Nicholas Cayzer, remained determined to fight it out with the Greeks, especially since 1968 had seen the appearance of even more opposition in the trade, in particular from the private Italian line of Ignazio Messina. In the view of the majority, this was not the time to show weakness.[52] Despite this Conference determination, it was clear by the end of 1968 that the government's changed attitude was going to make it more difficult and more costly to beat off Hellenic. It was also not entirely clear who would bear the main financial burden of the struggle (though the Lines had their private fears).

[49] CAL, Lemon to Lines, 8 Nov. 1968.
[50] Ibid.
[51] CAL, Joint Meeting Minutes, 25 Nov. 1968.
[52] Ibid.

The London Lobby Against the Arms Embargo

In late 1967, while the Conference was setting out on the road of 'reappraisal' and locking horns with the Hellenic opposition, the British Lines had another issue on their minds: the campaign being waged with increasing vigour by the pro-South Africa business lobby in London to persuade Harold Wilson's Cabinet to lift its comprehensive arms embargo on the Republic. The British Lines naturally supported this campaign, though not because of any anxiety to recover valuable arms shipments: under the new OFA, as noted in the previous chapter, these were in future to be carried by South African flag vessels for security reasons (indeed, this had already been the case with the eight Buccaneer aircraft reluctantly released by the Labour government in 1966[53]). Instead, they were concerned that failing to lift the embargo at this juncture—which saw Pretoria wishing to make its first major new arms purchases in Britain since the introduction of the ban—would prejudice South Africans against the rest of Britain's exports and thus reduce the quantity of high-rated Southbound cargo available for shipment.[54] In December 1967, as is generally known, the campaign to have the arms embargo lifted almost succeeded, with seven members of Wilson's Cabinet in favour (including George Brown at the Foreign Office, Denis Healey at Defence, George Thomson at Commonwealth Relations, and Anthony Crosland at the Board of Trade), and six others wavering—including Wilson, who was clearly not hostile in principle.[55] What contribution did the pro-South Africa lobby, in which the British Lines (led by the Cayzers) played a very prominent part, make to this near success?

The Cayzers had long been a politically active Conservative family.[56] Although none of its members was in Parliament in the

---

[53] The first 4 were shipped from Hull by Safmarine's *SA Van der Stel* and the last 4 by its *SA Langkloof*: CAL, Safcon (Southbound), Minute Book 68, 12 July, and 13 Sept. 1966.

[54] Fears for the fate of Britain's 'civil trade' with South Africa were widely shared by British business men, see G. Berridge, *Economic Power in Anglo-South African Diplomacy: Simonstown, Sharpeville and After* (London, 1981), 156–60.

[55] B. Castle, *The Castle Diaries, 1964–70* (London, 1984), 336–42; and R. Crossman, *The Diaries of a Cabinet Minister, 2, Lord President of the Council and Leader of the House of Commons, 1966–68* (London, 1976), 476 f. and 603–5.

[56] Sir Nicholas Cayzer's grandfather, Sir Charles Cayzer (the founder of the Clan Line), was MP for Barrow-in-Furness from 1892 until he lost the seat in 1906; Lord Rotherwick, his uncle (the first Chairman of B & C)—prior to his elevation to the peerage, of course—was MP for Portsmouth South from 1918 until 1939; and his cousin, the third Sir Charles Cayzer, was MP for the City of Chester from 1922 until his death in 1940.

1960s, Ian Lloyd, a South African who had been on Dr Norval's Board of Trade and Industries in the early 1950s, and had been Director of Research and Economic Adviser at B & C since 1956 (retaining the latter post until 1983), had entered the House of Commons as a Conservative in 1964. (Sir Nicholas's son-in-law, Michael Colvin, also became a Conservative MP, in 1979, and, like Ian Lloyd, joined the right-wing '92 Committee' of Tory back-benchers;[57] in 1981 Sir Nicholas Cayzer himself entered the House of Lords as one of the three life peers created by Mrs Thatcher in that year.) The Cayzers were also one of the largest corporate contributors to the central funds of the Conservative Party (prior to 1972, indirectly via British United Industrialists), as well as to free enterprise pressure groups such as the Economic League—and remain so (see Appendix XI). With such a long-standing and substantial commitment to right-wing politics on the part of his family, as well as a major direct interest in the South Africa trade, it is hardly surprising that Sir Nicholas Cayzer—though no friend of apartheid—should have played a prominent role in the pro-South Africa lobby in London.

The most important constituent parts of the lobby were the London office of the South Africa Foundation, a subtle 'man-to-man movement' formed at the end of the 1950s,[58] and especially the broadly based UK–SA Trade Association (UKSATA), launched with Foundation encouragement in late 1965.[59] Sir Nicholas Cayzer put a lot of money into both of these organizations, and was indispensable to the success of UKSATA,[60] of which he was the first President. He was also a Vice-President of the SA Foundation, while Fred Bamford, Chairman of Safmarine, was a member of its Executive Committee and allowed himself to be pressed by the B & C Chairman to take over the presidency of the South Africa–Britain Trade Association, UKSATA's sister association in the Republic.[61]

[57] *The Times*, 25 May 1984.
[58] Major-General Sir Francis de Guingand, *From Brass Hat to Bowler Hat* (London, 1979), 107.
[59] Private papers of W. E. Luke, UKSATA: The Chairman's Speech at the Annual Council Luncheon on 27 Oct. 1969, 'Toast of the Guests', Appendix C. On the various elements in the pro-South Africa lobby, see also First *et al.*, chap. 10; and J. Barber, *The Uneasy Relationship: Britain and South Africa* (London, 1983), 67–74.
[60] Information supplied to the author by W. E. Luke.
[61] Private papers of W. E. Luke: Report by Mr W. E. Luke, Chairman United Kingdom–South Africa Trade Association and British National Export Council Southern Africa Committee. Visit to Southern Africa and the South African Republic 24 Jan–23 Feb. 1967. 4 Apr. 1967.

There is no doubt that this lobby was energetic in opposing the arms embargo in 1967 and had excellent access to both the Labour government and the Trades Union Congress. This was assisted by the strength and breadth of its corporate support, and by its intimate links with the Confederation of British Industries (CBI) and the British National Export Council (BNEC): UKSATA's Chairman, William Luke, was a member of the Council of the CBI and Chairman of the Southern Africa Committee of the BNEC, as well as being Chairman of the London Committee of the SA Foundation. George Brown, Anthony Crosland, Ray Gunter (subsequently described by Luke as 'one of the best Ministers of Labour we have had this century'[62]), Vic Feather, and even Harold Wilson all accepted personal representations from Sir Nicholas and William Luke.[63]

The UKSATA Chairman subsequently claimed a certain amount of credit for bringing the Labour government so close to lifting the arms embargo, and his view was endorsed in the left-wing polemic, *The South African Connection*, which was published in 1972.[64] However, both of these sources had an interest in coming to this conclusion: William Luke to justify the importance of their continuing membership to his corporate subscribers (his statements on this theme were made to Annual General Meetings of UKSATA); *The South African Connection* to illustrate the (axiomatic) malevolence of British business, not to mention its authors' theory of the state. In fact, existing evidence on the subject suggests that, while the pro-South Africa lobby may have marginally heightened the sensitivity of the Foreign Office, the economic ministries, and—not least—the TUC to the effects on civil trade with South Africa of confirming the arms embargo, the lobby was substantially preaching to the converted.

What seems to have happened is that in June 1967 the Defence and Overseas Policy Committee of the Cabinet (OPD)—chaired by Harold Wilson—decided to explore with the South Africans the possibility of lifting the embargo. This was not because its members had been bullied, duped, or corrupted by the pro-South Africa lobby, but because they saw in this issue the possibility of a quid pro quo for assistance in getting a settlement in Rhodesia—the most serious

---

[62] Private papers of W. E. Luke, UKSATA: The Chairman's Speech at the Annual Council Luncheon on 27 Oct. 1969, 'Toast of the Guests', Appendix C.
[63] First *et al.*, 218; and information supplied to the author by W. E. Luke.
[64] 219.

foreign policy problem confronting the Wilson government.[65] George Brown saw the South Africans soon afterwards, but no definite agreement emerged and the Foreign Secretary seems no longer to have been sanguine about South Africa's ability to help with pressure on Ian Smith,[66] though his anxiety at least to retain South Africa's neutrality in the affair contributed to his decision to support the lifting of the embargo.[67]

However, there were others in the OPD—including Wilson—who thought the possibility of a quid pro quo worth pursuing further.[68] Moreover, since shipping had been diverted to the Cape following the closure of the Suez Canal in the June War, the argument that Britain should sell arms for 'external defence' to South Africa in order to sustain its inclination as well as its ability to protect Western shipping at the Cape had gained ground.[69] As a result, further discussions were held between the two governments in September–October 1967,[70] and it seems clear that, for its consummation, a major change in British policy awaited only further preparation of the ground by Brown and his allies in the Cabinet and the Parliamentary Labour Party. In November their hand was further strengthened when the continued drain on Britain's reserves, coupled with a forecast of another massive balance of payments deficit for 1968, forced the government to execute a volte-face of at least equally dangerous political implications—the devaluation of the pound.[71] This made the large South African arms order look even more attractive and heightened fears in the economic ministries—where it can be safely assumed that no one needed the assistance of UKSATA to read the statistics of Britain's stake in the Republic, or of the increasing threat to it from the non-embargoing states, France and Italy—about the ripple effects of a refusal to lift the arms ban. At Defence, Denis Healey appears to have seen arms sales to South Africa as a way of ameliorating the severity of defence cuts,[72] as well—presumably—as a way of beefing up the South Africans for the greater role in Western defence which Britain's remaining cuts would nevertheless require them to play. By the end of 1967, then, which also happened to be the deadline set by the South Africans for a

[65] Castle, 338; and G. Brown, *In My Way* (Harmondsworth, 1972), 164.
[66] Crossman, 477.   [67] Castle, 261.
[68] Crossman, 477.   [69] Brown, 164.
[70] Castle, 338; and Berridge, 158.
[71] S. Brittan, *Steering the Economy: The Role of the Treasury*, rev. edn. (Harmondsworth, 1971), 356 f.
[72] Castle, 337 and 341.

British decision on the arms embargo, the Wilson government had political, strategic, and economic reasons of its own for taking seriously the possibility of lifting it. At a meeting of the OPD on 8 December there was a majority for this course.[73]

In the end, to the fury of the pro-South Africa lobby, which believed that its objective was 'in the bag',[74] the embargo was confirmed, and on 18 December Harold Wilson announced in the House of Commons that there was to be no change from the policy instituted in November 1964. This ended ten days of the most bitter—and public—strife which the Labour Cabinet had yet seen, and had two immediate causes: firstly, the failure of the South Africans to pressurize the Rhodesian rebels into a settlement—'South Africa hadn't done its part', Barbara Castle records Wilson as telling the Cabinet on 15 December, 'and to sell out on this issue, for nothing in return, was intolerable';[75] and secondly, the decision of the Prime Minister—described by Richard Crossman in September as being 'miserable and unhappy and divided in his mind' about this affair[76]—to come out against lifting the embargo partly so that he could exploit the opportunity provided by the issue to isolate and drive out of his Cabinet the two powerful Ministers whom he considered to be challenging his leadership—George Brown and Denis Healey.[77] In the event, Wilson succeeded in harnessing the Parliamentary Labour Party to this strategy and reasserted his authority in Cabinet.[78] In the following March George Brown resigned. As one of the Prime Minister's own back-benchers charged in the subsequent three-hour adjournment debate on the issue (in which Ian Lloyd, still relatively inexperienced, made no significant intervention), arms for South Africa had been sacrificed on the altar of 'party management'.[79] This, of course, was not the whole story. The diplomatic costs of lifting the arms embargo, especially within the Commonwealth, obviously weighed heavily with the government, a fact which William Luke bitterly complained of in a subsequent private encounter with Harold Wilson. 'I don't think, sir, that any British Prime Minister, even a Socialist one, should allow himself to be pushed

[73] Ibid., 336.
[74] Information supplied to the author by W. E. Luke.
[75] Castle, 338.
[76] Crossman, 477.
[77] Castle, 336 f.; and Crossman, 603 and 607.
[78] Castle, 341 f.
[79] *House of Commons Debates*, 19 Dec. 1967, c. 1119.

around by the Afro-Asian bloc', said Luke; to which Wilson replied: 'Nobody pushes me around, especially right-wing Conservatives'.[80]

To conclude, it seems that the impact of the pro-South Africa lobby on the centre-right members of the Labour Cabinet in 1967 was at most marginal, while the influence of the latter was in the end insufficient to have the embargo lifted. Of course, when the Tories returned to power in 1970 the ban was lifted on arms for 'external defence' (though in practice few were sold as a result of the predictable furore—at home and abroad—which the decision aroused),[81] and in this the pro-South Africa lobby undoubtedly played a larger part. Its connections with the Conservatives were obviously much better and it had devoted considerable attention to educating them on the question for some years before the general election.[82] 'Heath', remembers William Luke, 'was not really sympathetic but he had to listen to Sir Nicholas, not least because of his contributions to the Conservative Party funds.'[83]

The Question of the Tariff Currency

While the Lines and the government had been grappling with the intrusion of Hellenic Lines into the trade, and the South Africa lobby in London had been trying to persuade the Wilson government to lift the arms embargo, a quite new problem for the Conference had blown up. In November 1967 sterling was effectively devalued by 16.67 per cent against the dollar (and all other currencies which retained their IMF parities—which was most of them and included the South African rand), and the question arose as to whether it should remain the currency in which the tariff of the Europe–South Africa trade was calculated. This issue was to cause a bitter split within the Conference, and was also to divide the Conference and the South African government.

The acute differences within the Conference over the tariff currency issue surfaced at the emergency Joint Meeting called to discuss it on 23 November 1967. The problem for the Conference was that while the devaluation of sterling meant that all of the lines would lose income in real terms, the variations in their countries of origin and

---

[80] Information supplied to the author by W. E. Luke.
[81] D. Hurd, *An End to Promises: Sketch of a Government 1970–74* (London, 1979), 55.
[82] First *et al.*, 218–21.
[83] Information supplied to the author by W. E. Luke.

patterns of trade meant that some would lose much more than others. In general, the Continental Lines and the South African Lines stood to suffer the most, and the British Lines—with most of their expenses in sterling—the least. Consequently, the Continental Lines and Safmarine demanded an increase in freight rates of the full 16.67 per cent, preferably disguised by a change from sterling to either the dollar or the rand as the tariff currency. The British Lines, however, fearful of the reaction to an increase of this size on the part of their own shippers and government, and inclined to regard the suggestion that sterling should be dropped as nothing but an insensitive red herring, would not countenance a tariff increase of more than 12½ per cent, a standard which had already been adopted in certain other trades. This, said Sir Nicholas Cayzer, would be 'rough justice' but justice nevertheless.[84] The British Lines also refused to consider a suggestion of different increases for different sectors of the trade, which the Continental Lines and Safmarine offered as a counter-proposal, and which Sir Nicholas said would 'break up the Conference'.[85] At the end of a long day, the Continental Lines and Safmarine—who stood to suffer most from a failure to take any decision at all—were forced to accept the British position: the Lines would ask the South African government to approve a 12½ per cent devaluation surcharge on the sterling tariff in both directions. (In the event, this was unacceptable to the government, which forced the Lines to adjust to devaluation by introducing surcharges which further discriminated in favour of the Northbound trade—10 per cent Northbound and a full 15 per cent Southbound.[86])

There is no doubt, though, that the Continental Lines and Safmarine resented the British compromise and were determined not to be placed in a similar position again. The only way to do this was to get rid of sterling as the tariff base, the impetus for which increased as rumours circulated throughout the winter of 1967–8 that there would be a second sterling devaluation.[87] This weakened the resistance of the British Lines, while the notion that the US dollar should replace sterling was strengthened by a shift of opinion in favour of the American currency as the tariff base in other major conferences. The case for the dollar was based on its stability as a reserve currency, a

[84] CAL, Joint Meeting Minutes, 23 Nov. 1967.   [85] Ibid.
[86] CAL, Notes covering Meetings held in Forum Building, Struben Street, Pretoria, 27–8 Nov. 1967 (3 meetings); and Joint Meeting Minutes, 16 Feb. 1968.
[87] Brittan, 377 f.

status which the rand did not have, and which the British government clearly did not intend sterling to retain for long.[88] Secondly, the dollar—unlike the rand if not unlike sterling—was used for commercial and financial transactions across the world. Thirdly, the dollar—unlike both the rand and sterling—was a neutral currency for the South African Conference, that is to say, none of its members would obtain any special advantage from its use as the tariff base. This last point, pressed by DOAL at a Special Committee convened by the Conference to discuss the tariff currency in January, clearly made an impression on the British lines,[89] and by the time of the next Joint Meeting, in February 1968, they no longer offered any serious resistance to a change to the dollar; agreement on this course of action was thus easily achieved.[90]

The Conference had assumed that it did not need the South African government's consent to change the tariff currency, and at the Joint Meeting in February had agreed that Lemon should merely 'notify' Steyn of its decision. This is not surprising since—though Lemon himself subsequently *asserted* to the contrary[91]—it was by no means obvious from either the OFA or its Supporting Letters that the Lines were under any obligation to obtain government consent on this matter. Unfortunately for the Conference, though, the government had different ideas. Worse still, March 1968, when Lemon was due to visit South Africa in order, amongst other things, to 'notify' Steyn of the Lines' decision, was probably the least propitious moment in the entire post-war period to attempt to sell the virtues of the dollar to anyone, and least of all to the South African government. For in this month the dollar, which had been looking less and less solid as the US balance of payments deteriorated during the 1960s, came under such intense pressure against gold that on 15 March the 'gold pool' (created in 1961 to stabilize the free market) was exhausted, and the Bank of England was obliged to close the London Gold Market altogether. Two days later the Western central banks, led by the US Federal Reserve, announced that they had, *inter alia*, effectively demonetized gold. This led to open war between the Federal Reserve and the South African government, for whom monetary demand for new-mined gold

[88] Ibid., 379.
[89] CAL, Notes of Meeting of Special Committee held at 18 London St, EC3, at 2.15 p.m. on Mon. 29 Jan. 1968.
[90] CAL, Joint Meeting Minutes, 16 Feb. 1968.
[91] CAL, Lemon to Lines, 20 Mar. 1968 (Note 3).

had always been paramount and an increase in its official price a long-coveted objective. The so-called 'gold war' between Washington and Pretoria was not settled until the end of the following year.[92]

It was in such circumstances, then, that Lemon came away from Cape Town in late March without securing Steyn's blessing to a change in the Conference's tariff currency from sterling to the US dollar, and feeling strongly that the Lines should not try to 'bounce the government on this issue'.[93] And, although Steyn gave the dollar's current instability as the reason for his opposition,[94] there is little doubt that the principal reason was the start of the gold war with the United States: over the following months the most important priority of South Africa's foreign economic policy was to weaken the dollar and, *ipso facto*, strengthen gold. Significantly, as subsequently emerged, it was Diederichs's Ministry of Finance, rather than Steyn's own Department, which was the major obstacle to the Conference's desire to change to the dollar. Following Steyn's stalling action of March and his announcement in May that, 'after very thorough consultation with the Treasury', it had been decided to retain sterling as the tariff currency,[95] the Lines began to cast around for another solution.

From time to time since sterling's devaluation, the government, with the support of Safmarine, had rather half-heartedly canvassed the rand as an alternative tariff base. So strong was the hostility of the major Continental Lines to sterling that at the Joint Meeting in May they themselves came out for the rand, but the British Lines would not accept it, and the issue had to be shelved.[96] Then, in July, DOAL, fearing another sterling devaluation, proposed that the rand should be introduced in the Northbound trade and the dollar in the Southbound, but the British Lines rejected this as well.[97] In November Steyn again listened to a Conference deputation putting the case for wholesale change to the dollar, but once more he refused to accept it, bringing the conversation to a close by revealing that 'it was the Minister of Finance, Dr. Diederichs, who had been dead against changing from sterling to dollar Tariff Currency base when the question was last

[92] On these events, see Berridge, 160–2; and I. Davidson and G. L. Weil, *The Gold War* (London, 1970).
[93] CAL, Lemon to Bedford (telex), 15 Mar. 1968.
[94] CAL, Notes covering Discussion held in Marks Building, Parliament Street, Cape Town, at 2.30 p.m. on Wed. 6 Mar. 1968.
[95] CAL, Joint Meeting Minutes, 28 May 1968.   [96] Ibid.
[97] CAL, Paproth to Lemon (telex), 26 July 1968; and Joint Meeting Minutes, 11 Oct. 1968.

raised'.[98] There the matter rested for two and a half years, until it was picked up again by the Continental lines in May 1971. The South African Conference was stuck with sterling as its tariff currency, though most of the major conferences had by this time changed over to the dollar.[99] The South African government had demonstrated its power over the Conference in yet another area.

[98] CAL, Lemon to Lines, 8 Nov. 1968.
[99] CAL, *Aide-mémoire* for Conference Delegation in Discussion with Mr G. Steyn, regarding Tariff Currency Base, 29 Oct. 1968.

6

THE OFA IN DANGER
1969–1972

THE next four years saw what was probably the high point of white South Africa's post-Sharpeville complacency: prosperity continued; the 'outward-looking policy' was successfully extended beyond the Republic's immediate neighbours; a firm grip was held on local security by its *entente* partners in Rhodesia and the Portuguese colonies; and a more friendly administration had been installed in Washington under President Nixon. However, the same satisfaction did not colour Pretoria's attitude towards its relationship with the South African Conference. This was largely because of the growing number of outsiders in the trade and the diplomatic and domestic political problems which this caused for the government as a result of its obligations to the Lines under the OFA, which continued to run until the end of 1976. For the moment, Hellenic remained the outsider which was the major cause of concern.

The Intensification of the Hellenic War

In 1969 the Hellenic War went from bad to worse for both the Lines and the government. In South Africa itself trouble mounted at the beginning of the year when local stevedores, threatened by the Lines with the loss of Conference business (their bread and butter) if they continued to handle Hellenic vessels, told the Greek line that its ships would no longer be serviced after the expiry of their contracts on 31 March.[1] Despite their compliance, the stevedores were unhappy with the Conference-inspired boycott of Hellenic, and the Chairman of the Stevedore's Association in Durban gave public vent to their feelings. This produced such bad publicity for the Conference in the last week

[1] CAL, Lemon to Lines, 12 Feb. 1969.

of January,[2] that Lemon considered dropping the boycott altogether.[3] However, in the absence of any sounds of displeasure from Steyn, and with Callimanopulos facing real difficulties when the boycott took effect on 1 April, the Lines decided to stand firm.[4] In the last week of February, though, their determination began to wilt rapidly, largely as a result of the intervention of the Greek government, and a new sensitivity to the Greek point of view on the part of the South Africans.

Greece was still relatively unimportant to South Africa at the end of the 1960s and, under the junta, not a country with which the Republic wished to be too closely identified. It is perhaps significant that Athens was not included in Vorster's tour of right-wing European states in June 1970. Nevertheless, relations between the two countries seemed to be improving. Both were staunchly anti-Communist, both were treated as outcasts by Western Europe, and both had mutual friends in roughly the same category—Spain, Portugal, and Israel. Moreover, anxious to diversify its trade, South Africa was looking to Greece as a country in which there was scope for a modest increase in the Republic's exports. It is also probable that Pretoria was considering Greece as a possible point of access to NATO arms.[5] In January 1967 the South African Minister of Economic Affairs had visited the country,[6] and, while South Africa's exports to Greece had remained static in 1967, they had doubled in 1968.[7]

In the light of these considerations, then, it is not altogether surprising that, having received a formal protest from the Greek government over the stevedores' boycott of Hellenic Lines on the morning of 21 February 1969, the South African Foreign Minister, Dr Hilgard Muller, summoned Steyn at once to his office. Hellenic Lines, Muller informed him, was the shipping company of a country with which South Africa had friendly relations. Furthermore, he pointed out, the affair had wider implications, for government approval of the Conference-inspired boycott of Hellenic's vessels was inconsistent with South Africa's long-standing opposition to attempts to influence

---

[2] 'Stevedores' "No" to Hellenic Lines', *Daily News*, 24 Jan. 1969; 'Ban on Greek Ships Shocks Stevedores', *Sunday Express*, 26 Jan. 1969; 'Concern over Shipping Ban', *Natal Mercury*, 28 Jan. 1969; and 'That Boycott . . . A Matter for ASSOCOM?', *Daily News*, 29 Jan. 1969.

[3] CAL, Lemon to Lines, 12 Feb. 1969.

[4] CAL, Joint Meeting Minutes, 14 Feb. 1969.

[5] R. Jaster (ed.), *Southern Africa: Regional Security Problems and Prospects*, Adelphi Library 14 (Aldershot, 1985), 52.

[6] *House of Assembly Debates*, c. 2732-3 (18 Mar. 1969).

[7] UN, *Yearbook of International Trade Statistics, 1970–1971* (New York, 1973).

trade unions, dock workers, or other services to boycott the handling of *South African* goods, and this was obviously a matter to which the government attached great importance. Having reported Muller's view to Austin, the local Conference Chairman, on the evening of the same day, Steyn concluded by telling him that in the light of these considerations the government would like the Conference to rescind its instructions to stevedores 'immediately'.[8]

The size of the South African Conference, of course, meant that it could never take an important decision 'immediately', and while Lemon was consulting Principals the Greek junta dramatically stepped up the pressure on Pretoria. On the morning of 5 March Steyn received a cable from the South African Ambassador in Athens saying that unless the South African government had made the Conference rescind its instructions to stevedores by 7 March at the latest, 'the Greek government would take reprisals against South Africa's total export trade to Greece'. The Secretary for Commerce again issued an urgent summons to the local Conference Chairman and repeated his request for the calling-off of the boycott, adding significantly that 'We don't want a first class international row. After a very long process of hesitation the Greek Government has just agreed to appoint a full scale Ambassador to South Africa and we would not like to see this appointment withdrawn as a result of the escalation of the Hellenic problem.'[9]

As it happened, the increased Greek pressure and Steyn's second demand were both unnecessary, for by the time Lemon received this news he was putting the finishing touches to a telex to the local Conference Chairman asking him to inform Steyn that the Lines had agreed to rescind their instructions to the stevedores: the boycott was off.[10] However, apart from the South African Lines, the Conference felt very bitter about Steyn's action, a feeling which Lemon fully shared. The Lines had agreed to call off the boycott with great reluctance, the Secretary for Commerce was informed, because it was a normal commercial practice employed by shipping conferences against outsiders, and because Callimanopulos would be greatly encouraged by what had happened.[11] Indeed, the Lines felt badly let down by the government and, as a result of a misunderstanding

[8] CAL, Austin to Lemon (telex), 24 Feb. 1969.
[9] Ibid., 6 Mar. 1969.
[10] CAL, Lemon to Austin (telex), 6 Mar. 1969.
[11] Ibid.

between Lemon and Austin as to how much of the former's telex of 6 March should be shown to Steyn, did not conceal it.[12]

In view of the lengths to which Steyn felt he had already gone to defend the Conference position, the suggestion in Lemon's telex of 6 March that the government was not keeping its side of the bargain and was leaving the Lines to battle on their own greatly incensed him, and he informed Austin that he was quite happy to wash his hands of them. For good measure he added that it was essential that an early solution to the Hellenic problem should be found, and gave a thinly disguised clue as to what sort of a solution that should be by also informing Austin that he would not tolerate the stevedores withholding contract (i.e. cheap) terms from Hellenic,[13] which Lemon had hoped might be possible as a poor second-best to the boycott.

However, despite its sensitivity to Greek pressure over the stevedores' boycott, the South African government—which liked neither Callimanopulos himself nor the trouble which he had caused—was by no means inclined to force the Conference to admit Hellenic at any price. Indeed, on 18 March, J. F. W. Haak, the Minister of Economic Affairs, in reply to probing by an Opposition MP, made a statement in the House of Assembly which the Lines were right to find encouraging.[14] While it was true, the Minister said, that South Africa had informed Greece that it would welcome the introduction of a direct shipping service between the two countries in the interests of expanding trade (as Callimanopulos had frequently claimed), Hellenic was exceeding what South Africa had had in mind by initiating sailings from Trieste as well. Moreover, it was landing goods in the Republic 'at prices which had a disruptive effect on certain local manufacturing industries', and the government had no intention, therefore, of withdrawing its threat to deny import licences to receivers who patronized this cut-rate service.[15] In early May Haak gave an even stronger defence in the House of Assembly of the government position, adding to his reasons for opposing Hellenic's tactics the government's contractual commitment to the Conference, the worrying possibility of a further increase in Northbound rates if Hellenic's erosion of the Lines' Southbound earnings could not be curbed, the need to defend the position of the South African members of the Conference, and (by implication) the need to acknowledge the

[12] Ibid., 10 Mar. 1969.   [13] CAL, Austin to Lemon (telex), 7 Mar. 1969.
[14] CAL, Lemon to Lines, 31 Mar. 1969.
[15] House of Assembly Debates, c. 2732–3 (18 Mar. 1969).

interests of Italy in the shipment of Italian goods under the Italian flag.[16]

Shortly after the first of these two ministerial statements in support of the Conference, Callimanopulos himself visited South Africa for direct talks with Steyn at the latter's invitation. (The Secretary for Commerce had become frustrated at the ignorance in shipping matters of the local Greek diplomatic representative.[17]) During discussions over 20 and 21 March Steyn intimated to the Greek shipping magnate that he might be given an ultimatum to get out of the trade altogether within three weeks. In that event, Callimanopulos replied, he would personally arrange for the whole matter to be raised with the Security Council of the United Nations, and the diplomat accompanying him—demonstrating that the acquaintance of Greek diplomacy in South Africa with the provisions of the UN Charter on the functions of the Security Council was as inadequate as its acquaintance with shipping—confirmed that this was indeed a subject which could ascend to these heights. After this evidently sobering exchange of bluster and threats, Steyn and Callimanopulos got down to serious talking, and at the end of their long discussions Steyn remained convinced that the Lines should settle with Hellenic on the best terms available. Amongst the proposals put forward by Callimanopulos, the one that Steyn found most attractive was the idea that Hellenic should be allowed to continue loading from the Adriatic for a further six years. Thereafter trade between Greece / Eastern Mediterranean and South Africa would have expanded sufficiently for the Greek line to be able to withdraw from the Adriatic trade and make a living from Greece and the Eastern Mediterranean alone. Having secured Haak's support for his position immediately after the departure of Callimanopulos on the morning of 21 March, Steyn summoned Lemon—who was also in South Africa—to his office, and informed him of his decision. The unhappy Conference Chairman told Steyn that he would have to report back to the Lines.[18] Meanwhile, Callimanopulos set off for his headquarters in New York 'looking confident'.[19]

It was not only in South Africa that the campaign being waged by Callimanopulos, with the energetic support of the Greek government, was putting the Lines on the defensive in the Hellenic War. They were

[16] Ibid., c. 5713–15 (9 May 1969).
[17] CAL, Austin to Lemon (telex), 24 Feb. 1969.
[18] CAL, Lemon to Lines, 31 Mar. 1969.
[19] *Travel and Trade News Pictorial*, Apr. 1969, 20.

disappointed in other quarters where they had looked for sympathy. In October 1968 Callimanopulos had used the occasion of CENSA's annual meeting with the European Shippers' Council to launch a major attack on the South African Conference's 'instigation' of government intervention against Hellenic in the South Africa trade, making much of Steyn's famous letter to importers.[20] On 30 January 1969 he continued the attack at the CENSA meeting in Paris, now adding the stevedores' boycott to his indictment of both the Conference and the South African government. It was here that the Lines' difficulties in Europe began to parallel those which they were already experiencing in South Africa, for though CENSA proposed to take no action in the matter, it unanimously condemned the South African government's 'interference with the free flow of trade', and regretted the Lines' refusal to resort to the CENSA Conciliation Panel.[21] This was a blow to the Conference, which was particularly worried that the Consultative Shipping Group (CSG)—which had expressed its concern when the CENSA motion was put before it at the joint meeting on the following day—would persuade its twelve member governments to intercede on behalf of Hellenic.

While the Lines were attempting to head off diplomatic protests to the South African government by individually 'educating' their own ministries,[22] the Greeks were busily broadening their campaign. The Greek government reported the affair to the Maritime Committee of the OECD, and Callimanopulos wrote to the Chairman of the House Committee on Merchant Marine and Fisheries in the US Congress. It was also widely believed that he would take the issue to the Shipping Committee of UNCTAD. Not only was the line-up of their critics likely to grow, but the Lines were unsuccessful in persuading their own governments to refrain from lodging protests with the South African government against its interference with the free flow of trade. Even the British Board of Trade, customarily sympathetic to its shipowners and well disposed towards closed conferences, would not approve the action taken by the South Africans against Hellenic in order to protect the Conference under the terms of the OFA.[23] By

[20] CAL, Statement made by Mr P. G. Callimanopulos, representing the Association of Greek Shipowners at the Plenary Annual Meeting of the CENSA/European Shippers Council held in Hamburg, Germany, on 24 Oct. 1968, 31 Oct. 1968 (privately circulated).
[21] CAL, Gurr (Dep. Conference Chairman) to Lines, 3 Feb. 1969, and Lemon to Lines, 29 Apr. 1969.
[22] CAL, Joint Meeting Minutes, 14 Feb. 1969.   [23] Ibid., 27 June 1969.

September 1969, as Steyn angrily reported to Lemon, most of the European diplomatic missions in Pretoria (including that of the United Kingdom) had registered 'strong protests against the unfriendly attitude our Government has allegedly been adopting towards Hellenic Lines'.[24] With the attitude of European governments and other European shipowners at best neutral and at worst hostile, with Steyn's resolve to support them eroded by mounting pressure from the Department of Foreign Affairs, and with existing tactics making no serious impression on the Greek line's determination to stay in the trade, it is hardly surprising that by the middle of 1969 the Lines were reluctantly inclined to consider a peace settlement to the Hellenic War on the terms favoured by Steyn: admission to the Adriatic for a period of five or six years.[25]

The subsequent attempt to reach agreement with Hellenic, however, was complicated by a parallel exercise with another outsider, the Italian line, Ignazio Messina, which in the previous year had also applied to join the Conference, claiming rights from Marseilles as well as from Italian ports on the Tyrrhenian Sea. This application had been turned down by the Lines on the grounds that, *inter alia*, the Italian flag was already represented in the trade by Lloyd Triestino.[26] However, in the subsequent tussle with Messina the Conference had to take account of the fact that Italy was a country which was of some importance to South Africa, and certainly more so than Greece. Though in quantitative terms Italy could not be classed as one of South Africa's major markets, it nevertheless ranked sixth in this respect in 1968. Moreover, while Italy had agreed to observe the voluntary arms embargo imposed on South Africa by the UN in 1964, its interpretation of the ban had not been excessively strict, and in 1968 it was the Republic's fifth most important source of imports.[27] Italian money and expertise was also in the process of committing itself to the South African-backed Cabora Bassa project in Mozambique,[28] while Italy—like the other major NATO powers—opposed the introduction of economic sanctions against South Africa and in general adopted an abstentionist posture on South African questions at the United Nations. It is therefore not difficult to understand why Steyn should

[24] CAL, Steyn to Lemon, 23 Sept. 1969.
[25] CAL, Joint Meeting Minutes, 27 June 1969.   [26] Ibid., 11 Oct. 1968.
[27] UN, *Yearbook of International Trade Statistics, 1970–1971.*
[28] K. Middlemas, *Cabora Bassa: Engineering and Politics in Southern Africa* (London, 1975), 67–9.

have had little hesitation in giving his blessing to Messina's application when the Italian Ambassador to Pretoria intervened on its behalf in the middle of 1969.[29]

Under pressure from Steyn, and also now from Lloyd Triestino itself (which was apprehensive of the powerful commercial and political support enjoyed by Messina in Italy and had decided to drop its opposition to the rival line),[30] the Lines decided to seek a settlement with the Italian line. Moreover, partly because it was insisted on by Lloyd Triestino (the most intimately affected party), and partly because Lemon believed that an agreement with Messina would strengthen his hand in bargaining with Hellenic, the Conference opened discussions with the Genoa line first, in June 1969. The Messina negotiations, however, were not immediately successful, and it was soon clear to the Lines that they would not necessarily be able to delay opening talks with Hellenic until discussions with the Italians had been concluded. This was confirmed by information from Steyn in late September that Athens would lay a formal charge against South Africa for a breach of GATT principles if the threat to deny import licences contained in his October letter was actually carried out. Steyn also informed the Conference that the government was not prepared to proceed with its threat, and added for good measure that he had 'reason to believe that our importers are well aware of this fact'.[31] With the key element in the Conference's defence against Hellenic's incursion crumbling, Lloyd Triestino dropped its opposition to negotiation with Hellenic prior to a settlement with Messina, and at the Joint Meeting on 7 October it was decided that 'further negotiations should be pursued without delay with Hellenic'. Subsequently, Lemon suggested to Steyn that he should participate in the talks in order to tie Callimanopulos more tightly to any agreement which they might produce.[32]

Before any negotiations could be organized, however, there were further developments on the diplomatic level. In November the Greek Ambassador approached Steyn again, at least twice, and proposed that the Hellenic affair should be settled by the exclusion of the Adriatic from the South African Conference altogether. Instead of the existing arrangement, he suggested that a new Conference should be created to

[29] CAL, Austin to Lemon (telex), 2 June 1969.
[30] CAL, Joint Meeting Minutes, 11 Oct. 1968.
[31] CAL, Steyn to Lemon, 30 Sept. 1969.
[32] CAL, Lemon to Steyn, 15 Oct. 1969.

cover not only the Adriatic but also Greece itself and the Eastern Mediterranean. The trade of this Conference should be shared between Hellenic, Lloyd Triestino, and Safmarine, the first two each having 40 per cent and the last 20 per cent. The Ambassador also appealed for an early settlement of the Hellenic dispute because of the 'serious prejudicial effects' which it was having on Greek–South African relations. While Steyn later told Lemon that this proposal had been 'smartly rejected',[33] the Secretary for Commerce was sufficiently impressed by the urgency of the Greek representations (which were made with the South African Secretary for Foreign Affairs in attendance) that he offered to fly out to Athens at short notice to negotiate a settlement at government level, albeit on the basis of the idea that Hellenic would have rights in the Adriatic for five or six years only.[34] In the event, this offer was not taken up by the Greeks, who simply failed to issue their Ambassador with a reply to his suggestion. As a result, Steyn was pleased to learn from Lemon in mid-December that the Lines had been approached by Hellenic's Vice-President, Theodore Pangos, and that direct negotiations between the two parties were likely to commence in the New Year.[35]

Indeed, talks took place between Lemon and Pangos in London during late January and early February 1970, but came to nothing. Lemon offered the Greeks only 10,000 tons of general cargo from Trieste, and added insult to injury by stating that they could only be Associate Members while serving their 'apprenticeship'. Hellenic replied that they would countenance nothing less than the formation of a pool for the Adriatic trade in which they would have a 40 per cent share, together with exclusive rights to Greece, the Eastern Mediterranean, and the Black Sea.[36]

Following the failure of these negotiations, the Greek junta renewed its pressure on Steyn, informing the Secretary for Commerce at the end of February that Athens would only settle for Hellenic's admission to the Conference 'as full members without restriction', even if Callimanopulos himself was prepared to settle for less. While Steyn remained anxious for a settlement of the Hellenic problem, he was

[33] CAL, Memorandum of Discussions with Mr G. J. J. F. Steyn at London Airport on 15 and 17 Dec. 1969.
[34] CAL, Austin to Lemon (telex), 8 Dec. 1969.
[35] CAL, Memorandum of Discussions with Mr G. J. J. F. Steyn at London Airport on 15 and 17 Dec. 1969.
[36] CAL, Notes of Discussions with Mr Pangos, 20, 21 and 22 Jan., and 2 and 3 Feb. 1970; and Lemon to Lines, 23 Feb. 1970.

irritated by the size of the Greek demands and also by the preference of the junta for conducting such technical negotiations through its diplomatic service. He also subsequently stated to Lemon that if more shipping was needed in the Adriatic it should be provided by the Italian and South African lines. As a result, Steyn adopted a tougher attitude towards the Greek Ambassador, informing him that his demands were unacceptable and that in any case it would be better if negotiations were now conducted directly between Hellenic and the Lines, to whom he could not dictate.[37]

Reinforced in his hostility to the Greeks by what he took to be a new and 'sinister' attitude of maritime expansionism on the part of their government,[38] and encouraged by Steyn's reaction, Lemon himself now determined to wait for Callimanopulos to come to him. Before this happened, negotiations with Ignazio Messina were successfully concluded in April, and on 1 June 1970 the Italian line formally entered the Conference. This was followed by what Lemon had been waiting for: Callimanopulos proposed that talks should resume. These took place on 21 September but swiftly collapsed. Confirming Lemon's growing conviction that Hellenic was weakening, Callimanopulos had reduced his demand for participation in the Adriatic to 25 per cent, but the Conference Chairman felt that 10 per cent would be 'nearer the mark', and that was that.[39] The Hellenic War continued.

In the middle of the following year, 1971, Hellenic received a fillip to its cause when the Lines announced a cut-back in services following a major rationalization agreement arrived at under pressure from the South African government (discussed later in this chapter). In July Hellenic issued a notice stressing that the frequency of its own sailings was undiminished and that more modern vessels would soon be added to the service.[40] This undoubtedly worried the Lines.[41] Moreover, since the failure of negotiations the previous September, Callimanopulos had continued his general propaganda campaign against the Conference, and the Greek government had kept up its pressure on the South African Department of Foreign Affairs, issuing political as well as commercial threats (Foreign Affairs was now particularly worried that

[37] CAL, Austin to Lemon (telex), 1 Mar. 1970; and Note of Discussion with Mr Steyn in Pretoria on Fri. 20 Mar. 1970.

[38] CAL, Lemon to Lines, 3 Mar. 1970.

[39] CAL, Notes of Discussion at Cayzer House, 3.30 p.m., 21 Sept. 1970; and Joint Meeting Minutes, 6 Oct. 1970.

[40] *Natal Mercury*, 26 July 1971.

[41] CAL, Lemon to Lawrence, 9 Aug. 1971.

Athens might make things more awkward for South Africa at the United Nations).[42] Nevertheless, the Lines took comfort from signs of Callimanopulos's increasing anxiety to settle, and also from the clear evidence that neither CENSA nor the CSG countries would press their support for Hellenic any further. In addition, another Greek line, Meandros, had entered the trade during 1971, with more modest needs than Hellenic's, and the Conference had entered negotiations with it, hoping to satisfy Greek aspirations more cheaply and eliminate, or at least weaken, Hellenic's political support.[43] Above all, while in October 1970 and again in August 1971 Steyn had asked Lemon to be more generous to Callimanopulos,[44] he had not insisted that the Lines should settle on Hellenic's terms. For all of these reasons, then, the Conference, supported by Steyn, maintained that Callimanopulos must reduce his demands and that there was little point in further talking until he did. In June 1972 the Greek magnate again called on Lemon but, encouraged by the receipt of honours from the Italian government and the merchants of Trieste (for services to their commerce),[45] Callimanopulos was still in no mood to compromise. Still, therefore, the Hellenic War continued.

Loading the Southbound Rates Further

While the freight war with Hellenic was proving costly to the Conference, and the devaluation of sterling—despite the subsequent introduction of devaluation surcharges—was also eroding earnings, especially those of the Continental Lines, the fact remained that with the South African economy booming in the late 1960s and early 1970s the trade—particularly Southbound—was very buoyant. Indeed, it was so buoyant that in early 1968 the Lines discovered that they had generated a *surplus* of 3.3 per cent in the year ended 30 September 1967,[46] and they remained in surplus in 1968 as well. They therefore decided not to press the government for an interim Freight Review in that year, though they had felt that this would be necessary at the time

[42] CAL, Joint Meeting Minutes, 16 Feb. 1971; and Discussion with Mr Steyn, Pretoria, 26–7 Aug. 1971.
[43] CAL, Joint Meeting Minutes, 19 Oct. 1971.
[44] CAL, Lemon to Lines, 19 Oct. 1970; and Discussion with Mr Steyn, Pretoria, 26–7 Aug. 1971.
[45] CAL, Callimanopulos to Lemon, 17 Apr. 1972; and *Il Piccolo* (Trieste), 24 Mar. 1972.
[46] CAL, Joint Meeting Minutes, 2 Apr. 1968.

of the Review in April 1967.[47] However, the Lines could not avoid a Review in April 1969, since this was scheduled under the new OFA, and, despite Lemon's efforts to retain the whole of the surplus against the difficult days ahead which he anticipated, he was obliged to concede a general *reduction* of 5 per cent on Northbound tariff rates, with the fearful implications which this contained of agitation for a commensurate reduction from shippers in the Southbound trade. This reduction was granted as a result of intense pressure from Steyn, who maintained that South African exporters (especially in citrus) were facing acute difficulties in European markets and that, failing such a demonstration that the Formula could work in the interests of shippers as well, he might find it difficult to restrain the hostility which was now mounting in South Africa towards both the Conference and the OFA.[48]

The pressure for reductions in Southbound rates which the Lines had feared did not materialize, and, all in all, they did not feel able to complain unduly at the results of the 1969 Freight Review. However, the high level of investment in 'new transport techniques' which, as we shall see, the government was pressing them to undertake, was fuelling their dissatisfaction with the Formula return of 8 per cent on capital employed, and they had warned Steyn that they would soon be seeking its upward revision.[49] Furthermore, by the beginning of 1970 the fortunes of the Conference began to dip, as Lemon had anticipated. Cost inflation had now well and truly taken off, and all the signs were that it was going to get worse. By March the Lines were already pressing a reluctant Steyn for an interim Review in the next few months, as well as for a fresh examination of the Formula itself.[50] It would be much more politic, Lemon pointed out to Steyn, to put rates up now by a relatively small amount and again by a similar amount in 1971, than to leave them unaltered in 1970 and then face the prospect of trying to introduce a massive increase the following year in order to recover a huge cumulative deficit of £7 to £8 million.[51]

Steyn accepted Lemon's argument, and an interim Freight Review

[47] Ibid., 2 June 1967.
[48] This veiled threat was made at the third session of the negotiations: CAL, Notes covering Discussions held in Marks Building, Parliament Street, Cape Town, at 10.00 a.m. on Tue. 29 Apr. 1969.
[49] Under the terms of the OFA, the Lines were entitled to seek a review of the Formula after three years, i.e. after 22 August 1969.
[50] CAL, Note of Discussion with Mr Steyn, Fri., 20 Mar. 1970.
[51] CAL, Lemon to Lines, 20 May 1970.

was held in early June. However Steyn returned an uncompromising refusal to the Lines' request that their rate of return on capital should be gradually increased from 8 per cent to 12½ per cent, claiming that anyone involved in shipping was lucky to receive a more or less guaranteed 8 per cent (plus depreciation), and that no increase could be based on the need for future funding of new transport techniques because the government—although extremely interested in them—had as yet made no decisions. On the question of freight rates, Steyn was more forthcoming, although he still by no means satisfied the Lines. To cover the estimated deficit up to the end of September 1971, they had asked for an overall increase of 14 per cent, and had to settle for 7½ per cent only on Northbound rates (though the government did finally agree that this would include the much protesting fruit industry as well). As a result, they were forced to put up Southbound rates by the much higher margin of 12½ per cent, and, even so, calculated that the revenue generated by these increases (£5.3m.) would still leave them about £2m. short of the target needed to provide them with an 8 per cent return by the end of September 1971.[52]

To the consternation of the Lines, June was not the last time in 1970 when they had to go to the government to ask for something on account. Between the June Freight Review and the Joint Meeting of the Conference in early October, costs—particularly those of fuel oil—shot up again, and during October and November the Conference Chairman repeatedly pressed Steyn to help the Lines in the face of this 'unprecedented inflation'.[53] Furthermore, Lemon urged strongly that the discrimination in favour of the Northbound trade which the government had traditionally either imposed or made unavoidable should not apply to the further interim freight rate increases which he was now seeking.

Naturally, Steyn was appalled at the prospect of yet another interim increase, but he was aware that rapid inflation was now a world-wide phenomenon; he also claimed to be personally sympathetic to the Lines' case against the discrimination between the two sectors of the trade. But, in the event, Steyn's sympathy was not enough. In early December the South African Cabinet approved an interim increase in Northbound rates of only 6 per cent; it also 'approved' an increase in

[52] CAL, Notes covering Discussion held in Forum Building, Struben Street, Pretoria (4–5 June 1970, 4 meetings).
[53] CAL, Lemon to Lines, 23 Nov. 1970 (reporting on talks with Steyn in South Africa earlier in the month).

Southbound rates of 10 per cent (under the OFA, of course, increases in Southbound rates, except for essential plant and raw materials, were none of its business). 'Please tell Ted [Lemon] that I really did my best not to discriminate between Northbound and Southbound but the Cabinet would not listen to me', Steyn informed Austin on 4 December.[54] Even with the increases approved by the Cabinet, the Conference would suffer a deficit of £2.5m. on the Formula Year 1971, and carry a cumulative deficit of £6.5m.[55] Furthermore, the increases had only been granted on condition that, prior to the Biennial Review in April 1971, there would be a conference between the parties to the OFA in order to discuss ways in which the constantly rising costs in the *Northbound* trade could be contained.[56] (This was principally a reference to rationalization of the Lines' sailings.)

There is no doubt that the South African government was by this time under terrific pressure from the fruit interests to do something about freight costs to Europe, as they were also from the canners, who had been complaining bitterly that the Lines had been falling down on their obligation to lift all of their production (with some justice, thought Lemon).[57] It did not help, as the Conference Chairman pointed out to the Lines, that the new Minister of Economic Affairs, S. L. Muller, was MP for Ceres, a constituency in the middle of the canned fruit production region.[58] In the circumstances, then, the Conference felt that it had no alternative but to accept this small increase in Northbound rates and gird itself to press for a full restitution of its financial position in the Biennial Review in April, using that occasion also for a renewed effort to bring to an end the now glaring discrimination between the Northbound and Southbound trades.[59] If it were to make significant progress on either of these points, however, it would need to make serious efforts to meet the government on rationalization.

The 'Rationalization' of the Service

Following the condition laid down by the government for the freight rate increases approved in December, talks on rationalization were

---

[54] CAL, Austin to Lemon (telex), 4 Dec. 1970.
[55] CAL, Joint Meeting Minutes, 8 Dec. 1970.
[56] CAL, Austin to Lemon (telex), 4 Dec. 1970, and 7 Dec. 1970.
[57] CAL, Lemon to Lines, 23 Nov. 1970.
[58] Ibid.   [59] CAL, Joint Meeting Minutes, 8 Dec. 1970.

held in Cape Town on 17 and 18 March 1971. During these discussions the Conference accepted Steyn's argument for rationalization, though Lemon repeated its forebodings that a reduced service would increase the opportunities for exploitation by opposition lines. Apart from their realization that rationalization was a condition of further freight rate increases, the Lines were also swayed by Steyn's claim that the advent of containerization would mean that they would have to operate as a consortium, so they might as well get used to the greater co-operation that rationalization would entail.[60] In the event, a rationalized service was soon worked out—saving 911 port calls at the European end of the trade and 2,077 at the Southern African end, as well as some sailings[61]—and was introduced as early as May. To even out any inequalities thrown up by the rather hasty introduction of the new system, a money-pooling scheme was also established on the basis of existing shares in the trade, and was to last until the middle of the following year, by which time it was hoped the redivision of the trade—'reappraisal'— would have been concluded and a more permanent money pool created.[62] With money pooling as well as the joint scheduling of services—all under the lash of government-imposed rationalization— integration of the Conference service had advanced very considerably indeed.

This quick action by the Lines to rationalize their service impressed Steyn, as Lemon had hoped it would. At the Biennial Review held on 27 April the Lines asked for increases of 11 per cent in both directions to enable them to earn their 8 per cent during 1971-2, plus 3½ per cent overall in order to eliminate the cumulative deficit (now estimated at the somewhat lower figure of £5m.) over two years. In short, they wanted 14½ per cent in both directions. Following some procrastination by the Cabinet which, in view of the importance now attached to the subject, wanted to give more attention than usual to Steyn's advice, the Conference was delighted to learn (on 20 May) that it had been granted general increases *in both directions* of 12½ per cent. This was better than Lemon had expected.[63] Steyn, he thought, had done them proud, a claim confirmed by the anger subsequently directed at the Secretary for Commerce by both the fruit interests and the Federated

[60] CAL, Marks Building, Cape Town, Meeting of Representatives of the SA Government and the SA Conference Lines, Wed., 17 Mar. 1971, reconvened Thur. 18 Mar. 1971.
[61] CAL, Rationalization, Cape Town, 30 Apr. 1971.
[62] CAL, Joint Meeting Minutes, 26 Mar. 1971.   [63] Ibid., 27 May 1971.

Chamber of Industries (FCI).[64] There seemed no doubt at this point, then, that the government was still prepared to honour its part of the bargain at the heart of the OFA.

The Resumption of the Safmarine Advance

Rationalization of the Conference service had not only opened the way to higher freight rates, but had also helped the Lines to resist Safmarine's campaign to overthrow its ten-year Agreement of 1963 before its full term had elapsed. Nevertheless, by the end of 1972, via the so-called 'reappraisal' exercise, Safmarine had won the right to escalate its share of the trade quite significantly over the next five years. The Lines' willingness to countenance this, as promised in the OFA negotiations of 1965–6, helped to hold the Conference and the government together through these difficult years.

It will be recalled that in September 1968 the Conference had granted Safmarine the right to increase its Southbound sailings from the West Coast UK from fourteen to eighteen, but had omitted to elicit from it a formal understanding that this did *not* mean that it was now entitled to increase its total sailings from Northern Europe as a whole from twenty-four to twenty-eight. If Safmarine wished to take up its new West Coast UK rights, then it would have to *reduce* its North Continent sailings from ten to six. As well as either overlooking or simply ignoring this, Safmarine had in any case only accepted its increase in West Coast UK rights as a 'temporary palliative' pending the long-promised completion of the 'reappraisal' of all sailing rights in the different sectors of the trade. Neither had it been pleased at the flat 'no' which it was given to other demands, including admission to the trade between the West Coast UK and Lobito in Angola, and between Europe and the ports in Northern Mozambique between Chinde and the Rovuma River (the latter falling within the range of the East African Conference, of which of course Lemon was also Chairman).[65]

Evidently feeling that its alliance with the B & C Group was not paying all of the dividends for which it had hoped, and that Sir Nicholas Cayzer required further education on Safmarine's entitlement to entry into these other trades, representatives of the national lines had met Sir Nicholas in Cape Town in March 1969. At this meeting

[64] CAL, Lawrence to Lemon (telex), 25 May 1971, and 9 July 1971.
[65] CAL, Lemon to Smith (Safmarine), 22 Oct. 1968, and Smith to Lemon, 1 Nov. 1968.

they had outlined their concept of 'a Southern African economic group', which was, they had claimed, 'their particular area of influence'. This group comprised 'South Africa including South West Africa, Rhodesia, Malawi, Mozambique and Angola (and possibly Zambia)'. Malawi and Mozambique were included in the zone because 'South African finance and effort were being expended in those countries', while Rhodesia was included because of 'the special relationship now existing with South Africa owing to the current political situation'.[66] This thinking was undoubtedly influenced by the IDC, the dominant force in Safmarine, which was encouraging South Africa's northward economic expansion in order to assist the 'outward-looking policy'.[67]

Sir Nicholas Cayzer had readily assented to Safmarine's claims for a preferential position in the European trades serving the 'Southern African economic group', and—thus encouraged—the national carrier had stepped up its pressure on the Conference, combining a demand for more rights in the North Europe–South Africa trade to be implemented from 1 September[68] with an announcement that the frequency of its Mediterranean service would be increased at the same time.[69] That Safmarine's patience with the Conference should have expired at this juncture is not surprising since 'reappraisal' had been under way for two years, and, although it had made progress on pooling, a basis for the redivision of the trade was still not in sight.[70] Furthermore, Safmarine was worried that other South African interests, including the giant Anglo-American Corporation, would put their own ships into the European trade, on the argument that national flag participation was insufficient—'precisely the point we have made for some years', Safmarine had expostulated.[71]

Despite this new pressure, however, Safmarine's demands were still resisted by the Conference. Reappraisal might be taking a long time but it was still in progress, and it would hardly be helped by an attempt at a major reallocation of rights under the *existing* system. Lemon's own hostility to Safmarine had also deepened in the second half of 1969 when it became evident that during 1967 and 1968 the national line had been exceeding the sailings provided for in its current

[66] CAL, Meeting between B & C and Safmarine, Cape Town, 17 and 20 Mar. 1969.
[67] K. W. Grundy, *Confrontation and Accommodation in Southern Africa: The Limits of Independence* (Berkeley, 1973), 48 f.
[68] CAL, Safmarine to Lemon, 26 June 1969.   [69] Ibid., 25 June 1969.
[70] CAL, Joint Meeting Minutes, 27 June 1969.
[71] CAL, Safmarine to Lemon, 26 June 1969.

Agreement, and was now refusing to reduce its North Continent sailings in order to take up the increase in West Coast UK rights which it had been recently granted and yet remain within its overall ceiling of twenty-four.[72] On 10 November 1969, therefore, the Conference Chairman had refused the Safmarine application once more; for good measure, he had also turned down its application to the East African Conference for participation in the Europe–Northern Mozambique trade.[73]

By the end of 1969, then, relations between Safmarine and the Conference Chairman had reached a fairly low level. Not only had the national line taken the view that the Conference was not honouring the spirit of the new OFA provisions on increased South African flag participation, but it also implied that it had been misled by Lemon in 1968 (albeit inadvertently) into thinking that it had actually been granted a net increase in North Europe rights, and was not now inclined meekly to surrender them.[74] This dispute was so serious that in February 1970 Lemon aired the possibility that it would have to be resolved by arbitration.[75] Nevertheless, at Cape Town in March the affair seems to have been smoothed over, though just how this was achieved is not clear from Conference records; Safmarine was certainly not granted any improvement on its Agreement of 1963.

One reason why Safmarine may have been disinclined to pursue its agitation after March 1970 was that since 1966, by one means or another (including, of course, its entry into the mail service), it had achieved additional sailings in the North Europe trade, and had also found room for the employment of its expanding fleet on the Mediterranean run. In practice, therefore, South African flag participation had been allowed to increase quite significantly. At the end of 1970 Lemon had told Steyn that in the Southbound trade—where its participation was highest—the South African flag carried 40 per cent of the trade from the United Kingdom (a slight exaggeration) and 30 per cent from the North Continent.[76] In addition, there is no evidence from the Conference records that Steyn had been particularly anxious to support Safmarine or, for that matter, the three South African

[72] In the Agreement Year ended 30 June 1969 Safmarine despatched 4 sailings in excess of its entitlement: 16 from the West Coast UK and 12 from the North Continent: CAL, Lemon to Safmarine, 17 and 30 Oct. 1969.
[73] Ibid., 10 Nov. 1969.
[74] CAL, Safmarine to Lemon, 3 Nov. 1969, 11 Dec. 1969, and 23 Jan. 1970.
[75] CAL, Lemon to Lines (excluding Safmarine and Springbok), 3 Feb. 1970.
[76] CAL, Lemon to Lines, 30 Dec. 1970.

companies which had attempted to put ships into the Europe–South
Africa trade in this period for the first time: Arden Hall in 1969 (which
he had encouraged Safmarine to torpedo by lobbying the Minister of
Economic Affairs[77]), Anglo-American also in 1969 (which he had told
Lemon he 'hoped . . . could be persuaded to stay away'[78]), and
Concorde Shipping Company in 1970 (which he had only supported at
the last minute and with great reluctance because it had 'influential
friends'[79]). Clearly, Steyn had been aware that at a time when one of
his top priorities was to convince the Lines of the need for an overall
reduction in sailings—'rationalization'—it was not a good idea to be
seen to be *simultaneously* pressing for more South African flag
sailings—even though there was no necessary tension between the
two. Steyn may also have realized that containerization was on the
horizon—as we shall see in the next chapter—and that this would
throw the whole trade into the melting pot. In this ultimate
rationalization, Safmarine would get its full deserts.

Both Steyn and Safmarine may have been relatively quiescent in
their campaign for an increase in South African flag rights in the trade
during 1970, but this did not by any means indicate that they had
abandoned it,[80] and, following the introduction of the rationalized
service in the middle of 1971, Safmarine, with Steyn's support,
recommenced its agitation. Rationalization, especially in the Southbound
trade from the North Continent, was operating to its disadvantage,
claimed Safmarine; and so was the money-pooling scheme which had
been introduced for the 1971–2 period. Its Chairman, Marmion
Marsh, told Lemon that Safmarine was considering withdrawing from
the new scheme altogether.[81] Although at the Joint Meeting in October
Safmarine was given the necessary assurances and this minor storm
quickly blew over,[82] in the continuing discussions on the redivision of
the trade—where shares of liftings and earnings were the currency of
debate rather than sailings—the national line assumed a very tough
position.

In the trade between the UK and South Africa, where in 1971–2

[77] CAL, Lemon to Austin (telex), 24 May 1969.
[78] CAL, Memorandum of Talks that took place in the Office of the Secretary of
Commerce in Forum Building, Pretoria, on Mon. 4 Aug. at 10.30 a.m. and on Wed. 6
Aug. at 11.00 a.m.
[79] CAL, Joint Meeting Minutes, 27 May 1971.
[80] E.g. CAL, Steyn to Lemon, 14 Dec. 1970.
[81] CAL, Marsh to Lemon (telex), 22 Sept. 1971.
[82] CAL, Joint Meeting Minutes, 19 Oct. 1971.

the South African flag group lifted about 35 per cent Southbound but only 20 per cent Northbound, Safmarine demanded an increase to 45 per cent of the Southbound trade over the next five-year cycle, rising subsequently to 50 per cent. There were no cross-traders in the UK-RSA trade, said Safmarine, and it was therefore entirely proper that ultimately there should be a 50:50 division between the South African and British flags in this sector. Safmarine was not anxious to increase its share of the poorly paying Northbound trade.[83] The British Lines, however, felt that they had strong 'historical' claims to a larger percentage than Safmarine, and quite rightly resented Safmarine's unwillingness to carry its fair share of national exports. As a result, they made a counter-proposal of 40 per cent *in both directions* by the end of the next six years, with this figure remaining the South African flag group's permanent share. After much argument and further bluster from Marsh about Safmarine removing itself from the rationalized service and the money-pooling arrangement,[84] a settlement in the UK-RSA trade was finally reached on 13 December 1972, and constituted a clear improvement for Safmarine. Over the five-year period starting (retrospectively) on 1 July 1972, Safmarine would steadily achieve 41.15 per cent of Southbound liftings in the UK-RSA trade, and 37.15 per cent of Northbound liftings; in the UK-Mozambique trade it would achieve 20 per cent Southbound and 18 per cent Northbound.[85]

In the important North Continental sector, negotiations over trade shares were even more difficult, though the most serious dispute was between the Continental Lines and the British Lines over the division of what remained after the share to be achieved by the South African flag group by 1977 had been agreed. (Since the British Lines were cross-traders in the North Continent–Southern Africa trade, the Continental Lines felt that the British should make the main sacrifice to allow for the escalation of the South African share.) In 1971–2 the South African flag group's share of the Southbound trade from the North Continent to South Africa and Mozambique was 28.35 per cent of liftings and 30.46 per cent of earnings; for the Northbound trade, the figures were 20.20 and 20.95 per cent respectively.[86] However, as

---

[83] CAL, Lemon to British Lines, 2 Oct. 1972.

[84] CAL, Marsh to Lemon, 12 Oct. 1972.

[85] Southampton was excluded from this Agreement; the shares were to apply to both East and West Coasts of the UK: CAL, Meeting, 13 Dec. 1972, Cayzer House, between Conchair and Mr Marsh, and Mr Poulter.

[86] CAL, Lemon to Lines in the North Continent Trade, 20 Jan. 1975.

in the UK trade, the South Africans eventually wanted almost 50 per cent of the Southbound trade from the North Continent (50 per cent of that to South Africa and 33 per cent of that to Mozambique), though they were much less anxious to shoulder an increased burden in the Northbound trade.[87] By the end of 1972 the broad principles of a compromise between all three flag groups in the North Continent trade had been achieved, although it was not until two years later, in December 1974, that all of the details were finalized. Under this agreement, the South African flag group would increase its share of Southbound liftings from 28.35 per cent in 1971-2 to 35.60 per cent in 1976-7, and of earnings from 30.46 per cent to 36.57 per cent. In the Northbound trade, however, its share would remain virtually static, rising from 20.20 per cent of liftings and 20.95 per cent of earnings to only 20.97 per cent in both cases.[88]

In the final sector of the trade, the small but complicated Mediterranean sphere, where the British, Dutch, and West Germans represented the cross-trading interest, Safmarine made similar demands.[89] However, agreement on new shares here proved impossible,[90] and it must be assumed that in the years between 1971 and 1977 the South African flag group did not advance significantly on the respectable shares which it had already achieved by 1970: 29.1 per cent of liftings and 29.9 per cent of earnings in the Southbound trade to South Africa, with 13.4 per cent and 16.7 per cent, respectively, Northbound; and 24.8 per cent of liftings and 25.5 per cent of earnings in the Southbound trade to Mozambique, with 17.7 per cent and 16.4 per cent, respectively, Northbound.[91]

By the end of 1972, therefore, Safmarine had, after a long struggle, considerably strengthened its position in the Europe–South Africa trade. Moreover, the fact that the national line had more or less been conceded escalation to 40 per cent in the more lucrative sectors of the trade by 1977, when, it was now being assumed, 'new transport techniques' of one sort or another would be introduced, made it axiomatic that its share in the 'new era' would be nothing less than this.

[87] CAL, Notes of Meeting of the British and North Continental Lines serving the North Continent held in the Dorchester Hotel, London, on 22 Feb. 1972.

[88] CAL, Lemon to Lines in the North Continent Trade, 20 Jan. 1975.

[89] CAL, Notes of Meeting of European Lines serving the Mediterranean held in Cayzer House on 15 Feb. 1972.

[90] CAL, Draft Minutes of Meeting of Principals in the Mediterranean–South African Trade (in both directions), 16 June 1976.

[91] CAL, Reappraisal–Mediterranean, 3 Mar. 1972.

Portuguese, and Other, Outsiders

Rationalization might have been expected to reduce the *costs* of the Conference but, as Lemon had repeatedly warned Steyn, it would also reduce its attractiveness from the service point of view and thus make it more vulnerable to outsiders (as well as encourage shippers to charter their own vessels), thereby reducing the *revenue* of the Lines. In short, rationalization was likely to prove a mixed blessing. Trade subsequently slackened; freight rates in the open market dipped alarmingly;[92] and in the second half of 1971 the freshly exposed Conference found the problem of opposition more acute than ever.

At the same Joint Meeting—in October 1971—at which the Lines had been warned of the incursion of Meandros and of an increase in Hellenic's activities, they were also informed by Lemon of the likelihood of opposition in the North Europe trade from Empresa Insulana Navegacao (EIN) of Lisbon. This line, the oldest in Portugal, had run into great difficulties and had recently been acquired by the Portuguese government, which was currently attempting to rationalize the country's merchant marine and increase its foreign earnings.

For their part, the Lines regarded the possibility of an EIN intrusion as unwarranted, not only on the usual commercial grounds but on national ones as well, since two Portuguese lines, Companhia Nacional de Navegaçao (CNN) and Companhia Colonial de Navegaçao (CCN)—the latter, like EIN, government controlled—were already members of the Conference. CNN and CCN not only ran the Conference trade between Portugal itself and Southern Mozambique, but also had a small stake in the trade with North Europe. Moreover, hostility already existed towards the Portuguese as a result of what was widely regarded as the flagrant flag discrimination practised by Lisbon when trading with its overseas territories, such as Mozambique. All trade between metropolitan Portugal and the overseas territories was reserved by law to Portuguese shipping, while in addition all cargo carried in Portuguese bottoms *from metropolitan Portugal* was entitled to a 20 per cent customs preference in the colonies. What further angered the Conference was that Portuguese vessels bound for Mozambique were able to secure cargo unfairly from North Europe—i.e. cargo of *non-Portuguese origin*—by 'naturalizing' it through fictitious transhipment in Lisbon *en route* south, thereby making it eligible for

---

[92] This was mainly a result of a drop in Japanese demand for chartering: *Fairplay*, 13 Jan. 1972.

the 20 per cent customs preference on arrival in the colony.[93] This issue had been taken up by the British and other governments in the OECD, but the Portuguese had refused to budge. It is not surprising, therefore, that the Lines should have taken an extremely jaundiced view of this new threat. EIN intrusion, Lemon advised Steyn, could provoke a freight war in the North Europe trade which 'would make our trouble with Hellenic in the Mediterranean trade look like a skirmish'.[94]

The prospect of a freight war with EIN in the vital UK–North Continent trade came perceptibly closer in November 1971, when it became evident that the Conference member, CCN, had been obliged by the Portuguese government to team up with EIN, and that both would be entering the trade—with or without Conference approval—in the new year.[95] The EIN/CCN threat was underlined further by a personal visit to Lemon by the Portuguese Ambassador to London, who left the Conference Chairman with no doubts as to the determination of his government to see its lines enter the South Africa trade.[96]

Steyn had himself received diplomatic representations from the Portuguese on behalf of EIN as early as March 1971, and had told them that he had no objections to EIN entering the trade between Portugal and South Africa, provided—as he had earlier told Hellenic—that they did not undercut Conference tariff rates.[97] Furthermore, after resisting strong pressure from Lemon throughout the remainder of 1971, in March 1972 Steyn informed the Conference Chairman that EIN/CCN should be allowed to cross-trade between North Europe and South Africa as well.[98] In adopting this attitude, Steyn admitted to Lemon that political considerations—'our special relationships with the Portuguese government'—were uppermost in his mind.[99]

Relations between Portugal and South Africa had not always been warm. In the second two decades of the twentieth century the Union had not bothered to conceal its contempt for the way in which the Portuguese administered their African empire, nor its desire to annex that part of it in which its interests were deepest—Southern

[93] CAL, Lemon to Steyn, 25 Apr. 1972.   [94] Ibid., 14 Sept. 1971.
[95] CAL, Lemon to Lines, 29 Nov. 1971.
[96] CAL, Ambassador Antonio Leite de Faria, *Aide-mémoire*, London, 23 Nov. 1971.
[97] CAL, McCarthy to Lemon (telex), 7 July 1971.
[98] CAL, Joint Meeting Minutes, 27 Mar. 1972.
[99] Ibid.; and McCarthy to Lemon (telex), 7 July 1971.

Mozambique.[100] Though the latter issue had been submerged by the 1960s, there remained differences of national style which both found irritating,[101] and differences over domestic racial policy which were at least the source of some mutual public discomfort.[102] Nevertheless, assisted both by the development of South Africa's 'outward-looking policy' in the second half of the 1960s, and the rise of black insurgency in the African colonies of Portugal which bordered the South African sphere, by the early 1970s each had come to look to the other as a vital partner in economic and defence relationships. The Cabora Bassa dam project in Mozambique—set in motion in the late 1960s—was the most notable expression of economic collaboration between the two countries, while the increasingly intimate defence relationship was seen most clearly in the regular conferences held on the security position in Mozambique.[103] In 1970, Lisbon had been Vorster's initial stop on his somewhat furtive trip to Europe, the first made by a South African Prime Minister since the Republic left the Commonwealth in 1961. From roughly the middle of 1971 until the middle of 1973, following the opening of a second front in the Tete province by the black national liberation movement in Mozambique, FRELIMO, South Africa's awareness of the protection afforded by the Portuguese army was at its most acute, and its general sympathy for Portugal therefore at its most complete. Morever, South Africa's disposition to demonstrate its friendship for Portugal was strengthened by its desire to compensate for Rhodesia's tactless criticisms of the performance of the Portuguese army in Mozambique.[104]

It was against this political background that Steyn had asked the Conference to admit EIN/CCN not only to their national trade with South Africa but also to the cross-trade with North Europe. However, he was clearly in a dilemma: on the one hand he was under pressure to introduce more tonnage into the trade in order to help shore up a vital *entente*; on the other, he was anxious to support rationalization in order to reduce costs and thereby halt, or at least slow down, the escalation in freight rates. In a futile attempt to live with this dilemma he had asked the Lines to look favourably on EIN/CCN, but had omitted to add any inducement to his request. The Lines consequently ignored it,

---

[100] L. Vail and L. White, *Capitalism and Colonialism in Mozambique: A Study of Quelimane District* (London, 1980), 205–11.

[101] Middlemas, *Cabora Bassa*, 27 and 58 f.

[102] *The Times*, 8 June 1970.

[103] Middlemas, *Cabora Bassa*, 27 f. and 283.   [104] Ibid., 286–90.

and introduced fighting rates against the Portuguese as well as against the other outsiders.

As a result of the increase in Hellenic's activities in the second half of 1971, the modest threat from Meandros, and the certainty that the Portuguese would appear in the trade in the new year, Steyn had come under fresh pressure from the Lines for further help against the opposition. However, while he was still prepared to urge support for the Conference within the South African business community—for example, by writing to ASSOCOM and the FCI[105]—he no longer seemed willing to take more vigorous action on its behalf. Moreover, he kept the hands of the Conference itself tied by continuing to refuse it *carte blanche* in the use of fighting rates. As a result, a Special Meeting of the Lines was called in early December 1971 in order to decide what to do. This council of war was opened by Lemon with an ominous roll-call of existing intruders and others on the horizon. The Lines were not being confronted by 'the odd tramp competition', said the Conference Chairman, but by 'determined opposition being mounted from various sources'. In the light of this it was agreed that Steyn should once more be asked to provide the Lines at the very least with a free hand in the use of fighting rates, and in the hope that he would agree an 'Action Committee' was appointed.[106]

The appointment of the Action Committee did not prove futile, for on 9 December Steyn at last met the Lines' minimum demand, granting them authority to use fighting rates without reference to his office. However, he did not do this without serious misgivings and was subsequently described by Lemon as 'somewhat despondent and, indeed, depressed' about the whole position.[107]

What Steyn pretended to fear most of all was that major resort to fighting rates would be self-defeating since, under the OFA Formula, the shortfall in revenue to which this would lead would require an *increase* in rates. However, this was only a debating point since, obviously, the Lines could either delay asking for the increases until after the opposition had been beaten off, or they could retain fighting rates (which were selectively applied) while simultaneously implementing general increases. Steyn's real fear was slightly different: this was the belief, already voiced by Haak in the House of Assembly in May 1969, that since it was in the Southbound trade that the main opposition

[105] CAL, Joint Meeting Minutes, 19 Oct. 1971; and *SA Shipping News*, Oct. 1971.
[106] CAL, Special Joint Meeting Minutes, 2 Dec. 1971.
[107] CAL, Lemon to Lines, 13 Dec. 1971.

challenge was being mounted, and, therefore, where most fighting rates had to be offered, the Lines would look for their compensatory increases in the *Northbound* trade alone. It was really for this reason that Steyn attached three particularly important conditions to his latest gesture of support: firstly, that the new freedom would only apply to shipments effected up to 30 June 1972; secondly, that the Lines would only be able to debit the Formula with 50 per cent of the revenue sacrificed by the use of fighting rates; and thirdly, that revenue thus lost on the Southbound trade could not be used to justify increases on the Northbound trade.[108] The implications of his concession for freight rates in the Northbound trade were also responsible for Steyn suggesting to Lemon that 'if an out and out war eventuated, then the Formula arrangement must be suspended'.[109]

Despite the conditions attached to Steyn's offer, Lemon thought that the Lines had achieved 'a major step', and the Action Committee was soon quoting rates in the Southbound trade which were on average 15 per cent below tariff rates and in some instances up to 27 per cent below. Shortly afterwards, Steyn relented further and allowed the Lines to quote fighting rates as far ahead as they felt necessary.

Relieved though they were at having their hands untied by the government in the face of the increasingly serious challenge from outsiders, the Lines continued to believe that the problem of opposition would never be resolved in the current recession without firmer government action to *compel* South African shippers, importers, and receivers to patronize Conference vessels exclusively. This belief was further strengthened when, after five months of rate-cutting, there were no signs that the most worrying of the new intruders, EIN/CCN, was being driven off. On the contrary, the Joint Meeting of the Conference in June 1972 was told that the Portuguese were doing quite well in the South Africa trade and that CCN—which in early January had been expelled from the Conference for going into opposition with EIN[110]—was extending its activities by introducing a service between South Africa and the Mediterranean.[111] The Lines consoled themselves with two thoughts: firstly, that at least the Smith regime in Rhodesia had been successfully warned off patronizing EIN/CCN because of the spotlight which would inevitably fall on their

[108] CAL, Steyn to Lemon, 17 Dec. 1971.
[109] CAL, Lemon to Lines, 13 Dec. 1971.
[110] CAL, Lemon to CCN, 10 Jan. 1972.
[111] CAL, Joint Meeting Minutes, 29 June 1972.

illegal traffic if it became involved in a freight war;[112] and secondly, that Steyn had persuaded ESCOM to *instruct* all those who tendered for its business to ship exclusively with the Conference[113]—though, as the SALines Chairman observed at the June Joint Meeting, until the government made the rest of the statutory corporations fall into line as well there was no chance at all that private industry in South Africa would respond to Steyn's promptings.[114]

By 1972, then, it was obvious that the opposition in the trade was presenting a serious threat to the whole relationship between the Lines and the South African government. The Lines were deeply dissatisfied with the support which Steyn was giving them, while the Secretary for Commerce was becoming more alarmed at the implications of the Formula for freight rates in general and Northbound freight rates in particular. When in March it had become clear that, although in the current Formula Year the Lines were operating at a small surplus, the Formula Year ended 30 September 1971 had produced a deficit as high as £7.7m. (bringing the cumulative deficit to £9.7m.), it was evident that a reckoning could not be postponed for long. Fearing that if they failed to press for further increases now they would be left irretrievably in arrears at the end of the OFA period, the Lines begged Steyn for yet another interim Freight Review.[115] Though he reluctantly agreed to this, the Secretary for Commerce warned Lemon that Cabinet hostility to the OFA—which had been simmering for some time—was now at such a pitch that the Review could well spell the end of the historic contract.[116]

It is not difficult to understand the attitude of the Cabinet Committee on Economic Affairs. Since the end of the 1960s South Africa had faced mounting inflation and balance of payments deficits. In an attempt to rectify the payments position, import controls were introduced in November 1971, and in December the rand was devalued by 12.28 per cent; to combat inflation, restrictive fiscal and monetary measures were introduced. Following these moves, the balance of payments improved in the first half of 1972 (the deficit in 1971 had been a record), but the higher cost of imports following rand devaluation made it more difficult to control inflation. Nevertheless, in the middle of 1972 the authorities were under pressure to relax import

[112] Ibid., 27 Mar. 1972.   [113] CAL, Lemon to Steyn, 13 June 1972.
[114] CAL, Joint Meeting Minutes, 29 June 1972.
[115] Ibid., 27 Mar. 1972; and Lemon to Steyn, 6 Apr. 1972.
[116] CAL, Steyn to Lemon (telex), 14 Apr. 1972.

controls and stimulate the economy.[117] It was against this background that the Cabinet Committee saw the Lines' demand for yet another substantial round of tariff increases—a demand made despite the fact that outsiders were crowding into the trade and both private and public sectors in the Republic were imploring the government to drop its hostility to the cut-rate services they were offering. In other words, just as the government thought it had got things right, along came the spoiled Conference Lines proposing to throw a spanner in the works.

The size of the spanner became evident to the government at the 'Special Freight Review', which was held in early June. The Lines would need, said Lemon, either 15 per cent effective from September or 10 per cent in September followed by another 10 per cent a year later—in fact, probably 10 per cent a year until the end of the OFA in 1976. Not surprisingly, Steyn replied: 'You couldn't have selected a worse time in the history of this document to come forward with what you want to do now. You could not have selected a worse time', he repeated, 'and I speak on the authority of seven Cabinet Ministers.'[118] Elaborating on why this should have been so, he said that 'Such an increase in rates . . . must necessarily intensify the pressures of inflation with which we are faced and at the same time it must largely dilute to our export trade the benefits of devaluation which we had hoped to reap in the interests of the balance of payment.'[119] The Lines would have to wait for a while, he informed their delegates, before the government announced its decision.

It was not until 20 July that the Lines learnt officially from Steyn that the government had decided to grant them increases of 7½ per cent in each direction, effective from 30 October.[120] Of course, they did not like this at all and believed that they would need another 10 per cent in April. But at least the government—as in the Biennial Review of the previous year—had not discriminated against the Southbound trade. Presumably this was partly because exports were no longer in the doldrums and it was anxious to avoid importing inflation.

This further increase in freight rates, and the deeper Cabinet hostility to the OFA which the Conference demand had provoked, had concentrated Steyn's mind on the problem of opposition in the trade as

[117] Standard Bank, *Annual Economic Review: South Africa*, Dec. 1972.
[118] CAL, Notes covering Discussions held in Marks Building, Parliament Street, Cape Town, at 9.00 a.m. on Thur. 1 June 1972.
[119] Ibid., at 8.30 a.m., Fri. 2 June 1972.
[120] CAL, Lawrence to Lemon (telex), 20 July 1972.

never before. In August he informed Lemon that he was prepared to fly to Lisbon himself and take up the matter of EIN/CCN opposition with the Portuguese at the highest possible level.[121] Shortening a planned trip to Brazil, the Secretary for Commerce descended on Lisbon on 7 September and remained for two days, accompanied by Marsh of Safmarine, and with Lemon and R. Brennecke of DOAL in the wings (the Continental Lines, who were suffering most from the opposition in the trade, were afraid that Lemon and Steyn were going to do a deal with the Portuguese at their expense and insisted on Brennecke's attendance).

Although in August Steyn's position had still been that the Portuguese outsiders should be admitted to the Conference, by the eve of the Lisbon trip political considerations were obviously weighing less heavily with him than the general problem of opposition. On 1 September he telexed Lemon that he was having 'second thoughts about the admission of the two Portuguese outsiders to the Conference seeing that this may not provide a solution to all or even the largest part of problems of the Lines'.[122] He was also, of course, aware of the majority view in the Conference that the admission of EIN/CCN could even—by encouraging other outsiders—make these problems worse. In the event, while Steyn seems to have remained reconciled to the possible entry of the Portuguese for political reasons, he took a tough line in Lisbon, hoping either to scare them off or, failing that, to establish a climate in which they would be inclined to sue for peace on terms which the Conference could swallow.

Steyn certainly had a weighty audience in Lisbon: Ambassador Calvet de Magalhaes, Secretary General of Foreign Affairs (already well known to the South Africans as a result of his leading role in the negotiations on Cabora Bassa[123]); Admiral Gomes Ramos, Chairman of the Maritime Board; and Dr Thomas Breiyner Anderson, Director General of Economic Affairs. However, Steyn brushed aside the Portuguese claim for preferential treatment for their shipping on the grounds of their *entente* with Pretoria, and told them that EIN/CCN activities were disrupting South Africa's vital trade with Europe, damaging the interests of the Republic's own merchant marine, costing the government money, and threatening to wreck rationalization. As a result, he said, these activities must cease.[124] Nevertheless, Steyn

---

[121] CAL, Steyn to Lemon (telex), 23 Aug. 1972, and 29 Aug. 1972.
[122] Ibid., 1 Sept. 1972.   [123] Middlemas, *Cabora Bassa*, 26 and 59.
[124] CAL, Lemon to Lines, 11 Sept. 1972.

did not make any threats, and the Portuguese, while protesting their anxiety to avoid harming their relations with South Africa, showed no inclination to fall in with his demands. Though Lemon subsequently claimed that Steyn had 'read the riot act to the Portuguese government',[125] it was obvious from the talks which the Conference Chairman had with EIN/CCN representatives immediately following Steyn's intervention, that the latter had not even succeeded in persuading Lisbon to scale down its lines' demands.

Steyn himself was under no illusions about the effectiveness of his *démarche* in Lisbon and asked Lemon to visit him in November for urgent discussions. Opposition in the trade, Steyn informed Lemon, was now at a level vastly in excess of anything contemplated at the time of the signature of the current OFA in 1966, and, as a result, the Formula was not working as envisaged. In particular, he continued, repeating the argument of a year earlier, since most fighting rates had been introduced in the Southbound trade, 'the Northbound trade was taking the brunt of the consequences of opposition'. In any case, the fighting rates were ineffective and were likely to remain so—'the opposition continued and, in fact, was increasing its hold on the trade'. It was in this light, Steyn informed Lemon, that he had been appointed Chairman of a committee to investigate the OFA, consisting of the heads of the seven government departments 'most concerned with the economic life of the country'. Steyn did not seem to Lemon to be suggesting that the OFA should be scrapped, but rather that it should be modified, as provided for under the 'changed circumstances' clause in the Agreement. However, the only substantial idea which Steyn proposed was that membership of the Conference should be reduced form the 'excessive' number of twenty-two so that the freight rates thrown up by the Formula should cease to reflect the inefficiencies inevitably found in such a variety of operations.[126] The committee of seven, by implication, would come up with more far-reaching proposals.

In reply to Steyn, Lemon ducked the issue of a reduction in Conference membership and, on the opposition, shifted his ground somewhat by seeking to minimize the latter's extent—in terms of its percentage share of the trade, if not in terms of its effects on the Lines'

---

[125] CAL, Lemon to Lawrence (telex), 12 Sept. 1972.
[126] CAL, Lemon to Lines, 20 Nov. 1972: Discussion with Mr Steyn in Pretoria 13–14 Nov. 1972, No. 1—Opposition in the Trade.

revenue, which he admitted.[127] He also reminded Steyn of the advantages of the OFA to South Africa, pointing out that, in its absence, there would be no *guarantee* of shipping for South Africa's overseas trade, especially for its exports, and that the latter would cease to be subsidized by the Lines. (At this stage Lemon told Steyn that 'it would pay the Lines in many instances to ballast ships back from South Africa to Europe rather than take a Northbound cargo'.) In addition, he slipped in the telling point that the Lines simply would not make the massive investment in new transport techniques, which—as we shall see—was now being anxiously sought by the government, if they were not to be provided with 'security of tenure' in the trade. The answer, repeated Lemon, was *to get rid of the opposition* and, if South African shippers and importers could not be legally compelled to use the Conference (as Steyn had reaffirmed), then informal pressure to this end should be stepped up. In the case of the statutory corporations, the government should go beyond the letter of the OFA and direct, rather than merely exhort them to support the Conference.[128]

It is clear that Steyn did not attempt to deny the general advantages of the OFA for South Africa, and that Lemon's confidence was properly placed when he subsequently reported to the Lines that 'I have no doubt in my own mind but that he will not be easily moved away from this concept'.[129] However, it is also clear that the meeting did not produce any further agreements between the Conference and the South Africans as to how to cope with the opposition. Steyn repeated that he was already doing everything he could as far as the statutory corporations were concerned, while Lemon had to admit that, since almost all of their traffic was now being carried by the Conference, they were not really the problem.[130] As for EIN/CCN, Steyn, whose Lisbon *démarche* had provoked an official protest at Foreign Minister level, merely confirmed that politics dictated the necessity for a peace settlement. Lemon also saw that there was no way around this, and at the Joint Meeting in December it was agreed to

[127] Between December 1971 and 30 June 1972 the Lines had lost an estimated £543,000 in fighting the opposition in the Southbound trade and £14,000 Northbound. As % of the total freights which would have been earned in the absence of fighting rates, these losses amounted to 2.54% Southbound, and 0.6% Northbound: CAL, Lemon to Nichol, 18 Aug. 1972.
[128] CAL, Lemon to Lines, 20 Nov. 1972: Discussion with Mr Steyn in Pretoria 13–14 Nov. 1972, No. 3—Statutory Corporations; and Lemon to Steyn, 6 Nov. 1972.
[129] CAL, Lemon to Lines, 20 Nov. 1972.
[130] Ibid.: Discussion with Mr Steyn in Pretoria 13–14 Nov. 1972, No. 3—Statutory Corporations.

make an approach to the Portuguese flag group as a whole.[131] But
Steyn insisted that the Portuguese, whose ships were short of cargo
outwards to Mozambique but full on the return leg and who therefore
only wanted to participate in the lucrative Southbound trade from
North Europe to South Africa, should be made to carry their share of
the Northbound trade as well. He added that no deal should be struck
with them without his prior approval.[132]

The OFA and the CENSA Code

Another matter which was discussed by Lemon and Steyn at their
crisis talks in November 1972 was whether or not the South African
Conference should adopt the Code of Practice for Conferences which
had been agreed between CENSA and the ESC at Genoa in October
the previous year, and which came to be known as the 'CENSA Code'.
Whilst it did not contain any radical ideas, it codified the best
conference practices which had been adopted since the early 1960s in
an attempt to forestall more radical action by UNCTAD. These
consisted mainly of more consultation with shippers' councils and, as a
corollary of this, the provision of more information to shippers on
conference affairs. Adoption of the Code was voluntary, but after its
announcement all conferences came under considerable pressure from
CENSA, ESC, and the CSG governments to endorse it. This was the
more necessary since, unfortunately for the traditional maritime
powers, the underdeveloped countries were just as offended by the
assumption that a code drafted without their participation would be
acceptable to them, as they were by the provisions of the CENSA
Code, which they naturally regarded as inadequate. As a result, as Juda
says, the CENSA Code 'inflamed rather than soothed passions' in the
Third World, and at a meeting in Lima in November 1971 its
representatives called for the drafting of a new code under UNCTAD
auspices. After UNCTAD prompting the following year, the UN
General Assembly voted to convene a major conference for the
purpose of drafting such a code.[133]

Under considerable pressure from CENSA and the ESC, not to

---

[131] CAL, Joint Meeting Minutes, 12 Dec. 1972.
[132] CAL, Lemon to Lines, 20 Nov. 1972: Discussion with Mr Steyn in Pretoria
13-14 Nov. 1972, No. 1—Opposition in the Trade.
[133] L. Juda, *The UNCTAD Liner Code: United States Maritime Policy at the Crossroads*
(Boulder, Col., 1983), 8.

mention national associations of shipowners and shippers together with their governments, many lines in the South African Conference were anxious to subscribe to the CENSA Code. However, the nature of the relationship between the Conference and the South African government which was expressed in the Ocean Freight Agreement made this impossible: the OFA and the CENSA Code were creatures of different worlds. Whereas the CENSA Code held that the liner trades should be controlled by shipping conferences in consultation with shippers, with the balance of power resting squarely with the former and with no provision for government participation, the OFA enshrined the right of the South African *government* to control all important matters in the South Africa trade, albeit in consultation with the shipowners in the Conference; shippers, whose rights had been increased in the CENSA Code, were largely ignored in the OFA (of course, South African shippers in general were indirectly represented by the government in the OFA, and perishables exporters were directly represented by the PPECB, but *European shippers* were utterly excluded from the OFA). The South African flag lines in particular had pointed out how the OFA would make it difficult for the Conference to adopt the CENSA Code when Lemon had canvassed opinion on this question at the beginning of 1972.[134]

The Lines were clearly in a quandary. On the one hand they were just as anxious as the other CENSA members to take the wind out of UNCTAD's sails by making the Code work and were instinctively sympathetic to its hostility to government regulation; on the other hand, government regulation was a fact of life in the South Africa trade, and Lemon in particular was acutely aware that Steyn would not welcome a CENSA-sanctioned challenge to it from European shippers. Thus pulled in opposite directions, the Lines took the only rational course available to them: they stalled. Indicating to CENSA their intention to act in the *spirit* of the Code, they did not formally accept or reject it.[135] However, in the second half of 1972, with the growing likelihood of a rival code being produced by UNCTAD, pressure on conferences to adopt the CENSA Code mounted (indeed, by the end of the year over forty conferences—including some major ones—had already subscribed to it),[136] and Lemon had decided to seek Steyn's guidance at the crisis talks in November.

In Pretoria, Lemon found Steyn poorly briefed on the whole

[134] CAL, Joint Meeting Minutes, 15 Feb. 1972.   [135] Ibid., 29 June 1972.
[136] OECD, *Maritime Transport 1972* (Paris, 1973).

question of the CENSA Code and its embryonic rival, the UNCTAD Code, and partly for this reason found it easy to win the support of the Secretary for Commerce for his preferred course of action. The Conference, said Steyn, 'should not rush into adopting the Code . . . [and] should stall unless and until such time as the present contractual arrangements as expressed in the Ocean Freight Agreement were revised, if there is any revision'.[137] With this, and despite Lemon's apprehension at the reaction in Western Europe,[138] prevarication on the CENSA Code was confirmed as the policy of the South African Conference.

[137] CAL, Lemon to Lines, 20 Nov. 1972: Discussion with Mr Steyn in Pretoria 13–14 Nov. 1972, No. 7—General items applicable to both Southbound and Northbound Trades—Code of Conference Practice.
[138] Ibid.

7

BOXING IN THE GOVERNMENT
1973–1974

As if the opposition to the Conference was not already bad enough by the end of 1972, the following year started with an intrusion before which the others paled into insignificance. This was the entry into the trade of the specialized container company, Enterprise Container Lines (ECL), which on 25 January 1973 despatched its first sailing from Rotterdam.[1] Though ECL was controlled by Norwegian interests (Skjelbreds Reederi of Kristiansand), it had been registered in South Africa and was headed by R. D. Robertson, previously the South African Foreign Trade Organization's containerization expert.[2]

Although the Conference initially regarded the intrusion of ECL with a certain amount of complacency, this was not to last for long. The Lines had been under pressure from the South African government to explore the possibility of 'new transport techniques' since 1965, and at the beginning of 1973 they were still not in a position to put forward firm proposals. Having proved that it could run an efficient operation based on the most promising of the new techniques, ECL put at risk the Conference's long-term interests, for it had been obvious for some time that the future of most trades lay with shipping freight in large metal boxes in specially designed cellular vessels, that is to say, with 'containerization'.

New transport techniques had been an undercurrent in relations between the Conference and the government since May 1965, when the South Africans, anxious as always to explore every means of reducing the costs of shipping in the trade with Europe, had urged their joint study.[3] Shortly thereafter the Lines had established their own study group, and during the protracted negotiations on the new OFA a decision on the creation of a joint working party had been one of the few important ones quickly arrived at.[4] In the meantime, B & C,

---

[1] *Fairplay*, 22 Feb. 1973.   [2] *Fairplay*, 21 Dec. 1972.
[3] CAL, Kotzenberg to Bevan, 7 May 1965.
[4] 6th Meeting, 1st series. This agreement was written into the new OFA as cl. 7, p. 9.

which had been seriously interested in containerization since 1960,[5] had teamed up with three of Britain's other biggest liner groups, P & O, Alfred Holt, and Furness Withy, to form a new company—Overseas Containers Limited (OCL)—to develop container traffic and other modern transport techniques.[6]

The Conference as a whole, however, had not been able to generate much enthusiasm about introducing containers into the South Africa trade, for by 1967 it had concluded that this would be feasible but not economically viable—at least not for a very long time. It was said that Northbound cargoes from South Africa were not really suitable for containerization, and that there would be few savings to be made in the Republic's ports since they did not suffer the high labour costs and trade union militancy which were encouraging containerization on other routes. However, the main reasons for the lack of Conference enthusiasm had less to do with the merits of the issue than with background circumstances. First of all, there had been the extraordinary complexity of the problem and the daunting prospect of securing agreement on new proposals in a conference with so many members and such divergent interests. Secondly, it was unfortunate for the Lines that this question had surfaced just as they became preoccupied with the more immediate and almost equally complex problems of opposition and reappraisal. Thirdly, they had shown an understandable desire to see how the container service currently being introduced between Europe and Australia worked out, since Australia had a similar trade with Europe to South Africa. Finally, they were very concerned that over-hasty introduction of containerization would jeopardize existing investments in conventional tonnage, including—as far as B & C was concerned—the mail ships and the refrigerated cargo ships.[7]

For all of these reasons, it was not until March 1968 that the joint working party called for in the new OFA had actually been set up, following pressure from Steyn in the previous October.[8] In the light of the Conference attitude, Steyn had wisely insisted that the government should take charge of the working party and had put at its head the influential Professor W. F. J. Steenkamp. The other members came from the PPECB, the SAR&H, and the Department of Commerce;

[5] *The Times*, 2 Sept. 1965.
[6] CAL, N. M. Forster, 'South African Containerisation' (internal report), Mar. 1969.
[7] CAL, Joint Meeting Minutes, 20 Oct. 1967.
[8] Ibid., 21 June 1968.

D. B. Lawrence, the local Conference Chairman, was the only Conference representative on it.[9]

The Steenkamp Report

As it happened, Steenkamp had also proceeded relatively slowly and had not reported until August 1970, several months after a visit by his group to Australia. As expected, though, he had come out strongly in favour of containerization, classifying the other new techniques which had been canvassed as nothing more than optional transitional stages on the road to its achievement. The 'container movement', Steenkamp had concluded, 'has acquired revolutionary momentum', and, since it was proceeding quickest in South Africa's main markets and was being joined by the Republic's rivals, especially Australia, South Africa would have to join in as well, whether it liked it or not.[10]

But, Steenkamp had said, it was not merely a case of South Africa having to put its trade into boxes in order to ensure its acceptance; there would also be direct benefits, such as the faster turn-round of ships.[11] Nor was the capital cost of the new methods likely to prove daunting, he had claimed, since the greater part would consist of investment in the boxes and new vessels, and this would be borne by the shipping companies. The capital to be found by the government for port and inland facilities (about 20 per cent of the total) would be 'by no means large in relation to the means a country like South Africa possesses', representing about R20m. for a five-ship fleet.[12] In the light of these and other arguments Steenkamp had been able to conclude that 'the new transport system promises to arrest the continuous post-war rise in transport costs and hence in freight rates'.[13]

Following from this analysis, Steenkamp's recommendations had not been surprising. The most important from the point of view of the Conference were that 'Containerisation should be introduced into the South African trade at the earliest possible date', and in order to ensure that the SAR&H could proceed with developing the infra-structure, the shipping companies should also submit their proposals 'at the earliest possible date'. Interestingly, he had also added that the Railways should 'seriously consider the desirability of leasing the container berths and their stacking areas to the shipping companies,

[9] CACT, Report of the Working Group investigating New Cargo Handling and Packing Methods, 38 f.
[10] Ibid., 42-6.   [11] Ibid., 56-60.   [12] Ibid., 73 f.   [13] Ibid., 73.

provided they will be operated without discrimination'.[14] On 24 August
Steenkamp was publicly endorsed by both the Ministry of Economic
Affairs and the Ministry of Transport.[15] The next move belonged to
the Lines.

The Seizing-up of the Conference, and the EPB

Unfortunately for the Lines, they had not been able to agree among
themselves on the sort of proposals to put to the government. Indeed,
the Continental Lines had suggested that containerization was not
necessarily appropriate to their sphere of the trade, and had expressed
resentment at the bias of the Conference's own studies towards it.
Lemon had repeatedly warned the Lines of the government's
impatience and of the importance of not appearing to be dragging their
feet, but a conclusion to their studies had still been nowhere in sight by
the Joint Meeting in December 1972. With obviously mounting
anxiety, Lemon had told the Lines that he had undertaken to produce
something for Steyn by the middle of 1973.[16]

This was the situation when ECL independently introduced
containers into the trade in January 1973, and thereby added to the
pressure on the Lines. At the eleventh hour, in June, the Conference's
Steering Committee on containerization managed to produce a report,
and at two Joint Meetings held in quick succession in the first half of
July it was agreed that containerization should be introduced and that
it should be controlled by an integrated Conference operation—not
least because Steyn had made it clear that South Africa would accept
nothing less.[17] But the Conference was still unable to reach agreement
on the key decisions of when and precisely how containerization
should be introduced. Its decision-making procedure had seized up,
and the deadline with Steyn slipped by.

It was not surprising that by this time the exasperation of those
member lines most anxious to proceed quickly with containerization—
including B & C and Safmarine—had become unbearable. In their
view the unanimity rule on matters of major principle which was
traditional in the Conference had—in an organization of this
size—finally proved itself too serious an impediment to the taking of
necessary radical decisions. Accordingly, B & C and Safmarine,
together with Nedlloyd, DOAL, and Ellermans, took the only action

[14] Ibid., 76 f.   [15] *Commerce & Industry*, 39.2, Oct. 1970.
[16] CAL, Joint Meeting Minutes, 12 Dec. 1972.   [17] Ibid., 2 July 1973.

left open to them: they grabbed the reins themselves and set up their own, informal group to complete quickly the study of containerization and drive firm proposals through the Conference under the implicit threat that they would go it alone if the others would not agree. The Executive Planning Board (EPB), as the new group was styled, was placed under the chairmanship of R. J. Marsman of Nedlloyd and the vice-chairmanship of N. M. Forster of B & C. Its sense of urgency was reinforced by alarm at the escalating level of quotations for new container ships and by the notice served by Steyn in October that the substance of a new agreement with the Lines on containerization would have to be negotiated early in the following year; in preparation for this, he would need to know their proposals by December.[18] In the event, the EPB reported to Lemon on 11 December.

The EPB Report was firm and succinct. It predicted that by 1977 demand for containerization would cover almost three-quarters of the Southbound trade from the UK and the North Continent. That being so, it recommended the introduction as soon as possible—'(it is hoped by 1977)'—of a fleet of ten cellular container ships operating on a schedule of just over five days' frequency. The residual trade from North Europe should be carried by existing conventional vessels, together with four or five newly built Roll-on Roll-off ('Ro-Ro') ships. A cellular container service should also be introduced into the trade from the Mediterranean (three or four vessels, depending on the reopening of the Suez Canal), while as for the Northbound trade, the EPB felt that both cellular and Ro-Ro vessels should be built with perishables capacity; the mail service should 'either cease to exist or be severely curtailed'.

The EPB Report also contained some thoughts on the shape of the new Ocean Freight Agreement which would be appropriate to the 'New Transport Era'. Amongst other things, it noted that 'With regard to the return on capital . . . 15% would certainly be the minimum to be considered in present financial conditions bearing in mind the very substantial commercial and political risks involved in the construction of highly specialised custom built ships for this trade'; and that 'Maximum possible protection must be provided against outsider incursion'. In conclusion, the Report observed that 'The main services will be on integrated and jointly agreed schedules with a return to each shipowner commensurate with his capital investment'.[19]

[18] CAL, Lemon to Lines, 15 Oct. 1973.
[19] CAL, Marsman to Lemon, 11 Dec. 1973.

Feverish discussion among the Lines followed the delivery of the EPB Report, though the main argument—which in the light of the difficulties of 'reappraisal' was hardly surprising—was over the question of shares in the new container service rather than the character of the service suggested by the EPB, upon which there was broad agreement. In particular, having established that, in line with UNCTAD thinking on the cargo shares of national lines and the results of 'reappraisal', the South African flag group would be allowed four of the ten cellular vessels to be employed on the North Europe run, the British and Continental Lines could not agree on the division of the remaining six. Nor was there enthusiasm for Safmarine's claim that, in return for dropping an initial demand for 50 per cent of the new service, the South African flag group should be permitted 41 per cent of earnings on the basis of only 40 per cent of liftings.[20] However, although these matters were to be the subject of further internal wranglings, at least by the time of the Joint Meeting in February 1974 the Conference had agreed that Lemon should negotiate a settlement on containerization with the South Africans based broadly on the EPB Report. Indeed, in one respect this Report was sharpened up: in return for the massive capital investments which the new service would require—estimated by the Lines at about £300m.[21]—the Conference was determined to press the government for a return on capital of 12½ per cent on written down replacement cost (Steyn had already accepted that *depreciation* would be allowed on a replacement basis, with a 15-year life for the new ships and 7½ for the boxes[22]), or 15 per cent on written down historic cost, with revision after the first six years of the new OFA.[23]

The Memorandum of Understanding, February 1974

It was now possible to bring the issue of containerization in the South Africa trade to a successful climax. During 21 and 22 February 1974, in Cape Town, Lemon and Steyn negotiated a 'Memorandum of Understanding . . . regarding the introduction of a New Technique of Ocean Transport in the Trade between South Africa and Europe'.

[20] CAL, Joint Meeting Minutes, 13 Feb. 1974.
[21] On present trends, N. M. Forster calculated that the delivered price of a container ship in January 1977 would be about £15m.: CAL, Ship Capital Costs, 9 Oct. 1973. The figure of £300m. appears in an annex to the EPB Report of 11 December.
[22] CAL, Joint Meeting Minutes, 13 Feb. 1974.   [23] Ibid.

This Memorandum was ratified in March and was in fact a new Ocean Freight Agreement in all but name. It did not try to cover every point of detail in the traditional manner of the OFA, for there was no time for this now (in any case, the current OFA did not formally expire until the end of 1976), but if containerization was to be introduced into the trade at least by 1977, there had to be agreement on the main points: this is what the Memorandum achieved.

What the Memorandum of Understanding revealed was that the Lines had sold the EPB Report's package to the government at a very good price. As already agreed, depreciation on the vessels and containers in the new service was to be calculated on replacement cost at 6.33 and 13.33 per cent respectively. As anticipated, Steyn had not accepted replacement cost as the basis for calculating the return on the Lines' capital, but they still received a respectable 12½ per cent on historic cost (instead of 15 per cent). Moreover, it was accepted that freight rates (which would normally be reviewed *annually*, but also in the interim in 'exceptional circumstances') would be so fixed as to enable the Lines 'to aim' to earn their 12½ per cent over the following *year*, and in any event by the end of the 'initial period'.[24] The government also agreed that it would 'not require the Contractors to accept a return more than 2½% below the level of 12½% in any period of twelve months'.[25]

In contrast to the current OFA, under which the agreed rate of return was only to be achieved over the ten-year period as a whole, with the very real prospect of a large deficit accruing which the government would find politically impossible to make good at the end, here was the government unambiguously agreeing to a floor of 10 per cent for the Lines' rate of return in any twelve-month period of the agreement. In addition, the 12½ per cent was itself guaranteed to the Lines over the shorter 'initial period', following which the financial provisions could be renegotiated. In these circumstances, it would clearly be much more difficult for the government to avoid paying its debts. To reassure the Lines further, the duration of the agreement was extended from the traditional ten years to fifteen, and the escape clause providing for 'changed circumstances' would only come into

---

[24] This was defined as 'the period which terminates on the date on which the new technique ships to be introduced to the service have on average been in service for six years': CAL, Memorandum of Understanding, Annexure F, para. 3, Cape Town, 22 Feb. 1974.
[25] Ibid., para. 9.

operation after the 'initial period'[26] (under the current OFA the escape clause could be invoked at any time). The new OFA, then, would run from the beginning of 1977 until the end of 1991, by which time the new vessels were expected to be on their last legs. For good measure the Lines insisted on the insertion of a clause stipulating that any surplus *or deficit* arising under the current OFA which was not cleared by the end of 1976 would be carried forward to the new OFA.[27]

Of course, the Lines did not quite get everything they wanted in the Memorandum of Understanding, especially with regard to outsiders: the clause on 'Protection for the Contractors' merely reiterated that the government would use its 'best endeavours' to preserve the Conference position.[28] Furthermore, the Steenkamp Report suggestion that the container berths and stacking areas might be leased to the shipping lines—which would really have enabled the Lines to squeeze any outsiders seeking to break into the container traffic, such as ECL—was not taken up. The SAR&H was to remain in control of the berths, even though the inland depots, it is true, were to go to private enterprise (which *did* permit some Conference influence, as we shall see). Finally, the government once again insisted on its right to load Southbound freight rates if this was required by the South African economy.[29]

Nevertheless, on the whole the Memorandum of Understanding represented a major achievement for the Conference and demonstrated the bargaining power of its capital, experience, and technical expertise on the one hand, and the government's anxiety to see the introduction of containerization on the other. The obsolescence of the Mail Contract, confirmed by the EPB Report, had also seriously weakened the government's hand. The government might still be unhappy with the current OFA but, clearly, if the 'committee of seven' appointed to investigate it had ever been given a brief to consider whether an OFA *in principle* was consistent with South Africa's interests, this had now been forgotten. Moreover, as the clause in the Memorandum on the Lines' cumulative deficit made apparent, the Conference had used its new bargaining power to prevent the government seeking any substantial departure from the *operation* of the current OFA as well. In short, the whole atmosphere had changed completely: nothing more was heard of the 'committee of seven', and the government was now the real supplicant. Pretoria had been well and truly boxed in.

---

[26] Ibid., Annexure H, para. 2.   [27] Ibid., Annexure F, para. 13.
[28] Ibid., and Annexure G.   [29] Ibid., Annexure F, para. 10(a).

8

'BEDEVILLED BY POLITICS'
1973–1977

By the time that the Memorandum of Understanding providing for the containerization of the Europe–South Africa trade was negotiated in February 1974, the Conference had its eyes set firmly on the 'new era', due to begin in 1977. However, before that date a great deal was to happen in the relations between the Conference and the government, on which, even more than in the years between 1964 and 1966, external events—both in international politics and in the international world of shipping—were to have a large bearing. As a result, although it was during the 1960s that, in a moment of exasperation, a representative of one of the lines in the Conference exclaimed at a Joint Meeting that the South Africa trade was 'bedevilled by politics', the complaint was even more appropriate to the period between 1973 and 1977.

In world politics the development of greatest significance to South Africa's relations with the Conference was the weakening and final collapse of Portuguese colonialism between 1972 and 1975, especially in Mozambique, the southern half of whose coastline (including the major ports of Beira and Lourenco Marques) fell within the range of the South African Conference. The gaping holes in the cordon sanitaire between South Africa and Black Africa which this development produced caused Pretoria to redouble its efforts to defuse the threat from the north by diplomacy and the strengthening of economic links. In these efforts—which continued despite South Africa's military intervention in the Angolan succession struggle in 1975–6, and the collapse of its efforts to promote a settlement in Rhodesia in the same period—'transport diplomacy', as it came to be known, played a significant part and had, as we shall see, interesting implications for the South African Conference.

As for the high politics of shipping, the main event here affecting relations between the Conference and the South African government over the next few years was the passing of the UNCTAD Liner Code by the UN General Assembly in late 1974. This Code assigned a greater role to governments than the CENSA Code had done, and, most strikingly, held that the flag shipping of the countries at both ends of a trade should each be entitled to up to 40 per cent of the cargo carried within the conference controlling that trade, with only the remaining 20 per cent being available for cross-traders.[1] Amongst other things, the UNCTAD Code also provided that any 'national shipping line' was entitled to *full* membership of any conference which served the foreign trade of its country. It is true that the new Code did not become international law until 1983,[2] but the large vote in its favour, which included three major West European maritime states (France, West Germany, and Belgium), gave it considerable moral authority. This not only strengthened Safmarine's claim to a major share in the proposed container service, but also encouraged new outsiders with *national* claims to entry into the trade—as well as giving further encouragement to existing outsiders (such as Hellenic), who had already been leaning heavily on this sort of argument.

The Worsening Problem of Opposition

ECL had entered the trade with its container service in January, the Hellenic War continued in the Mediterranean sector, and in late 1974 Spanish intruders appeared for the first time in force. In 1973 itself, however, the outsider to which the Lines were required to devote most attention remained the Portuguese EIN/CCN.

During a visit to South Africa in March 1973, the Portuguese Foreign Minister, Dr Rui Patricio, had delivered a second protest against Conference hostility to his country's lines. In fact, a whole afternoon of discussion between Dr Patricio and South Africa's Foreign Minister, Dr Hilgard Muller, had been devoted to this subject.[3] As a result of this, Muller asked Sir Nicholas Cayzer (who also happened to be in South Africa at the time) to remember that the Portuguese were 'good allies' of the Republic's in the conflict with 'communist guerrillas' in Southern Africa,[4] while Steyn asked Lemon

---

[1] For a full analysis of the UNCTAD Code, see L. Juda, *The UNCTAD Liner Code: United States Maritime Policy at the Crossroads* (Boulder, Colo., 1983); and, for an excellent comparison with the CENSA Code and American practice, A. W. Cafruny, 'The Political Economy of International Shipping: Europe versus America', *International Organization*, 39.1, Winter 1985.

[2] Juda, 145–51.

[3] CAL, A. E. Lemon, Discussion with Mr Steyn, Capetown, 28 May 73.

[4] CAL, Cayzer to Muller, 11 Mar. 1973.

to 're-double' his efforts to reach a settlement with the Portuguese flag group.[5] Negotiations took place at regular intervals from the end of March, but, despite some progress (including agreement on a short-term truce in the freight war), it had proved impossible to bridge the gap between the two sides, and by November the negotiations had faltered once more.[6]

Following this further failure everything went quiet at the Portuguese end as EIN and CCN became preoccupied with merging their organizations. In February 1974 this was eventually brought off, and the Conference found itself faced with a new company: Companhia Portuguesa de Transportes Maritimos (CPTM). The Portuguese then increased their demands by making it clear that they expected to be given one of the ten cellular container vessels now proposed by the EPB for the North Europe–South Africa trade, and over which the British and Continental Lines had already fallen out![7] With the stalemate between the Conference and the Portuguese thereby reinforced, the Portuguese Ambassador was instructed to make further protests to Steyn. Reassured by the reply of the Secretary for Commerce that he 'would certainly not dictate to the Conference the terms on which the Conference must reach an understanding with the PFG',[8] but conscious of his anxiety for an understanding of some sort, Lemon resumed talks with the Portuguese on 2 April.[9] Once more, however, there was deadlock, and it was at this juncture that the cunning of history came to Lemon's assistance.

On 25 April, following serious reverses in its colonial wars in Africa, especially against FRELIMO in Mozambique, the Caetano regime in Portugal was overthrown by radical army officers. After the Lisbon coup, the entire Board of CPTM resigned and was replaced by a 'Management Committee' of employees and shareholders.[10] In view of the general chaos, it was not thought that anything more would be heard from the Portuguese for some time; nor was it. And in view of the avowed determination of the new government in Lisbon to relax the hold of metropolitan Portugal on its colonies, Lemon did not think that Steyn would be putting any more pressure on him to settle with the Portuguese flag group;[11] nor did he.

[5] CAL, Lemon to Lines, 16 Apr. 1973.   [6] Ibid., 14 Nov. 1973.
[7] CAL, Joint Meeting Minutes, 13 Feb. 1974.
[8] CAL, Lemon to Lines, 3 Apr. 1974.   [9] Ibid.
[10] CAL, Joint Meeting Minutes, 25 June 1974.
[11] CAL, Lemon to Lawrence, 28 May 1974.

Of course, the Lisbon coup only partly solved Lemon's problems with the Portuguese: even though Steyn's pressure for their admission had been removed, they remained in the trade as outsiders. Furthermore, the Conference tactic of admitting Meandros as a representative of the Greek flag in order to block Hellenic had foundered on the refusal of the junta to sponsor one Greek line at the expense of another,[12] and, with the disappearance of this pressure, Hellenic were in no mood to scale down their demands for participation in the Mediterranean run. On 22 May 1973 Callimanopulos stalked out of Lemon's office, announcing as he left that he would never come to see the Conference Chairman again![13] Despite subsequent efforts by Safmarine (not entirely appreciated by Lemon) to act as peacemaker, Hellenic remained in opposition to the Conference.

The container line, ECL, was also causing the Lines more concern by establishing itself firmly in the trade with the North Continent. In May 1973 ECL had applied to join the Conference but had been turned down out of hand,[14] and now the Lines were having to compete with it by carrying a small number of containers themselves.[15] Indeed, the Conference had to devote more and more time to meeting the challenge from this new and worrying interloper, for even after the successful negotiation of the Memorandum of Understanding it was to be three or four years before the Lines' own container service was introduced. The ECL service not only highlighted the apparent tardiness of the Conference in this respect, but suggested that by 1977 there might not be any container cargo left for the Lines' expensive new vessels to lift.

In 1974 ECL seemed to go from strength to strength, and there was a major scare when Volkswagen appeared to be about to switch to the rogue container line for the shipment of its knocked-down cars from West Germany, despite being emphatically warned against this by Steyn.[16] Volkswagen stayed with the Conference, but the Lines were aware that they had only narrowly escaped a major blow.[17] Safmarine was becoming particularly alarmed at the ECL threat and, in addition to pressing the Conference to carry more boxes,[18] threatened those

[12] CAL, Joint Meeting Minutes, 15 Feb. 1972, and 12 Feb. 1973.
[13] CAL, Lemon to Lines, 23 May 1973.
[14] CAL, Joint Meeting Minutes, 4 June 1973.   [15] Ibid., 22 Oct. 1973.
[16] CAL, Steyn to Lawrence, 17 Sept. 1974.
[17] CAL, Joint Meeting Minutes, 11 Feb. 1975.   [18] Ibid., 8 Oct. 1974.

South African firms canvassing for ECL with exclusion from the proposed container depots consortium, South African Cargo Depots (SACD).

To add to the woes of the Conference, it was learned in the middle of 1974 that there were serious moves afoot in ASSOCOM to set up a South African Shippers' Council on the lines of those in Europe. Many South African shippers were exasperated at the combined attempts of the Lines and the government to prevent them exploiting the lower tariffs of the outsiders, and to this was now added the fear that Conference interests were disproportionately represented in the plans for the new container service.[19] However, it would be some time before a South African Shipper's Council could be launched, and in the meantime the most serious new danger was the sudden appearance in October 1974 of Spanish intruders supported by Madrid.

For balance of payments reasons, Spain, already a substantial maritime state, had decided, like the *ancien régime* in Portugal, to foster the further expansion of its merchant fleet on international routes. To assist this policy, it had relaxed restrictions on the purchase of cheaper foreign tonnage for those Spanish owners who were members of transoceanic conferences.[20] Following this, Spanish outsiders promised to appear in strength in the South Africa trade, whose Conference had as yet no Spanish members. Indeed, bids to join the Conference were received from two separate Spanish sources in October 1974, while in the same month the Lines learned that a third service was being planned to commence in the new year. The two formal approaches to the Conference came from Consortium Line, which was owned by Naviera Garcia-Minaur, SA of Bilbao, and three lines (Companhia Naviera Marasia, SA, Ybarra y Cia., SA, and Companhia Transatlantica Española, SA) proposing a jointly owned company. The line which realized that asking the Conference for membership would be a waste of time was subsequently styled 'Naviera Celta' (or 'Navicelta'), and was formed by Naviera de Canarias, SA and—to the chagrin of the Lines, and especially Safmarine—the South African company, Freight Services Ltd., in which Anglo-American had a 53 per cent shareholding.

Consortium Line had already been in the trade between Spain and Northern Europe for seven years, and was proposing to make the Spain–South Africa run economic by picking up cargo in the United Kingdom and on the North Continent. Its application was formally

[19] *SA Shipping News*, June 1974.
[20] CAL, Lemon to Steyn, 28 May 1975.

supported by letters from the Spanish Embassies in London and Pretoria, the Spanish Chamber of Commerce in Great Britain, and the Director General of Navigation in Madrid. For their part, Marasia, Ybarra y Cia., and Transatlantica Española were proposing to make the Spain–South Africa run viable by picking up cargo in the Mediterranean, while Naviera Celta was sensibly proposing to ignore Spain altogether and operate exclusively from the North Continent. As a result, Naviera Celta, Lemon informed Steyn, was not—despite its nominal colours—a 'Spanish' service at all.[21]

While the Lines were prepared to see the Spanish flag enter the small trade between South Africa and Spain itself on UNCTAD terms, they were naturally hostile to the proposed Spanish cross-trading in their sphere, and had no difficulty in persuading Steyn of its commercial undesirability. Moreover, in his initial reaction to this question, it was commercial rather than political considerations which were clearly uppermost in Steyn's thoughts. It is true that Spain and South Africa had links: trade between the two countries was not entirely insignificant and was certainly more substantial than that between South Africa and Greece; furthermore, it was growing quickly. Between 1973 and 1975 South African imports from Spain (which included a small proportion of arms[22]) almost tripled in value, while in 1975 the Spanish market for South African goods more than doubled its size the previous year, standing at $94.2m.[23] In November 1974, the month after the Spanish applications were received by the Conference, a large Spanish trade mission visited the Republic.[24] In addition, South African Airways (SAA)—which was barred from overflying and landing in almost all OAU countries and had to go around the 'bulge' of Africa to Europe—had landing rights at Las Palmas in Spain's Canary Islands. These were likely to prove much more important if South African flights were denied refuelling stops at Ilha do Sal in the Cape Verde Islands (since 1973 a stop *en route* to the USA as well as to Europe[25]) after independence in July 1975.[26] Finally,

---

[21] Ibid.

[22] P. H. Frankel, *Pretoria's Praetorians: Civil Military Relations in South Africa* (Cambridge, 1984), 85.

[23] UN, *Yearbook of International Trade Statistics 1975*, vol. 1.

[24] *Africa Contemporary Record, 1974–1975.*

[25] *Africa Contemporary Record, 1973–1974.*

[26] In November 1974 a spokesman for the incoming PAIGC Transition Government in Cape Verde announced that there would be no talks with SAA on future contracts until after independence. For the time being, SAA stops would be allowed to continue: *Africa Contemporary Record, 1974–1975.*

Franco Spain had good right-wing credentials and pursued a relatively independent line in foreign policy. It is not, therefore, entirely surprising (though it seems to have surprised Franco's government at the time) that, in his search for new friends, South Africa's Prime Minister, John Vorster, should have included Madrid in his short 'private' tour of Europe in June 1970.[27]

On the other hand, it is also clear that relations between Spain and South Africa had hardly become intimate in the period since 1970. Anxious for the retention of the support of the Afro-Asian states against Britain at the United Nations on the Gibraltar issue,[28] and with African problems of its own (in the Spanish Sahara) which it did not wish to see exacerbated,[29] Franco Spain was not enthusiastic about identification with South Africa, and had, indeed, voted steadily against it on the question of apartheid at the UN.[30] Vorster's reception in 1970 (he had more or less invited himself) had therefore been extremely muted, and it is significant that when South African arms purchasers were in Madrid in October 1971 (a fact denied by the Spanish Foreign Ministry), it was widely reported that the delivery of the Spanish corvettes which they were seeking would be laundered through Portugal.[31] In short, relations between Spain and South Africa were clearly not as important or as intimate as they were with Spain's Iberian neighbour, Portugal, and it is for this reason that Steyn initially failed to support the Spanish lines' application to join the Conference.

Thus confident of Steyn's support, at its next Joint Meeting, on 11 February 1975, the Conference decided to reject the applications from Consortium and from the three Spanish lines proposing a jointly owned company. To be more precise, the Spanish applications to enter the non-Spanish trades within the Conference sphere were rejected, though this was tantamount to a comprehensive rejection, since the Spain–South Africa trade alone could not support a regular service (assuming 40 per cent for the South African flag, as well as 40 per cent for the Spanish, and 20 per cent for the cross-traders). As for Naviera Celta, it was decided in the first instance to bring pressure to bear against this outsider by warning its South African backer, Freight Services (already the object of Conference resentment for its support of ECL), that the time had come for it to choose: long-term profit by

[27] *Guardian*, 9 June 1970.
[28] *Christian Science Monitor*, 28 Oct. 1971.
[29] *Daily Telegraph*, 8 June 1970.   [30] *The Times*, 9 June 1970.
[31] E.g. *Christian Science Monitor*, 28 Oct. 1971; and *Daily Telegraph*, 21 Oct. 1971.

friendship with the Lines and participation in SACD, or short-term gains by association with the opposition.[32]

Though Freight Services initially resisted Conference pressure to drop Naviera Celta, Steyn himself came to the assistance of the Lines a few months later by refusing an import licence to a South African company, John Deere, which was patronizing the Spanish line. The Spanish government retaliated by informing the South African Ambassador that SAA landing rights at Las Palmas would be substantially cut and might even be withdrawn altogether. This was a worrying development for the South Africans, since on the eve of the independence of the Cape Verde Islands there were fears that the strategic airport at Ilha do Sal would be leased to the Soviet Union and that, as a result, SAA landing rights there would also be withdrawn.[33] Steyn found himself in very hot water with the Cabinet for provoking the Spanish action at Las Palmas,[34] and, on 2 June, he asked Lemon to consider admitting Consortium Line to the Conference as the representative of the Spanish flag. This, Steyn said, would help South Africa 'to calm down the Spanish government' and restore SAA's landing rights at Las Palmas to their previous level.[35]

The pressure from Steyn to admit Consortium proved to be only a hiccup in Conference resistance to the Spanish intrusion. As early as 4 July Lemon found the Secretary for Commerce much more relaxed about the matter and of the opinion that the Lines, who had reluctantly accepted the need to negotiate with the Spanish, but on a flag rather than on a line basis, should be in no hurry to proceed. This change in attitude surprised and puzzled Lemon, and probably had something to do with the decision of the government of the newly independent—and deeply impoverished—Cape Verde Islands to adopt a policy of non-alignment and continue to allow SAA to stop at Ilha do Sal,[36] as well as with improving prospects at this fluid juncture in Africa's affairs for a South African air corridor through West Africa,[37] though Steyn's explanation for his change in attitude was simply that there had been

[32] CAL, Joint Meeting Minutes, 11 Feb. 1975.
[33] Africa Contemporary Record, 1975-1976.
[34] CAL, Lemon to Lines, 5 June 1975.
[35] Ibid., 16 June 1975.
[36] Africa Contemporary Record, 1977-1978, and 1978-1979.
[37] It seems likely that at this point South Africa was optimistic about obtaining landing rights in both Ivory Coast and the Central African Republic: The Times, 19 May 1975, and 16 July 1975; and D. Geldenhuys, The Diplomacy of Isolation: South African Foreign Policy Making (Johannesburg, 1984), 117 f and 148.

no further pressure from Madrid.[38] In any event, Steyn was once more lined up with the Conference against the Spanish, and his office had reiterated that John Deere should make exclusive use of its vessels.[39] At the Joint Meeting in October Lemon was also gratified to be able to report that Freight Services had given notice of disengagement from Naviera Celta from the end of the year, and had also agreed that in future it would confine its support to the Conference.[40]

By 1975, which, in consequence of the set-back suffered by world trade as a result of the oil crisis, was the worst year for shipping since the Second World War, the problem of opposition in the South African trade was acute, with the Lines having to give most of their attention to EIN/CCN, Hellenic, ECL, and—though it was on the defensive by the end of the year—Naviera Celta as well. Sceptical of the prospect of further help from the South African government, at the Joint Meeting on 11 February 1975 the Conference reassessed its own 'counter opposition policy', as it was now called. High on the agenda, as it had been for the last two years, was dual rating. (Steyn had promised to take care of any legal complications under the Post Office Act, 1911, which might arise for B & C and Safmarine as a result of their involvement in any such scheme.[41]) However, largely because of the European shippers' continuing hostility to dual rating, this proposal was rejected once more and, despite Lemon's pessimism about the effectiveness of rate-cutting, the Lines were left with little alternative but to refine this strategy.[42]

Freight Rates and the Crisis over the Cumulative Deficit

Planning for the 'new era' of containerization and grappling with the worsening problem of opposition had not allowed the Conference to lose sight of the question of freight rates and the cumulative deficit. Following the Special Freight Review held in early June 1972, the Lines had been granted increases of 7½ per cent in each direction, but the floating of sterling on 22 June had brought about an effective devaluation of 9½ per cent by November, and in the light of this—as well as of their dissatisfaction with the size of the recent increases—the

[38] CAL, Lemon to Lines, 12 Aug. 1975.
[39] CAL, Sempill to Lemon (telex), 1 July 1975.
[40] CAL, Joint Meeting Minutes, 28 Oct. 1975.
[41] CAL, Lawrence to Lemon (telex), 24 and 26 July 1973.
[42] CAL, Joint Meeting Minutes, 11 Feb. 1975.

Lines felt justified in pressing Steyn for a 10 per cent devaluation surcharge on all rates. This was, in fact, accepted by the Cabinet (with the proviso that perishables should be excluded), and on 1 December the Lines were able to introduce the surcharge in *both* directions. Having expected a discrimination in favour of the Northbound trade (in the level of the surcharge as well as by the exclusion of perishables), Lemon was once more pleasantly surprised.[43]

In early 1973, with sterling continuing to depreciate against continental currencies, the cumulative deficit at the end of September 1972 standing at about £9m., and Lemon expecting the Lines' figures for current trading to be adverse, the Conference decided to press Steyn for an increase in the devaluation surcharge from 10 to 15 per cent, and for perishables to be included as well. However, while he was making his case in Cape Town in February and March, the Conference Chairman was rather disconcerted to learn from preliminary voyage results that not only had the Lines 'more or less' earned their 8 per cent return on capital in the Formula Year ending September 1972, but, with the figures updated to 31 January 1973, they were currently £3m. in *surplus*.[44] In these circumstances, Lemon was content to accept Steyn's offer of agreement on the surcharge (now conceived mainly as a device to erode the cumulative deficit), provided that the Biennial Freight Review scheduled for April/May 1973 was cancelled. At least an increase in freight rates via a devaluation surcharge had the advantage from the Lines' point of view of more or less immediate implementation (in fact this one was introduced on 9 April), whereas an increase in the tariff rates required the customary three months' notice.[45] Further sterling depreciation induced Lemon to start pressing Steyn in August for the devaluation surcharge to be raised to 20 per cent, an increase which was finally implemented on 31 January 1974.[46]

As in 1972 the Formula figures for 1973 turned out to be quite encouraging for the Lines—updating them to 31 January 1974 the Lines were once more running a surplus on current trading of £3.5m. The cumulative deficit, however, was now almost £10m. and, given the strong shipping market and the newly sensed government dependence

---

[43] CAL, Lemon to Lines, 20 Nov. 1972: Discussion with Mr Steyn in Pretoria 13–14 Nov. 1972, No. 2—Sterling Devaluation.
[44] Final results showed the Lines to have done even better. The surplus for 1972 was £0.48m., while including the figures up to 31 January 1973 brought it to £3.56m.: CAL, Lemon to Lines, 7 May 1973.
[45] Ibid., 4 Apr. 1973.   [46] CAL, Joint Meeting Minutes, 13 Feb. 1974.

on the Lines for the massive investment needed for containerization, it was decided to ask Steyn for an interim Freight Review.[47] This was held in early April 1974, and the Lines asked Steyn for an all-round increase of 10 per cent, which the accountants on both sides agreed would probably recover just over £5m. of the deficit by the end of 1975, leaving one year for the remainder to be recouped before the expiry of the current OFA. Despite the usual homilies on the evils of inflation, Steyn accepted the Lines' case,[48] and on 21 May the South African Cabinet gave its formal blessing to the increases.[49]

By the time of the Biennial Review in April 1975, however, it was clear that inflation had far outstripped the allowances made for it in calculating the 1974 tariff increases, and, instead of going down, the cumulative deficit had increased from £10m. to £11.5m. by the end of the Formula Year to 30 September 1974. Furthermore, the Lines were running in deficit on current account, and had sustained a further £2m. in losses with the figures updated to 31 January 1975. Since the savage inflation which had already upset their calculations was expected to continue, the Lines now asked Steyn for a 30 per cent increase in tariff rates (to be implemented in two stages) in order to enable them both to balance their books on current account *and* wipe out the cumulative deficit by April 1976.

Steyn did not reject this large claim out of hand, and did in fact acknowledge the government's responsibility for the cumulative deficit. But, with South Africa now in the grip of serious recession, and (under the impact of a weakening gold market and soaring oil prices) its current account deficit rising rapidly, it is not surprising that he should have indicated that the size of the deficit made it impolitic to try to recoup it from the freight rate structure in the time left in the current OFA. Coming away from the Freight Review with Steyn's view unclear and the Cabinet Committee appointed to decide the matter clearly hostile and prevaricating, Lemon felt that the suggestion of a lump sum to liquidate the cumulative deficit was likely, and that the Lines might also be offered freight rate increases of either 12½ or 15 per cent. If the offer should be less than 15 per cent, he thought that the Lines would need to claim an 'Intermediate Freight Review', probably in October.[50]

In May, after further foot-dragging by the Cabinet Committee, the

---

[47] Ibid.   [48] CAL, Lemon to Lines, 10 Apr. 1974.
[49] CAL, Lawrence to Lemon (telex), 21 May 1974.
[50] CAL, Lemon to Lines, 28 Apr. 1975.

Lines were eventually offered all-round freight increases of only 10 per cent to meet the current position,[51] and—as Lemon had surmised—a cash settlement to cover the cumulative deficit. However, the settlement offered, R12m. (£7.6m.), was roughly £4m. short of the cumulative deficit, and it was to be made in three instalments: R3m. on 15 July, R4m. on 15 March 1976, and R5m. on 1 July 1976.[52] With the proviso that it would need a further Freight Review later in the year (which was accepted by Steyn),[53] the Conference reluctantly accepted the 10 per cent, but—conscious of its contractual entitlement and fearful of creating a dangerous precedent—it flatly rejected the cash offer of R12m., demanding instead the full amount of the cumulative deficit.

By the middle of 1975, then, the argument over the cumulative deficit had brought relations between the government and the Lines to a dangerous pass, particularly since this coincided with the flare-up of the Spanish affair and the acquisition by Steyn of a new Minister, J. C. Heunis, who was not schooled in the advantages to South Africa of the Ocean Freight Agreement.[54] As a result, the Secretary for Commerce had informed the local Conference Chairman, Lawrence, 'that through the political pressures his capacity to protect our interests was likely to be very much reduced'.[55]

It was against this background that Steyn shifted his position on the cumulative deficit, and suggested that in order to regain the goodwill of the government the Lines should ignore his recent offer of a R12m. settlement and write off the cumulative deficit altogether.[56] This view was echoed by Safmarine and the local Conference Chairman, both of whom emphasized the following points: firstly, that the Lines were unpopular with the commercial fraternity in South Africa as well as with the government (this was a result of the deterioration in the service following rationalization, as well as the escalation in freight rates and the heavy pressure being brought to bear on shippers and importers to stop them using the cheaper services offered by outsiders); and secondly, that this unpopularity would reach danger level if a cash settlement of the cumulative deficit became public knowledge—which, in view of its size, they regarded as inevitable.[57]

[51] CAL, Sempill to Lemon (telex), 6 May 1975.
[52] CAL, Lawrence to Lemon (telex), 16 May 1975.
[53] CAL, Lemon to Lines (telex), 16 May 1975.
[54] CAL, Lemon to Lines, 5 June 1975.
[55] CAL, Lawrence to Lemon (telex), 19 May 1975.   [56] Ibid.   [57] Ibid.

Though Lemon was inclined at first to minimize these arguments, suggesting to Lawrence that he had caught Steyn 'in one of his most pessimistic moods',[58] he quickly accepted the request of the Secretary for Commerce that he should fly out to the Republic for urgent discussions.

Despite an agenda which included the tariff currency and the Spanish affair, the six-hour private talks held between Steyn and Lemon in Cape Town on 2 June were dominated by the question of the cumulative deficit. After recounting the story of the Spanish imbroglio, Steyn repeated his plea that in the interests of preserving the alliance between the Lines and the government the Conference should waive its right to recoup the cumulative deficit, confirming that a cash settlement could not be kept secret since it would have to be voted by Parliament. While he would have nothing to do with simply forgetting the deficit, Lemon was by no means insensitive to the serious drawbacks of attempting to recoup it by means of a cash settlement, and he urged Steyn to reconsider approaching the problem in the customary manner, that is to say, via increases in freight rates. If, said Lemon, the government were to grant the Lines increases of 15 or even 17½ per cent at the 'mini' Freight Review now agreed for early November, then it would not be entirely unrealistic to assume that the Lines might be all square at the end of the current OFA in December 1976. Such a solution, Lemon pointed out, would avoid the adverse publicity of a cash settlement, represent another step towards attaining the 'plateau' of higher freight rates which would be needed in any case at the beginning of the expensive new container era, and, from the Lines' point of view, would avoid the acute difficulty of deciding how to share out a cash settlement between the twenty-two lines in the Conference. Steyn was also opposed to a cash settlement because of the inevitability of adverse publicity for the OFA. In addition, he was impressed by the determination of the Conference not to be denied its full entitlement, and was anxious to leave a clean slate for his successor, when—as he seemed to envisage at this juncture—he retired around the end of the OFA period. So, Steyn accepted Lemon's argument, with the implicit proviso that whether the gambit worked or not—whether the Lines remained in deficit, or even in surplus at the end of 1976—the slate would be wiped clean at the start of the 'new era'. When Lemon left Steyn it was with the understanding

[58] CAL, Lemon to Lawrence (telex), 20 May 1975.

that the Conference Chairman would seek the agreement of the Lines to this proposal, and only when this was obtained would Steyn return to the Cabinet for its sanction. This would involve some loss of face for the Secretary for Commerce, since he had only recently told the Cabinet that allowing the Lines to recoup the cumulative deficit by increasing freight rates would be so injurious to South Africa's export trade as to be inconceivable.[59]

After a somewhat acrimonious discussion at the next Joint Meeting of the Conference, on 23 June 1975, it was agreed to pursue the strategy worked out by Lemon and Steyn, and on 4 July they were once more closeted together, this time in Pretoria. Here Lemon gave the Secretary for Commerce the Lines' reaction, and also informed him that he could not support the idea—once more floated by Steyn—that if the deficit were not eliminated through the freight rates by the end of 1976 then it should be written off. Steyn accepted this, and also pleased Lemon by telling him that he remained content with this plan of action and foresaw no difficulties in persuading the Cabinet of its virtues when it reassembled in early August.[60] It would not be until the 'mini' Freight Review in early November, however, that the Lines would know just how serious the government was about allowing them to recoup the cumulative deficit through the freight rates. And before then another issue which would affect this matter came to a head: the tariff currency question. This had been simmering since its reappearance in May 1971.

The Adoption of the Dollar Tariff Currency

Because of the disadvantage at which the Continental and South African Lines had been placed by the sterling tariff base of the Conference at a time when sterling was depreciating, the downward movement of the pound after June 1972 had once more made the tariff currency a major issue, both within the Conference and between the Conference and the South African government. It will be recalled that in 1968 the Conference had finally decided to change to the US dollar, but that this had been blocked by the government, currently engaged in hostilities with the American Federal Reserve. The issue had resurfaced briefly in May 1971, following the flotations of the Deutschmark and the guilder, but no conclusion had been reached.[61]

[59] CAL, Lemon to Lines, 5 June 1975.   [60] Ibid., 7 Aug. 1975.
[61] CAL, Joint Meeting Minutes, 27 May 1971.

However, by the second half of 1972 it had become clear that the
Continental Lines were suffering so badly that they would not be put
off as easily again. They were also of the opinion that, whatever the
tariff currency was, the Lines should *not* have to obtain the prior
approval of the South African government for a currency surcharge on
tariff rates following its devaluation; such surcharges should be
automatic and swift.

The problem for the Conference was that while it was generally
agreed that sterling should go, and that a strong, stable, and neutral
currency should be introduced in its place, the reputation of the US
dollar—which at one time had amply fitted this description—was by
1972 very low indeed. Furthermore, while South African hostility
towards it had abated, it had by no means disappeared altogether. As a
result, the arguments for and against all of the other possible
alternatives had been rehearsed once more, just as they had been in
1967 and 1968. Some had supported the wholesale introduction of the
Swiss franc, others the sectionalization of the tariff currency (for
example, using sterling from the United Kingdom, and other
currencies in the other sectors of the trade). The Continental
Lines—led by DOAL—urged the introduction of the Deutschmark
Southbound and the rand Northbound, while Lemon and the Lines'
accountants agreed with the latter, but favoured the US dollar
Southbound. The South African government, supported by Safmarine,
naturally pressed for a wholesale switch to the rand.

Unfortunately for the Continental Lines, Steyn could not be roused
to much interest in the tariff currency in the second half of 1972.[62] In
addition, the general uncertainty in the international monetary
situation made it difficult to make confident assumptions about the
future strength and stability of any of the major currencies, and thus
imposed a severe handicap on the internal Conference debate. If the
determination of the Continental Lines (in the event, ungratified) to
obtain relief from the currency position by having higher devaluation
surcharges imposed in the North Continental than in the UK sector
is added to these considerations,[63] it is not surprising that little
headway was made on changing the tariff currency in 1972 and 1973.
As for the idea that devaluation surcharges should be operated
automatically and immediately, Steyn was implacably opposed to this,[64]

[62] CAL, Lemon to Lines, 20 Nov. 1972: Discussion with Mr Steyn in Pretoria 13–14
Nov. 1972, No. 2–Sterling Devaluation.
[63] CAL, Joint Meeting Minutes, 22 Oct. 1973.   [64] Ibid., 4 June 1973.

clearly seeing it as an attempt on the part of the Lines to weaken the government's grip on freight rates.

By the beginning of 1974, however, there had been two significant developments in the matter of the tariff currency. Firstly, the Conference had finally come out again in favour of wholesale adoption of the US dollar, and secondly, Steyn, albeit with no great enthusiasm and protesting to the end the virtues of the rand, had indicated that he, too, no longer had any objections *in principle* to the use of this currency. Both of these developments were no doubt influenced by the improved position of the dollar over European currencies following the eruption of the oil crisis at the end of 1973;[65] while Steyn's attitude was also probably affected by the improvement in relations between Pretoria and Washington during the presidency of Richard Nixon. In the light of the soaring price of free market gold and other developments on the international monetary scene,[66] there was also a new confidence in South Africa that American monetary policy—though still supporting the demonetization of gold—would not have such serious implications for the price of gold as had been feared in 1968. Although by early 1974 there was agreement both within the Conference and between the Conference and the South African government that the US dollar should replace sterling as the tariff base, it was the middle of the year before Lemon was able to put detailed proposals to Steyn,[67] and it was to be another year before agreement between them was achieved.

One reason for the delay was the further attempt by the Conference to link this to the separate issue of automatic adjustment of freight rates in the event of currency fluctuations. Steyn remained adamantly opposed to this, and the Lines at last dropped their demand. (With a dollar, as with a sterling tariff currency, they would simply have to *persuade* the government of the merits of a surcharge in the event of adverse currency fluctuations.[68]) The more important reason for the delay, however, was the complex argument provoked by the justified suspicion of each of the parties that the other was attempting to gain a windfall from the conversion rates employed in the change-over. This was eloquent testimony to the lack of faith which each side now had in the fairness and efficiency of the OFA Formula arrangement: had this faith existed, the idea of a 'windfall' would have been meaningless in

[65] Samuel Montagu & Co. Ltd., *Annual Bullion Review 1973* (London, Mar. 1974), 7.
[66] Ibid., 7 f.   [67] CAL, Lemon to Steyn, 1 July 1974.
[68] CAL, Steyn to Lemon, 24 Oct. 1974.

the relationship between the Lines and the government, since any short-term gain by one party would have been recouped by the other via the Formula at the next Freight Review.

In the end, the argument over the conversion was settled in the private talk between Steyn and Lemon on 2 July 1975, when the Secretary for Commerce made it plain to the Conference Chairman that if the Lines wanted to change to the dollar then they would have to do this on his terms. To suit South Africa's exporters, these were as follows: firstly, that the conversion should be achieved by changing sterling into rands, and then rands into dollars (the Lines had wanted a straight conversion at £1 = $2.40);[69] and secondly, that South African shippers should have the option of paying the Conference either in the new tariff currency, or in the currency of the country of the shipowner in question—in the latter event at the (lower) buying rate for dollars of the shipowner's national bank.[70] Since they were anxious to have the dollar introduced—especially as it was now strengthening—the Lines accepted these conditions, even though Lemon calculated that they would cost the Lines 1.5 per cent of the revenue they would have earned on the conversion process preferred by the Conference.[71] On 14 July notice was given to the trade that the change-over would take effect on 1 September 1975, and that the conversion would take place on the basis of £1 = $2.3625. It was not explained to Southbound shippers that this quixotic rate was the result of the two-stage conversion insisted on by Pretoria; Lemon was not anxious to give further evidence to European shippers—already hostile to the Conference because of its poor record of consultation with them and its refusal to adopt the CENSA Code[72]—of the extent to which the South African government manipulated this trade to suit its own ends.

That the Lines should have received this fillip from the change to the dollar was just as well for at the same time the opposition in the trade was receiving a boost of its own, this time from the impending independence of Mozambique.

[69] The sterling–rand exchange rate was arrived at by taking the South African Banks' average buying rate for sterling over the three month period 15 Mar. 1975–15 June 1975, which established the figure of £1 = R1.6030454. The rand–dollar rate, on the other hand, was simply the official rate prevailing at the time: R1 = $1.4737: CAL, Lemon to Lines (telex), 20 June 1975.

[70] Ibid.

[71] CAL, Joint Meeting Minutes, 23 June 1975.

[72] CAL, Meeting with Representatives of European Shippers' Council at Berne on 13 Mar. 1974.

The Consequences of Mozambique's Independence

At the beginning of 1975 the leftward realignment of Mozambique following the coup in Portugal (Mozambique became fully independent on 25 June) had already given birth to a new aspirant to that part of the country's trade—the ports south of Chinde—which fell within the range of the South African Conference. This was the East Africa National Shipping Line Ltd. (EANSL), which had applied to the Conference for traffic rights through Lourenco Marques and Beira following the decision of one of its four shareholders, the Zambian government,[73] to re-route some of its trade through Mozambique. However, though this was a national carrier application, EANSL—already a member of the East African Conference—was not big enough to pose a serious threat to the Conference and, with Safmarine, Chargeurs Réunis, and CNN opposed to its admission, it was easily put off.[74] More worrying contenders for the trade of Marxist Mozambique than EANSL, however, were soon on the scene. These were the fleets of the Soviet bloc, which for several years had been engaged in a successful effort to break into the high-rated Western liner trades. Of course, political and strategic purposes, as well as the desire to earn foreign exchange, lay behind this push, and it was just beginning to cause serious alarm in the West.[75]

The first element of Comecon shipping to look towards Southern Mozambique was the 'Baltafrica' service operated by Polish Ocean Lines (POL) of Gdansk and VEB Deutsche Seereederei (DSR) of Rostock, which applied for admission to the trade at the beginning of the year. Like EANSL, Baltafrica was already a member of the East African Conference,[76] with rights in Northern Mozambique, and was regarded by Lemon as a powerful and responsible concern. He therefore recommended that the Lines should seek an accommodation with it.[77] On the understanding that Baltafrica would be restricted to

[73] The others were the governments of Kenya, Uganda, and Tanzania. In early 1975 EANSL owned 4 ships, which it operated in the trade between Europe and East Africa (Mombasa–Rovuma River range).

[74] CAL, Lemon to Lines, 17 Feb., 27 May, and 26 Aug. 1975.

[75] See, e.g. General Council of British Shipping, *Red Flag vs. the Red Ensign* (London, 1975); and Atlantic Council, *The Soviet Merchant Marine: Economic and Strategic Challenge to the West* (Washington, 1978).

[76] For an account of the manner in which it forced its way in, see I. Chrzanowski, M. Krzyanowski, and K. Luks, *Shipping Economics and Policy: A Socialist View* (London, 1979), 226 f. This is a work of Polish scholarship.

[77] CAL, Lemon to Lines, 17 Feb. 1975.

the trade between Mozambique on the one hand, and Poland and East Germany on the other, most members of the Conference were prepared to go along with this, but the same lines which had stood in the way of EANSL also blocked the entry of Baltafrica.[78] Being 'conference-minded', and probably because it was aware that only a small number of lines were involved, Baltafrica did not react to this rebuff by immediately going into opposition, but its patience could not be expected to last for ever.[79]

Even more alarming than the threat posed by Baltafrica was that from the 'Baltestafrica' service, which, without prior application or even notification to either the East African Conference (to which it was, of course, the greater danger),[80] or the South African Conference, commenced two sailings a month between North Europe and East Africa/Mozambique in late September 1975. Baltestafrica—or 'Besta Line' as it came to be known by the Conference in order to avoid confusion with Baltafrica—was run by the Baltic Shipping Line of Leningrad and the Estonian Shipping Company of Tallin, and was believed by Lemon—probably rightly—to have entered the trade in such unseemly haste because of the Soviet Union's urgent need to ship arms and other supplies to its friends in East Africa and Mozambique.[81] Given that political and strategic motives, as well as the desire to earn foreign currency, lay behind the general expansion of the Soviet merchant marine, Lemon was not convinced that ordinary commercial methods would be enough to beat off this new intruder. Nor did the Conference Chairman find Steyn in a helpful mood when he broached the subject in early October. Lemon tried to alarm Steyn by suggesting that South African cargo moving through Lourenco Marques might find itself in Soviet bottoms, and although Steyn replied that this would be 'anathema' to South Africans, he also indicated that it would be difficult for him to do anything about it in view of his government's anxiety to remain on good terms with the new government in Mozambique.[82] (South Africa had adopted a correct attitude towards the Machel regime and had been rewarded by a pragmatic response on

---

[78] Ibid., 27 May 1975.   [79] CAL, Joint Meeting Minutes, 2 Mar. 1976.
[80] OECD, *Maritime Transport 1977* (Paris, 1978), 54 f.
[81] CAL, Memorandum of Discussion over Lunch on Thur. 1 July, between Mr G. A. Maslov, Chairman and Managing Director of Sovinflot, Moscow; Mr A. G. Postnikov, Chairman of Anglo-Soviet Shipping Co. Ltd., London; and Mr A. E. Lemon, Chairman, and Mr R. Gaymer, Deputy Chairman, of the East African Conference, 2 July 1976.
[82] CAL, Joint Meeting Minutes, 28 Oct. 1975.

the practical level. Any other course would, in any case, have been economic suicide for Mozambique.[83]) As a result, at the Joint Meeting in October 1975 it was decided that there was nothing for it but to use all available commercial means against the Besta Line, and hope that the pressure currently being organized by Western governments against the tactics of the Soviet fleet would also have some effect.[84]

As the Lines had feared, their own efforts against the Russians were not successful: Soviet influence in Mozambique was growing rapidly,[85] and it was believed that a shipping agreement had been signed between Moscow and FRELIMO.[86] In June 1976 Lemon reported to the Joint Meeting that Besta Line was proposing to increase its sailings.[87] However, in the following month Western protests against Soviet tactics did bear some fruit in the form of the 'Leningrad Agreement', in which the Soviet Union agreed not to undercut other 'independent carriers', and to seek membership of liner conferences.[88] Western governments would not consider intervening until it had been shown that commercial accommodation was impossible.

As a result of the Leningrad Agreement, as well as the fact that commercial retaliation had failed to deter Besta Line, Lemon, as Chairman of the East African Conference, held exploratory talks with the Russians in London in July.[89] Further talks were arranged to take place in Leningrad at the end of October, and on 20 September Lemon wrote to the Lines urging them to take the opportuniry to examine terms for the entry of the Russians into the South African Conference as well as the East African one, though only in respect of the ports in Southern Mozambique of course. At the Joint Meeting on 19 October 1976 he reminded the Lines that some other conferences had already reached understandings with the Russians, and it was agreed that Lemon should raise Southern Mozambique in Leningrad.

The meeting in Leningrad concentrated on the East African trade and did not make much progress; a large gap appeared between the sailings demanded by the Russians and the sailings (purely token) offered by Lemon. However, the Russians reassured the Conference

---

[83] M. J. Azevedo, 'A Sober Commitment to Liberation?—Mozambique and South Africa 1974–1979', *African Affairs*, 79 (1980), 582.

[84] CAL, Joint Meeting Minutes, 28 Oct. 1975.

[85] K. Middlemas, 'Independent Mozambique and Its Regional Policy', in J. Seiler (ed.), *Southern Africa since the Portuguese Coup* (Boulder, Colo., 1980), 226.

[86] CAL, Lemon to Lines, 20 Sept. 1976.

[87] CAL, Joint Meeting Minutes, 25 June 1976.   [88] Juda, 44.

[89] CAL, Memorandum of Discussion over Lunch on Thur. 1 July . . . .

Chairman that they were conscious of the political dangers of getting involved with South African cargo through Maputo (as Lourenco Marques was now known), and seemed to Lemon to be anxious to forestall the intervention of Western governments by entering the conferences. So, although the Conference Chairman was pessimistic about the chances of reaching agreement, a further meeting was arranged to take place in Antwerp on 6 December.[90] Before this took place, however, the South African Conference met again and, led by the British Lines and Safmarine, made it clear to Lemon that the Russians would not be welcome, irrespective of the decision of the East African Conference. This was communicated to the Russians in Antwerp,[91] and in January 1977 negotiations for their entry into the East African trade also collapsed.[92] Besta Line remained in opposition, and the Lines left it to their respective governments to take the matter further.[93]

The appearance of Soviet bloc opposition had not been the only reason for the great increase in Conference concern about the ports south of Chinde following the political change in Mozambique. In the chaos which followed the Lisbon coup, the efficiency of Southern Mozambique's ports had declined to such a degree that many of the Lines' vessels had begun to avoid them, and a 30 per cent congestion surcharge had been introduced.[94] Despite the fact that berthing delays at Lourenco Marques had ended by early 1975 (largely because fewer vessels were calling there), the port remained slow-working and the Lines decided that the surcharge should be retained.[95] Although this was subsequently reduced to 15 per cent, it was not enough for Steyn, who asked the Lines to remove the surcharge altogether, and also to improve the Conference service to Lourenco Marques.[96]

There were, of course, commercial reasons for Steyn's attitude to Lourenco Marques. The traditional dependence of the Transvaal on this Southern Mozambique port, which was a key ingredient in the famous and long-standing Mozambique Convention,[97] was beginning

[90] CAL, Lemon to Lines, 1 Nov. 1976.
[91] Ibid., 13 Dec. 1976.   [92] Ibid., 31 Jan. 1977.
[93] CAL, Joint Meeting Minutes, 15 Mar. 1977.
[94] Ibid., 8 Oct. 1974.   [95] Ibid., 11 Feb. 1975.
[96] CAL, Lemon to Lines, 14 Oct. 1975.
[97] See L. Vail and L. White, *Capitalism and Colonialism in Mozambique: A Study of Quelimane District* (London, 1980), esp. 205–16; and S. E. Katzenellenbogen, *South Africa and Southern Mozambique: Labour, Railways and Trade in the Making of a Relationship* (Manchester, 1982), chaps. 6, 8, and 9.

to be eroded, and would substantially disappear the following year with the opening of the deep-water harbour at Richards Bay, some 160 kilometres north of Durban.[98] However, for the moment a substantial South African trade continued to rely on Lourenco Marques, and the surcharge made this more expensive. Furthermore, reduced employment of Lourenco Marques meant greater pressure on the Republic's own ports, which were themselves liable to serious congestion when trade was buoyant, and had also been the subject of surcharges in recent times;[99] Steyn expected the economy to pick up in 1976 and was worried that congestion at South African ports would return.[100] (For these reasons, Lourenco Marques had been included in the plans for the new container service.[101]) Nevertheless, this attitude to Lourenco Marques also had an urgent political edge: the Lines had run head-on into what was to become known as South Africa's 'transport diplomacy'.

The exploitation of transport links in the diplomacy between states was hardly a new phenomenon in Africa; nor, as we have seen, was it something of which the Lines themselves had had no experience, especially since 1966 when the South African government had elbowed its way into the Conference so that it could manipulate the Europe–South Africa shipping market for political ends. However, developments in Rhodesia, and in particular the collapse of the Portuguese empire in Africa, had forced the South African government to give particular attention, amongst other things, to the political significance of its transport—especially its rail—links with the states to the north as far up as Zaïre. The 'transport diplomacy' which began in earnest in 1975, then, while in some respects identical to the manœuvring in which Steyn had engaged with the Lines *vis-à-vis* Portuguese and Spanish shipping, was more urgent, more ambitious, and in practice associated exclusively with the states of Southern Africa (including Rhodesia).

The chief architect of South Africa's 'transport diplomacy' was J. G. H. Loubser, the General Manager of the SAR&H from 1970 until 1983. Loubser had a formidable reputation in South Africa as a public servant and was regularly consulted at the highest government levels

[98] Katzenellenbogen, 155.
[99] A 20% import surcharge at South African ports was reduced to 12½%, and a 10% export surcharge suspended, on 30 June 1975: CAL, Joint Meeting Minutes, 23 June 1975.
[100] CAL, Lemon to Lines, 14 Oct. 1975.
[101] CAL, Lemon to Steyn, 19 Feb. 1975.

on foreign as well as transport policy.[102] According to Loubser,[103] 'transport diplomacy' had three main objectives: firstly, to promote 'stability' in the neighbouring states, on the basis that this would reduce their hostility to South Africa; secondly, to foster a sense of common interests between the Republic and its black neighbours, out of which political *rapprochement* might eventually grow (a functionalist conception, as Geldenhuys rightly observes[104]); and thirdly—though Loubser was naturally more coy about this in his public utterances—to provide South Africa with a powerful pressure point against its neighbours should transport diplomacy fail in its first two objectives. Thus, South Africa should not only preserve the great dependence of the rest of Southern Africa on its transport networks (which is why he was hostile to Rhodesia's decision to close its border with Zambia in 1973), but selectively employ its unique blend of advanced technical knowledge with long experience of African conditions to provide aid to the transport authorities of its black neighbours. To avoid charges of paternalism and imperialism, this aid, Loubser felt, should only be given when asked for, it should only be provided if paid for at 'a fair price' (i.e. it should not be 'aid' in the generally accepted sense at all), and it should be so designed as to stimulate development. In short, it was Loubser's view that transport diplomacy was 'the strongest and most effective counter-measure against isolation and the best way of achieving the RSA's potential wealth-creating and stabilising role within the sub-continent'.

Therefore, when Lemon came under pressure from Steyn in October 1975 to remove the congestion surcharge from Lourenco Marques and improve the Conference service to it, it was against the background of transport diplomacy at the beginning of its heroic period. Not only had Vorster and Loubser, at the Victoria Falls conference in August, tried to persuade Smith and Kaunda to reopen the border between Rhodesia and Zambia so that the rail link between South Africa and Zambia could be restored,[105] but for some months before this the South Africans had been engaged in a high-level diplomatic operation to persuade FRELIMO itself to accept assistance from the SAR&H in normalizing the flow of traffic from the

[102] Geldenhuys, 154.
[103] The following exegesis is based on J. G. H. Loubser, 'Vervoerdiplomasie met Spesiale Verwysing na Suider-Afrika', *Politikon*, 6.2, Dec. 1979.
[104] Geldenhuys, 154.
[105] In the event, while Smith agreed Kaunda resisted, see Geldenhuys, 153, and 271 f. (n. 194).

Witwatersrand to Lourenco Marques[106] (so much for waiting to be asked), and this was already paying off. (Among other things, in April Mozambique had hired South African diesel locomotives.[107]) The 'spirit' of the Mozambique Convention was to be kept alive and this was to symbolize 'the white man's good intentions towards the black man in Africa'.[108] It is hardly surprising, then, that Steyn should have emphasized that the Lines and the government should do whatever they could to restore the normal pattern of traffic through Lourenco Marques. Indeed, so anxious was the Secretary for Commerce on this score that, when pressed by Lemon, he agreed that the cost to the Lines of the continued slow working at Lourenco Marques could be spread over the freight rate structure as a whole[109] (so much for assistance being paid for at 'a fair price'—or, for that matter, at any price at all). Shortly afterwards the congestion surcharge was removed.[110]

Conditions at Mozambique's ports remained difficult in the first half of 1976 and a significant number of South African shippers, even in the eastern Transvaal, were finding it cheaper to use Durban, despite the higher railage to that port. Furthermore, Portuguese residents in Mozambique had to decide by the end of June whether to take out Mozambique citizenship or leave the country, and South Africa confidently expected a mass exodus of those Portuguese personnel who remained,[111] including harbour pilots. It was against this background that on 4 May 1976 Neil Sempill, who had replaced Lawrence as local Conference Chairman in February, visited Maputo in order to investigate the position and warn the local authorities that the Lines were considering reintroducing the surcharge.

In Maputo Sempill met the Director of Transport in Mozambique, Engineer Alcantara Santos; the Port Director, Engineer E. Castro; and the Commercial Director of the Caminhos de Ferro de Moçambique (CFM), Dr A. Britto. To test what they had to tell him, he also spoke to local shipping people and the local office of the SAR&H. The impression of Maputo that Sempill formed as a result of these discussions was not entirely unfavourable. It was true, he felt, that—with the assistance of the SAR&H—the rail link between

[106] Loubser, 149.   [107] Ibid.; and Azevedo, 572–4.
[108] Loubser, 151.
[109] CAL, Lemon to Lines, 14 Oct. 1975.   [110] Ibid., 10 Nov. 1975.
[111] About three-quarters of the whites who had stayed in Mozambique after independence had already left by the end of 1975: Middlemas, 'Independent Mozambique and its Regional Policy', 218.

Maputo and the South African frontier had been improved, as Santos claimed, and it was also true that pilferage had largely been eliminated and that labour relations in the port were much better. Engineer Santos himself impressed Sempill as a competent man who was alive to his problems and was taking the right sort of steps to sort them out. On the other hand, shortages of skilled personnel—especially harbour pilots—remained serious, and Santos was unable to say when replacements for those who had already left and those expected to leave in June would be operational. Furthermore, Sempill had to admit that the best efforts of the CFM could well be undermined by failures in other essential services. Despite these cautionary notes, however, he concluded that: 'It is probable that the ports will survive and, unless the Lines continue to use them, the way will be left open for vessels of Comecon countries to lift what cargo is available. This applies', he felt, 'particularly in respect of Beira'.[112]

Sempill's conclusions were no doubt the source of some comfort to the South African government as well as to the Lines, for Pretoria was becoming alarmed at the possibility of a deterioration in its relations with Mozambique should South African shippers continue to be reluctant to use Maputo. Indeed, barely a week after Sempill's return from his exploratory mission, he was summoned to a meeting in Cape Town by the Department of Commerce, along with other representatives of the shipping community. The sole purpose of this meeting, which was chaired by Steyn and also attended by Loubser and Brand Fourie, the Secretary for Foreign Affairs, was to persuade the shipping community to make more use of Maputo on the now familiar grounds that this was in South Africa's political as well as economic interests.

The discussion at the Cape Town meeting was opened by Loubser, who admitted that harbour performance at Maputo could be put at no more than 60 per cent of its previous capacity, and that in any case South Africa only relied on the Mozambique port for the export of chrome ore (a reliance which would itself come to an end with the availability of a multi-purpose appliance at Richards Bay by 1979), and for the import of a certain amount of oil products. However, he maintained that the Mozambique authorities would 'not be happy' if South African traffic was restricted to these two relatively unremunerative commodities, and that it was therefore important for Maputo to be used for general cargo as well. He added that the rail link was working

[112] CAL, Sempill to Lemon, 7 May 1976.

well—which Sempill already knew—and claimed that any problems were sorted out directly with the Director of the CFM. Brand Fourie confirmed that technical, if not political, co-operation between the South African government and FRELIMO was good, and added that the Republic also depended on Mozambique for electricity from the recently commissioned Caborra Bassa project, as well as for the traditional supply of mine labour. In short, said Brand Fourie, 'it was imperative from South Africa's point of view that the existing relationship with the Mozambique Government be maintained and that South Africa must be seen to be using the port'. For his part, Steyn reminded the audience that a surcharge on cargo in and out of Maputo would have the effect of diverting traffic from the port, and was therefore something which the government 'could not countenance'.

Following this presentation, the shipping representatives readily agreed that, provided cargo was available, navigation was safe, and their vessels were expeditiously handled, they would continue to serve Maputo. But they expressed their worries about the harbour pilots and other matters, and Brand Fourie had to agree to relay these anxieties to the FRELIMO government 'with the utmost urgency'.[113] In the event, the dramatic deterioration at Maputo which some had feared would occur in June did not take place and—under constant pressure from Steyn[114]—the Lines continued to provide it with an adequate service, despite the fact that there was no dramatic improvement either.[115] Also, upon further appeal from the Secretary for Commerce,[116] they did not reintroduce a surcharge on the port. The South African Conference was certainly making its own contribution to South Africa's transport diplomacy in Maputo.

Intensifying the Search for an Effective Counter-Opposition Policy

With Soviet bloc opposition having been added to the ranks of the outsiders following the independence of Mozambique, the Lines were interested to learn at the end of 1975 that Steyn's Department had decided to promote a new Shipping Board Bill, though one quite

[113] CAL, N. D. Sempill, Notes of a Meeting arranged by the Department of Commerce held on 10 May 1976 to discuss the importance of Maputo to the South African Economy, 13 May 1976.
[114] CAL, Lemon to Lines, 12 July 1976.
[115] CAL, Minutes of Meeting between SAR&H, CFM and Association of Shipping Lines, held at Paul Kruger Building on Fri. 11 Mar. 1977, at 10.30 a.m.
[116] CAL, Lemon to Lines, 12 July 1976.

different from that which had so alarmed them two decades earlier. Apart from enlarging the Shipping Board—probably in an attempt to defuse the agitation within ASSOCOM for a South African Shippers' Council with a voice in the OFA[117]—this Bill gave the Board new and controversial powers to protect the Lines against outsiders. Under Clause 9 of the Bill outsiders were not directly outlawed, but the Shipping Board was given the power to prohibit an importer or exporter from having goods conveyed at rates which undercut the Conference. In the event of an infringement of this rule, the Department of Commerce would have the power to recover from the importer or exporter the difference between the Conference tariff rate and the outsider's rate.[118] This would not remove completely the incentive to use outsiders, especially when they offered sailings at times and to ports not covered by the Conference, but it would go a very long way towards this, for in general the Conference service was more reliable and it was abundantly clear that it was favoured by the government.

When the Shipping Board Bill was circulated for comment in November 1975 there was an immediate outcry over Clause 9.[119] The government quickly let it be known that the Bill was to be redrafted, and in early February 1976 Steyn informed Lemon that Clause 9 was to be dropped altogether, more or less admitting to the Conference Chairman that its inclusion had been a disingenuous manœuvre designed to reveal to the Lines, once and for all, that it was politically impossible for the government legally to enforce a Conference monopoly.[120] The Bill was passed by Parliament in April, without Clause 9.[121] Among other things, the new Act increased the representation of private commerce and industry on the Shipping Board, and introduced a representative from the Chamber of Mines for the first time (see Appendix V). Since ASSOCOM had meanwhile gone ahead and created its own long-threatened Shippers' Council anyway (even though Steyn had insisted that it keep its nose out of the Europe–South Africa trade[122]), the net effect of recent developments was to strengthen the hand of South African shippers and importers,

[117] Ibid., 16 June 1975.
[118] *SA Shipping News*, Jan. 1976.
[119] Ibid.; and CAL, Lemon to Lines, 13 Feb. 1976.
[120] CAL, Lemon to Lines, 13 Feb. 1976.
[121] *House of Assembly Debates*, c. 5313–20 (23 Apr. 1976).
[122] CAL, Lemon to Lines, 14 Oct. 1975, and 13 Feb. 1976.

and leave undiminished their inclination to support outside lines against the Conference.

Conference hopes, then, had been momentarily raised by the Shipping Board Bill and then dashed by its emasculation. The Conference Chairman's mood was not improved either by the receipt of an application from Jadranska Slobodna Plovidba (JSP), the Yugoslav line based in Split, at the end of 1975. Like Baltafrica, JSP was already a member of the East African Conference and now wanted its range extended down to Lourenco Marques.[123] Nor was Lemon encouraged by Steyn's indication that Russian ships themselves would not be barred from serving ports in the Republic if they should so desire.[124] Such was the situation on 16 February 1976 when, at Steyn's suggestion, Lemon made a grim stock-taking of the damage inflicted by the opposition on the Lines over the last twelve months.

The impact of the opposition remained most serious in the Southbound trade, Lemon wrote, especially from the Mediterranean, where outsiders had taken about 10 per cent of the trade (approximately 50,000 tons[125]), and—most serious of all—from the North Continent, where they had taken about 30 per cent of it (approximately 500,000 tons). Unless the position was reversed, he said, it was likely that the cumulative deficit would be increased rather than eliminated, and the vast capital investment of the Conference in containerization would be put in jeopardy. 'Altogether', Lemon concluded, 'the outlook for the Conference is grim'.[126]

What was to be done? This question was considered by the Joint Meeting on 2 March, at two special meetings of the Lines between March and June, and again at the Freight Review in September 1976. However, the only solid achievement of all this agonizing was Steyn's agreement to help with the collection of information on cargoes discharged by outsiders in South African ports.[127] On the eve of the 'new era', therefore, and despite Steyn's rejection of a further request from the Lines to allow them to debit against the Formula the full amount of revenue lost through the use of fighting rates, the Conference was left with no alternative but to introduce even more

[123] Ibid., 29 Dec. 1975.   [124] Ibid., 13 Feb. 1976.
[125] Lloyd Triestino subsequently claimed that this was a serious underestimation, maintaining that the figure was more like 120,000–130,000 tons, or 20–25% of the total trade: CAL, Joint Meeting Minutes, 2 Mar. 1976.
[126] CAL, Summary of the Situation in regard to the Opposition facing the Conference in the Trade, 16 Feb. 1976, attached to Lemon to Lines, 23 Feb. 1976.
[127] CAL, Joint Meeting Minutes, 19 Oct. 1976.

savage rate-cutting, and to hope that the new container service would tempt back lost customers.[128]

Towards 'the Plateau' of High Freight Rates

Having to grapple with a dollar tariff currency, come to terms with Marxist Mozambique, and agonize over the opposition, had not, of course, allowed either the Lines or the government to ignore the routine but vital matter of applying the OFA Formula to the level and structure of freight rates in the trade. Nor, as we shall see, had the opposition made quite the inroads into the earnings allowable to the Lines which was sometimes suggested by Lemon in his more gloomy moments—though this was partly a result of good fortune.

A 'mini' Freight Review in November 1975 had been granted by Steyn as a result of the Lines' unhappiness at the level of increases which they had been awarded in April, and, as agreed in July, had been envisaged as the occasion on which high tariff increases ($15-17\frac{1}{2}$ per cent) might be negotiated; it was hoped that their introduction in February 1976 would take care of the cumulative deficit of £11.5m. as well as keep the Lines in the black on current account. However, largely because of the change-over to the dollar on 1 September and its hardening against the currencies of account of the Lines, by the eve of the Freight Review the fortunes of the Conference had significantly improved. On 20 October Lemon was able to report that the Lines had achieved a surplus equivalent to about 1 per cent of revenue over the eight months from October 1974, and that, with the figures up-dated to 30 September 1975, this had risen dramatically to a surplus equivalent to 8.4 per cent of revenue ($15.586m.) for the Formula Year as a whole.

The windfall produced for the Conference by the strengthening of the dollar had led to a demand from Steyn, and to particularly angry demands from shippers in Europe, for the introduction of a negative 'currency adjustment factor' (c.a.f.), i.e. a reduction in freight rates. However, the refusal of the Conference to consider this, together with the (to Europeans) inexplicable rate of conversion from pounds to dollars which the Lines had employed, had led to an even further deterioration in relations between the Conference and ESC, which at the end of October threatened to mount a press campaign against the

---

[128] Ibid., 3 Feb. 1977.

Lines.[129] Worried about this reaction, and believing that the surplus would in any case see them through to the end of the current OFA in spite of future inflation, the Lines decided not to ask Steyn for any increases to cover the current position. However, this still left the cumulative deficit, which Lemon estimated at about 9½ per cent of revenue, and it was decided to ask Steyn in November for a general tariff increase of 10 per cent, to be introduced on 1 February 1976, in order to eliminate the deficit by the end of that year. This would be explained to shippers—who were ignorant of the cumulative deficit and would not be sympathetic if they did know about it—as an increase made necessary by the inadequate level of the devaluation surcharge which had been in operation prior to the change to the dollar.[130]

Unfortunately for the Lines, on 7 October 1975 a major government-sponsored anti-inflation campaign was launched in South Africa, with which Steyn, who was also government Price Controller, was much preoccupied.[131] This was due to last until 31 March 1976. It came as no surprise to Lemon, therefore, when the Secretary for Commerce used the anti-inflation campaign as an excuse to deny the Lines their requested increase. At the Freight Review which took place in Pretoria on 3 November, Steyn made much of the current surplus being earned by the Lines, and appealed to them to make a contribution of their own to the anti-inflation campaign. Steyn was quite resolute, and the Lines had to be satisfied with the promise of a further Review in February (rather than April), though any increases won then could not be introduced before 1 June 1976, leaving only seven months of the current OFA in which to recoup the cumulative deficit, now calculated at $22m. At least Steyn did not insist on the introduction of a negative c.a.f., and he also sugared the pill by agreeing that the Lines could tell shippers that South Africa had been responsible for the arbitrary (and, to shippers in Europe, unfavourable) rate of exchange which had been employed during the change from sterling to the dollar, as well as for the low devaluation surcharges which made it impossible to introduce a negative c.a.f. Conscious of their particularly low standing amongst shippers at both ends of the trade, the Lines quickly issued appropriate press releases. The South African notice also emphasized that in spite of the justification for increased freight rates, the Conference had

[129] CAL, ESC to Safcon (telex), 30 Oct. 1975.
[130] CAL, Joint Meeting Minutes, 28 Oct. 1975.
[131] CAL, Lemon to Lines, 14 Oct. 1975.

decided to defer its application 'following a request from the Government in terms of the Anti-Inflation Manifesto'.[132]

At the beginning of 1976, with the dollar remaining strong and the earnings of the Lines having therefore stayed high, Lemon considered it expedient to drop the claim for a Freight Review in February. The next Review, he agreed with Steyn, could be deferred until September, when the occasion would be employed to operate the budgetary procedure laid out in the new OFA (which was yet to be finalized) and determine the level of freight rates for the year commencing 1 January 1977.[133]

It is probable that Lemon's decision to drop the claim for a Freight Review in February was also influenced by his desire to avoid further provocation of the ESC, a delegation from which he had met at Schiphol Airport in early January in a (partly successful) attempt to reduce the high level of tension between them. At this meeting Lemon had promised to explore with Steyn the possibility of devising some sort of formal *modus vivendi* between the South African Conference and the ESC which would not infringe the OFA,[134] but he did not subsequently find any significant change in Steyn's attitude. The Secretary for Commerce remained apprehensive of the effects on South Africa's interests of any CENSA-style consultative procedures being devised by the Conference and the ESC[135]—as well he might have. As a result, by the end of 1976 relations between the Conference and the ESC were almost as bad as they had been at the end of 1975.[136]

Despite the opposition and poor trading conditions, the continuing strength of the dollar helped the Lines to maintain a generally comfortable level of earnings, which meant that at the Freight Review held in Pretoria on 22 and 23 September 1976 the Conference delegation was unable to ask for anything on current account, while it was calculated that the cumulative deficit would stand at only $10.1m. at the end of December and would require only a 5 per cent increase in freight rates to eliminate it altogether. In the circumstances the Lines felt it wise to make the most of the anticipated running-in costs of the container service to be introduced in late 1977 and the continuation of inflation, and, having added these considerations to the need to eliminate the cumulative deficit, the Lines asked Steyn for a general

[132] Ibid., 6 Nov. 1975.
[133] Ibid., 23 Feb. 1976; and Joint Meeting Minutes, 2 Mar. 1976.
[134] CAL, Lemon to Lines, 12 Jan. 1976.   [135] Ibid., 13 Feb. 1976.
[136] *Journal of Commerce*, 17 Dec. 1976.

increase in freight rates of 16 per cent.[137] They were subsequently pleased to learn that the Cabinet had granted an increase of 15 per cent[138] (Northbound as well as Southbound), which was introduced on 27 December 1976. The 'plateau' of high freight rates required to finance the new container service—increases of a similar order each year for the next three years[139]—was in sight.

The Opposition on the Eve of the 'New Era'

If 'the plateau' of high freight rates was in sight on the eve of the new era of containerization, it could not be said with quite the same confidence that a levelling-off in the growth of the opposition was in view. It is true that at the beginning of 1977 outsiders were taking no more Southbound cargo than they had been a year earlier.[140] On the other hand, new outsiders were still regularly entering the trade, and at the Joint Meeting on 15 March Lemon listed fourteen outsiders altogether.[141]

Nevertheless, there were glimmers of light in the otherwise gloomy opposition picture. The Yugoslav line, JSP, had been admitted to the Conference as an Associate Member at the end of 1976 with rights in Southern Mozambique limited to its national trade.[142] By early 1977 there was also strong evidence that Continental Lines SA, which had been in opposition for the last three years, was on the point of departure,[143] and, above all, there were indications that ECL was weakening.

During 1976 and early 1977 ECL had continued to fill its vessels, and had even expanded the ports which it served in North Europe.[144] Safmarine estimated that it was now carrying 16 per cent of the total breakbulk cargo in the trade and a full 83 per cent of all cargo moving in containers.[145] In an important propaganda stroke, ECL had also become the first South African company to adopt the CENSA Code.[146] In the face of this the Lines had been forced to resort to even

---

[137] CAL, Lemon to Lines, 27 Sept. 1976.
[138] CAL, Joint Meeting Minutes, 19 Oct. 1976.
[139] Ibid., 15 Mar. 1977.   [140] Ibid., 3 Feb. 1977.
[141] Ibid., 15 Mar. 1977.
[142] CAL, Lemon to Lines, 23 Dec. 1976.
[143] CAL, Joint Meeting Minutes, 21 June 1977.
[144] CAL, Lemon to Lines, 23 Feb. 1976; and *Journal of Commerce*, 24 May 1977.
[145] CAL, Joint Meeting Minutes, 3 Feb. 1977.
[146] *Journal of Commerce*, 24 May 1977.

more savage rate-cutting tactics and were discussing the possibility of buying it out.[147] It was probably fear of the new Conference container service that, in mid-1977, led ECL to approach the Lines (indirectly) with a view to an accommodation.[148] As the 'new era' was getting under way, Safmarine was engaged in exploring ECL's position.[149]

[147] CAL, Meeting of the COP Committee, 27 July 1976.
[148] CAL, Joint Meeting Minutes, 21 June 1977.
[149] Ibid., and 18 Oct. 1977.

9

'THE NEW ERA'
1977–1985

IN July 1977 the South African Conference introduced containerization. (Three months later the mail service—which had lasted for 120
years but was now obsolete—was brought to an end; thereafter the
mail itself was carried in boxes.) In return for the massive investment
which containerization had required, and which was normally estimated
afterwards at $1.5 billion,[1] the Lines looked forward to the substantially
increased rate of return which they had been promised: 12½ per cent
on historic cost. However, the new service was introduced in difficult
times for the South African government and for the trade.

  South Africa's racial problems had resurfaced in brutal fashion at
Soweto twelve months before the launch of containerization and had
contributed to the failure of the government's attempts to achieve
détente in Africa, to renewed demands for economic sanctions, to fresh
pressure on the government for reform from the Western powers, and
to the further weakening of the South African economy (already in
serious recession since late 1974). With its confidence badly shaken
once more, South Africa was on the eve of the introduction of 'total
strategy'.[2]

The New OFA

Though South Africa's political crisis of 1976–7 had not caused the
Lines to reconsider their investment in containerization, the recession
and its associated balance of payments difficulties had been reflected
in the failure of the traffic between Europe and Southern Africa to
come anywhere near the levels which had been projected in 1973–4.
As a result, nine cellular container ships were introduced in the North
Europe service instead of ten, and in the Mediterranean service three

---

[1] 'A Survey of Shipping', Supplement to *Financial Mail*, 17 July 1981.
[2] R. Davies and D. O'Meara, 'Total Strategy in Southern Africa: An Analysis of South
African Regional Policy since 1978', *Journal of Southern African Studies*, 11.2, Apr. 1985.

instead of four (see Table 2), though even this left the new operation still seriously over-tonnaged.[3] There had been no friction between the Lines and the government over the small reduction in the size of the container fleet, but arguments which had arisen between them in the course of fleshing out the Memorandum of Understanding into a new OFA—mainly to do with the new Formula, accounting procedures, the new tariff structure, and the rights and obligations of the PPECB—had been so serious that the new OFA was not signed until 15 June 1977, almost six months after the expiry of the old OFA. (Despite this, not a single question was asked when the new Agreement was tabled in both the House of Assembly and the Senate immediately afterwards.) In the interim, Lemon and Steyn had agreed to operate on the Memorandum of Understanding.[4]

TABLE 2 *The Container Ships*

Name	Owner	Flag	Where built
Southern Africa/UK and North-West Continent: Nine Cellular Vessels of 2,450 TEU Capacity			
City of Durban	EHCL	British	W. Germany
Table Bay	OCL	British	W. Germany
Ortelius	CMB	Belgian	Belgium
Transvaal	DAL	W. German	W. Germany
Nedlloyd Hoorn[a]	Nedlloyd	Dutch	Holland
SA Helderberg	Safmarine	S. African	France
SA Waterberg	Safmarine	S. African	France
SA Winterberg	Safmarine	S. African	France
SA Sederberg	Safmarine	S. African	France
Southern Africa/Mediterranean: Three Cellular Vessels of 1,338 TEU Capacity			
Africa	L. Triestino	Italian	Italy
Europa	L. Triestino	Italian	Italy
SA Langeberg	Safmarine	S. African	Italy

[a] Chartered out in the Far East trade on first coming into service.

Though the broad shape of the new OFA closely resembled the Memorandum, there were several important differences. Apart from the reduction in the size of the container fleet, while the new OFA retained the provision for a return of 12½ per cent on the first cost of

[3] *Fairplay*, 16 Feb. 1978.
[4] CAL, Lemon to Lines, 3 Dec. 1976.

both new technology and conventional vessels, it reduced it to 10½ per cent on the first cost of the containers themselves. Furthermore, where the vital question of the *period* over which the Lines might expect to earn this rate of return was concerned, there was no longer a specific reference to the fact that it would be the 'aim' to permit them to earn this over each twelve-month period (though it is true that this was implicit in the financial arrangements for reviewing freight rates), and the guaranteed floor of 10 per cent over each twelve-month period was now qualified by the phrase 'unless otherwise agreed between the Government and the Conference'.[5] On the other hand, though this was negotiated four months after the signing of the OFA, the government finally agreed to allow the Lines to debit the Formula with the full amount of the revenue lost in fighting the opposition, rather than only 50 per cent, as before.[6] In doing so it accepted the argument that, in the interests of keeping *all* freight rates in the trade as low as possible, maximum utilization of the new container service (with its custom-built ships and high ratio of fixed to variable costs) was desirable, and that it was therefore unfair that the Lines should be penalized for employing fighting rates in an attempt to achieve this. All things considered, then, including this late modification, the new OFA remained a distinct advance for the Lines over the old one.

Shares in the New Service and the Formation of SAECS

If acute differences between the Lines and the South African government had preceded the signing of the new OFA, there had been disagreements over the new container service of equal intensity within the Conference itself. By late January 1975, or thereabouts, Safmarine had won its demand for an 'edge' of 1 per cent in earnings over liftings in the Southbound trade from North Europe (having threatened to operate independently should this have been refused),[7] though this was not quite 41:40 since this trade carried some non-South African cargo. However, the argument between the British and Continental Lines over the latter's claim for four of the ten cellular vessels allocated initially to the North Europe run had not been settled until much later in the year, when the British Lines had at last capitulated. Neither had this British humiliation been much lessened when, in the light of the subsequently reduced traffic projections, the Continental

---

[5] OFA, 1977, 31.   [6] CAL, Joint Meeting Minutes, 18 Oct. 1977.
[7] Ibid., 27–9 Jan. 1975.

Lines had agreed to sacrifice one of their own allocated container ships
to bring the overall size of the North Europe fleet down from ten
vessels to nine (see Table 2); for they replaced this with two Ro-Ro
ships of the same value. It should not be forgotten, of course, that B &
C still held a 36 per cent stake in Safmarine,[8] which was to operate
four of the nine big ships on the North Europe run.

The 'new era' in the South Africa trade consisted not only in the
advent of a new shipping technology but also—as in other containerized
trades—in the introduction of a new style of organization to run it.
Growing out of the satellite planning committees of the Executive
Planning Board, which in the second half of 1973 had seized the
direction of the Conference's cumbersome machinery for planning the
new service, in early 1976 the Southern Africa Europe Container
Service (SAECS) had been formed. With responsibility for the co-
ordination of the operating and accounting procedures of the new
service (including the sharing of pooled revenue), SAECS had become
the power-house of the South African Conference.[9] Marsman of
Nedlloyd, who had chaired the EPB, was appointed the first Chairman
of SAECS, while A. F. Murray-Johnson of Safmarine was made its
first Chief Executive, thus establishing a pattern whereby the
chairmanship is always filled by the Continental Lines and the Chief
Executive by Safmarine. The increasingly less important chairmanship
of the Conference as a whole has remained in the hands of the British
Lines.[10]

Changes at the Top

The chairmanship of the Conference might have diminished in
importance since 1977 vis-à-vis the top positions in SAECS, but this
was by no means apparent in that year itself, especially since Lemon
retired on the very eve of the 'new era' and was replaced by the B & C
executive who had been one of the brains behind the EPB's container
planning: Neil Forster. This is another reason why 1977 was a
watershed in the history of the Conference, as well as why its decline
relative to SAECS was disguised.

[8] By virtue of its decision not to take up the major part of its entitlement to a
Safmarine rights issue in December 1979, B & C's direct interest in the South African
line was reduced to about 25%: B & C, *Annual Report 1979*.
[9] For fuller details on SAECS, see *SAECS News*, May 1977.
[10] P. Bower, *A Century of Service, 1883–1983: Europe/South & South East African
Conference Lines* (Cape Town, 1983), 77.

The differences between Lemon and Forster were enormous. It is true that Lemon had had to direct the Conference at a time when it was not only at its most unwieldy (having gained seven new members since the end of the Second World War), but also when it was facing problems of unprecedented number and complexity: opposition, rationalization, reappraisal, containerization, and political manipulation by the South African government, among others. However, his (not unusual) attachment to the necessity for Conference secrecy[11] and rather high moral attitude had hindered his diplomacy, and contributed in a small way to the unpopularity of the Conference at both ends of the trade. By contrast, Forster, who was a Cambridge graduate in Law and Economics, and had joined the Clan Line in 1952 and been Chairman of the Calcutta Liners' Conference from 1962 until 1966, was convinced that a lot of Conference secrecy was unnecessary, and was more alive to the importance in the present climate of carrying shippers—the Lines' customers—with him.

Forster did not take long to make his own position clear. Addressing the press in South Africa shortly after the inauguration of the container service, he said that the Conference had become bureaucratic, unapproachable, and insensitive to the interests of its customers. All of this, he continued, would change.[12] By November the *South African Shipping News* was already comparing the new Conference Chairman with the 'dynamic' Kobus Loubser, who, it said, had 'within weeks' of taking over the SAR&H made it 'approachable, co-operative and above all flexible'. In 1981 the *Financial Mail* confirmed that this was a fair comparison. The 'SA-Europe conference', it observed, 'has been transformed in the past few years. It is no longer the secretive, high-handed organisation it was in the days of Secretary for Commerce Joep Steyn and conference chairman Ted Lemon', adding that 'Neil Forster himself is credited with spearheading the change in image'.[13] Moreover, while this may not have been quite so popular with the South African government, Forster—whose brother was a senior civil servant at the Foreign and Commonwealth Office in 1977, and two years later was appointed British Ambassador to Pakistan—also had strong reformist views on apartheid and was not afraid to make them public.[14] Clearly the rising star of the British Lines, in 1982 Forster

[11] Consistent to the end, Lemon refused to talk to the author of this book, though he kindly commented on chaps. 4–8.
[12] 'New-look conference', *SA Shipping News*, Nov. 1977.
[13] 'A Survey on Shipping'.   [14] 'Letters to the Editor', *The Times*, 12 Mar. 1982.

was promoted to be Group Managing Director of the Cayzer empire, B & C, and in 1985 was elected Chairman of UKSATA.

The start of the 'new era' was also marked by important changes at the top at the South African end. In June 1977 the Minister of Economic Affairs unexpectedly announced that Steyn was to retire, and on 31 December the Secretary for Commerce left office. He was succeeded by his deputy, T. Van der Walt, whom the Lines found equally able and sympathetic. However, Van der Walt did not remain responsible for the OFA for long, for on 1 June 1980 its administration was transferred from the Department of Commerce to the 'Water Transport' division of the Department of Transport. The loss of expertise at the South African end which this change represented probably weakened the government in its dealings with the Lines. Certainly, A. B. Eksteen, the present Director-General of Transport, is by no means as familiar with the complexities of shipping as either of his predecessors.

The Resilience of the Opposition

The Conference hope that the new container service would undermine the opposition seemed at points in the first years of the 'new era' as if it might be borne out. This was because SAECS soon gained the reputation for being faster, more reliable, and more efficient than its rivals, because the outsiders (small operators on the whole) initially found it difficult to adjust to the greatly increased sophistication of the 'landside' container operation[15] (especially since this was dominated by SACD, virtually a creature of the Conference), and because at least for a time the government made life more difficult for some outsiders by its reluctance to grant them container operators' licences.[16]

The first and most prized scalp obtained by the Lines in the 'new era'—albeit with the help of a substantial pay-off—was that of ECL, which in June 1978 announced its withdrawal from the container trade.[17] Since Norwegian interests were behind ECL, Norway's recent decision to obstruct trade and financial dealings with South Africa on political grounds had probably not helped this line either.[18] The withdrawal of ECL in 1978 was followed by that of the Portuguese outsider, CTM, in early 1980[19] (though this was not the last that was

---

[15] *Journal of Commerce*, Aug. 1983.   [16] 'A Survey on Shipping'.
[17] See, e.g. *SA Shipping News*, July 1978; and Bower, 86.
[18] *Fairplay*, 22 June 1978.   [19] *SA Shipping News*, Mar. 1980.

seen of Portuguese opposition in the trade); and in the same year the
Conference nipped in the bud opposition from the recently formed
Royal Swazi National Shipping Company[20] by admitting it as a
member with slot charter rights in the SAECS operation. Thus
persuaded that it had no need of ships under its own control—either
owned or chartered—and with Safmarine acting as its agents through
its subsidiary, Freight Marine, Royal Swazi never really developed a
tangible existence. (Since Swaziland is one of the states which, for
political reasons, South Africa is particularly anxious to keep firmly in
its economic orbit, it can safely be assumed that Pretoria welcomed the
admission of Royal Swazi to the Conference, as indeed, for political
reasons, it had urged the Lines to grant at least observer status to
Botswana, Lesotho, and Swaziland in the negotiations which led to the
signing of the Memorandum of Understanding in February 1974.[21])
The Spanish opposition was eliminated in 1980 with the admission of
Consortium Line to the Conference as representative of the Spanish
flag,[22] and at the end of the following year even Hellenic (which was
now investing heavily in cellular ships) was finally brought within the
embrace of the Conference on tough terms: it had to abandon the
standard service which it had started in the North Europe sector in
mid-1979,[23] and, having withdrawn its conventional ships from the
trade, participate in the SAECS service to Mediterranean ports on a
slot charter basis only.[24] It was a sad irony for Hellenic, whose founder,
Pericles Callimanopulos, had died in 1979, that only two years after
making peace in its long and bitter freight war with the South African
Conference it should have got into desperate financial difficulties and
finally collapsed.[25]

Despite this thinning of the ranks of the outsiders in the period from
1977 until 1981, the opposition proved surprisingly resilient. Many
shippers in the trade were still prepared to put up with the poorer
service which it offered for the sake of lower freight rates, and, with the
world shipping market now seriously over-tonnaged as a result of the

[20] *Fairplay*, 6 July 1978.
[21] In the event, the obvious reluctance with which the Lines fell in with this proposal,
and an apparent oversight on Lemon's part, led to the exclusion of the 'BLS' countries
from these negotiations: CAL, Lemon to Lines, 22 Apr. 1974.
[22] *SA Shipping News*, Dec. 1980.
[23] Ibid., July 1979.
[24] It would also be allowed to provide feeder services to Mediterranean ports not
served by the big cellular ships: ibid., Dec. 1981.
[25] *Containerisation International*, Jan. 1984.

big expansion into container vessels and renewed recession,[26] there
were plenty of operators left who were willing to offer space at such
rates. Besides, although the Lines were able to put Ro-Ro ships into
Beira and Maputo in Southern Mozambique, container handling
facilities had not been developed at these ports, and the opposition
here (including Russian opposition) had not been confronted with the
challenge of the cellular ships.[27] (At the time of writing—December
1985—a container terminal at Maputo is due to be officially opened in
March 1986.[28]) As before, the South African government remained
unwilling to take further action against any of the outsiders, now
adding as a reason for this refusal the deterioration in South Africa's
international position following Soweto and the crack-down on the
Black Consciousness movement: no doubt bearing in mind the
reaction to Steyn's famous letter to importers in 1968, the government
felt that, with its friends abroad dwindling, it could not afford to
antagonize the governments of the outsider lines, governments of
countries which were still prepared to trade with South Africa.

Even while the ranks of the opposition were being thinned in
1977–81, new outsiders were entering the trade, and although they
have come and gone since 1977, outsiders have clung to a sizeable
proportion of the trade throughout the 'new era'. Today this stands at
about 20 per cent of the container traffic and 40 per cent of the
breakbulk cargo. The main outsiders at the moment are Maritime
Carrier Shipping (MACS) of Hamburg and the shadowy Mediterranean
Shipping.

Freight Rates: The Deceptive 'Plateau'

As can be seen from Appendix VIII, freight rates (excluding bunker
and currency surcharges) in the 'new era' have increased at the
unusually high annual average of 13 per cent. It is also evident that
over this period the South African government has not insisted on any
further discrimination in favour of Northbound freight rates, despite
the fact that South Africa suffered serious balance of payments
problems from late 1980 until the middle of 1982, and again from late

---

[26] OECD, *Maritime Transport 1981* (Paris, 1982).
[27] *SA Shipping News*, Aug. 1981.
[28] On the slowly improving position at Maputo from 1984 (following the Nkomati
Accords), see G. G. Maasdorp, *Transport Policies and Economic Development in Southern
Africa: A Comparative Study in Eight Countries* (Durban, 1984), 213 f.

1983 until the end of the third quarter of 1984.[29] However, the achievement of this 'plateau' of high freight rates is an extremely deceptive guide to the real earnings of the South African Conference. This is partly because inflation has been running at a very high level for most of the period, especially in Britain and South Africa, and partly because of a new weakness in the tariff currency—the dollar—in the first years of the 'new era'. It was not until late 1979 that the government finally agreed to the introduction of a positive currency adjustment factor (c.a.f.) to help the Lines with this difficulty; and, once they had established the principle of operating a c.a.f., they could hardly resist its application in a negative direction when the dollar began to strengthen in 1981 (by October 1985 the c.a.f. stood at −40.1 per cent). Above all, however, except for a short time in the early 1980s, the trade has been severely depressed, and outsiders have forced the Conference to resort to even wider and more substantial discounts on the published tariff. Since the government has so far refused direct cash assistance to the Lines, it is hardly surprising that they have been earning substantially less than the 12½ per cent promised in the OFA. The result is that a new cumulative deficit in terms of the OFA Formula has emerged, which, according to the present Conference Chairman, is 'well over one *billion* dollars'.[30]

The End of the OFA?

The current Ocean Freight Agreement runs until the end of 1991, but it is highly likely that it will not be renewed, even on the assumption that no radical political changes occur in South Africa before that time. The government itself will no doubt wish to retain as much formal control over this vital trade as possible (though it is true that in the present shipping market it has allowed the Lines to achieve almost complete *de facto* freedom in the fixing of freight rates),[31] but for the Conference the OFA is already a dead letter. The government has simply not been able to fulfil its promises, and the accounting procedures of the OFA are now regarded as obsolete. Moreover, the Mail Contract no longer exists to provide B & C with a compelling reason for giving freight concessions to the South African government. It is probable that the 'new era' in the South Africa trade will prove to be new in more ways than expected.

[29] *Standard Bank Review* (monthly).
[30] Information supplied to the author by N. M. Forster (emphasis in original).
[31] Ibid.

CONCLUSION

As far as South Africa's relations with Europe are concerned, the most important conclusions to emerge from this study concern the extent of the influence which has been obtained by its government over the shipping conference in the Europe–South Africa trade, and the consequences which have flowed from this. However, these conclusions also have a bearing on at least two important general questions of international political economy: firstly, that of the power of the multinational corporation relative to the state; and secondly, that of the problems entailed in using economic instruments of foreign policy.

The South African government exercised a significant degree of influence over the South African Conference from at least 1912, when what was in effect the first Ocean Freight Agreement was negotiated, until very recently. It achieved this by exploiting two circumstances: Union-Castle's extraordinary dependence on the South Africa trade and especially on the government Mail Contract (a dependence intensified by the generally depressed condition of the world shipping market after the late 1950s, but reduced in the early 1970s by the obsolescence of the mail service); and the control over the Conference which, until about the mid-1970s, the dominance of this trade by the mail line (subsequently B & C) delivered to it. In a nutshell, the South African government controlled Union-Castle and Union-Castle controlled the Conference.

It can hardly be said on the evidence of this study that the South African Conference has provided *direct* 'support for apartheid'. Nevertheless, major advantages for the Nationalist government have accrued from its control of the Conference. First, and perhaps of greatest lasting significance, the main obstacle to the development of a substantial merchant marine—the entrenched monopoly of European shipping capital in South Africa's most important trade—has been gradually removed. The growth of Safmarine, the national·carrier (which in the 1970s absorbed SALines, and whose Executive Chairman, Marmion Marsh, became Chairman of the massive Safren group in 1984 following the merger of Safmarine with Rennies Holdings), has undoubtedly been greatly assisted by the steadily increasing sailing rights which it has been granted in all sectors of

South Africa's trade with Europe. Neither should it be forgotten that this development has also been helped by the extremely important financial, managerial, and technical help provided to Safmarine by B & C. The South African merchant marine, which in 1947 disposed of less than 130,000 gross tons, had 273 vessels and stood at well over 600,000 gross tons in 1985 (in 1982 it had reached 776,153).[1] This large, modern fleet—comprising bulk carriers and refrigerated vessels as well as big container ships—is capable of carrying at least half of South Africa's total foreign trade and without doubt *all* of its *vital* foreign trade. As well as being of great economic value, therefore, it has been—and no doubt remains—indispensable to the secrecy and security required by the Republic's arms trade, and provides insurance against any future politically inspired attempts to interrupt South Africa's foreign-owned shipping services.

The second consequence to flow from the government's control of the South African Conference has been serious discrimination against Southbound freight rates in favour of Northbound ones. This has been designed to strengthen South Africa's balance of payments, to protect its home industries, and —quite possibly—to *subsidize* the politically influential agricultural sector. (Proving the latter point would probably require a major study.) This discriminatory principle had been written into the OFA from the beginning and was particularly evident in the decade following the Sharpeville crisis of 1960. As can be calculated from Appendix VIII, using an index starting with 1959 at 100, by 1971 Northbound rates had reached only 149.6 while Southbound rates had soared to 224.8. In other words, Southbound freight rates had been increased almost exactly two and a half times as fast as Northbound rates during this period.

The European Shippers' Council currently appears to be reconciled to the discrepancy between Northbound and Southbound rates because Southbound rates from Europe are at the moment no higher than rates to South Africa from other areas, and actually much lower than rates from the United States.[2] As a result, Europe's competitive position in the South African market is not adversely affected. The present Conference Chairman, Neil Forster, also now 'consults' with the ESC prior to each general rate increase. For their part, European governments and importers no doubt receive consolation from the fact that foodstuffs and raw materials from South Africa are that much

---

[1] Lloyd's Register of Shipping, *Statistical Tables* (annual).
[2] Information supplied to the author by Neil Sempill.

cheaper. However, none of this alters the politically surprising fact that during one of the periods of greatest international hostility to South Africa its export trade and domestic manufacturing were both being increasingly protected by high freight rates paid by European industry. The third consequence of government dominance of the South African Conference has been interference in the trade with Europe for political purposes. In particular, sailing rights and services have been manipulated in order to consolidate relations with friendly countries (especially Italy, Spain, and Greece) and seduce unfriendly ones (especially independent Mozambique). In the process, South Africa has further bolstered its defences against sanctions by placing greater reliance on the shipping of friendly countries and encouraging trade with them.

It is certainly true that the South African government has not always found it easy to use the Conference as an instrument of its foreign policy. The main reason for this in the late 1960s and 1970s was that granting new or additional sailing rights to the lines of friendly countries ran counter to the government's anxiety to reduce the total tonnage in the trade and thus slow down or even reverse the increase in freight rates, while any attempt to overcome this problem by reducing the sailing rights of unfriendly countries (such as Sweden, Holland, or Britain under Harold Wilson) would have represented an attack on the interests of influential supporters of the Republic within them. Moreover, new or additional rights could sometimes only have been extended at the expense of lines of *other* friendly countries (for example, Italy in the case of Hellenic Lines), not to mention Safmarine itself. In addition, there was always the worry that admitting *outsider* lines of friendly countries would only encourage other interlopers and thus increase the government's embarrassment over the general problem of opposition in the trade. For all of these reasons it is not surprising that it was 1980 before the Spanish flag was admitted to the Conference, and 1981 before Hellenic finally won entry. The increase in Portuguese rights to which the government attached so much importance in the early 1970s was never achieved—though in view of the overthrow of the Caetano government in 1974, Pretoria no doubt regarded this as a blessing in disguise. Nevertheless, the government did not find it too difficult to obtain entry into the Conference for the Italian line, Ignazio Messina, in 1970, while, in a different sort of case, it found it relatively easy to persuade the Lines to keep up their service (free of surcharge) to Maputo in the interests of Mozambique–South

Africa relations. This shows, then, that the liner trades can be manipulated for political purposes, but not without considerable difficulty. Moreover, rewards in the shipping market are evidently as difficult to disburse as punishments. How *efficient* the shipping market was as an instrument of South African foreign policy would require a study of the Republic's relations with each of the countries on which it was employed.

To sum up so far, the commanding position which the South African government achieved over the South African Conference in the post-war period—and the ignorance of, or indifference to this state of affairs on the part of European governments and the European Community—enabled Pretoria to make shipping in the Europe–South Africa trade serve South Africa's interests at the expense of Europe's. These interests were political as well as economic. This point is reinforced when it is remembered that the character of the bonds between the South African government, Safmarine, and the Conference (especially B & C) encouraged shipping interests to play a prominent role in the pro-South Africa lobby in London, and possibly in other European capitals, even though the influence of this lobby was not always as great as is sometimes supposed—both by the lobby itself and by its opponents.

This study clearly supports the anti-Marxist historiography of corporate–government relations, which stresses that corporate domination of governments is not axiomatic, but that corporations and governments are involved in a constant process of bargaining, with sometimes the one and sometimes the other having the upper hand. In the case of the South African Conference and the South African government, the former has sometimes had the upper hand, particularly when the government has been anxious for new tonnage for the trade. This helped the Lines to defeat the Shipping Board Bill in 1955, and extract favourable financial terms under the Memorandum of Understanding on containerization in February 1974. However, for reasons which have already been summarized in this Conclusion, it has usually been the government which has had the upper hand over the Conference, and in matters affecting South Africa's vital interests the government has *always* got its way (though it is true, as we have seen, that this has been in part because the Conference has been able to deflect much of the pain to European exporters). Even before the government's influence over the Conference on key issues was ratified in the 1966 OFA, this was true of the introduction of the Special

Immigrant Service in 1947, entry of the South African flag into the trade in 1949–50, and, of course, the structure of freight rates. The South Africans subsequently took from 1968 until 1975 to accept the pleas of the Conference that the tariff currency should be changed from the pound to the dollar, and then successfully insisted on a change-over on their own terms, even though there was no explicit provision for a government prerogative on this matter in the OFA.

Of course, the reply to this analysis will be: but what about the issues which the Conference succeeded in keeping off the agenda of its negotiations with the government? Is there not, it will be asked, on more subtle investigation, evidence that the government either *chose not* to raise certain issues because it anticipated insuperable opposition from the Lines, or did not raise certain issues because—having been effectively brainwashed by Conference propaganda over the years—it simply *did not occur to it* to raise them? In short, what of 'the hidden face of power'?[3] This is an important question. Perhaps a conclusion based largely on the written record of the most visible issues dividing the Conference and the government is indeed distorted. Perhaps the Conference 'in reality' had more power over the government than this record suggests. Neither should it be overlooked (though it usually is) that this methodological argument cuts both ways. Perhaps the government had 'a hidden face of power'. Perhaps, therefore, the government had even more power over the Conference than this account suggests. These issues require some brief consideration.

To take first the possibility that Conference power consisted of influence over the agenda of its discussions with the government. It is inconceivable that the latter drew its assessment of what was important from the Lines. Even the Smuts government, with its conservative Shipping Board, was not an innocent in shipping matters, as the record of the 1945 negotiations on the OFA and the Mail Contract amply reveal, and it became even less so with the birth of the national merchant marine and a national shipping press in 1946. It remains possible, however, that at least in the early years of this period, certain issues were kept off the agenda by the fear of insuperable opposition from the Lines—or at least from Union-Castle. State shipping, which was seriously considered by the South African government at the end of the Second World War but never took off, is

[3] S. Lukes, *Power: A Radical View* (London, 1974); and D. C. Bennet and K. E. Sharpe, 'Agenda Setting and Bargaining Power: The Mexican State versus Transnational Automobile Corporations', *World Politics*, 32.1, Oct. 1979.

an outside candidate, except that it was in effect *on* the agenda in 1946 and again in the early 1950s. Moreover, this seems to have been dropped less from fear of the Conference's reaction than from a shortage of second-hand ships at the end of the war and other domestic economic considerations. In the early 1950s Eric Louw used its revival as a pressure point on the Conference. More persuasive than this is the possibility that Union-Castle power was behind the failure of both the Smuts and National Party governments to put the Mail Contract out to tender, for though there were occasionally rumours to the contrary, whether or not Union-Castle should hold the Mail Contract was never a formal issue in the post-war period, only the terms on which it should hold it. And, certainly, the government would have been very hard pushed indeed either to put on a comparable mail service itself, or to find another line prepared to take on the job in the face of Union-Castle hostility. On the other hand, it would be astonishing if the government had not appreciated that the importance attached to the Mail Contract by Union-Castle was the secret of the government's own hold over the Conference, and amazing if it had not grasped, therefore, that it had everything to lose by placing the Mail Contract elsewhere. In short, if the Conference did have 'a hidden face of power' it was very expertly hidden indeed.

Just as the government failed to make an issue of Union-Castle's hold on the Mail Contract, so the Conference failed to make an issue of the Ocean Freight Agreement itself (as distinct from its terms), though in this case it seems that the failure was a genuine index of power. In the early 1950s, and again in the early 1960s, when the Lines were suffering more than usual from the government's control over freight rates, some thought was given to trying to break free from the OFA, the disadvantages of which seemed increasingly to be outweighing the advantages. However, knowledge of the importance attached by the government to control over freight rates, and apprehension at what might replace the OFA (as well as Union-Castle's fears for the Mail Contract) led the Lines on each occasion to put aside such thoughts. Having said this, there is no clue in the voluminous archives of the Conference that it failed to raise any other significant issue because it assumed that defeat was a foregone conclusion.

On balance, then, it is probably fair to say that consideration of the shaping of the agenda of Conference–government negotiations does not appreciably alter the estimate of relative power made on the basis of the results of those negotiations: much more often than not it was the government which evidenced more power. The South African Conference, for all its size and for all the wealth and expertise which it represented, was for most of this period a captive cartel. However, for reasons which were advanced at the end of the last chapter, whether this is currently the case, and whether it will ever be the case again, is open to very serious doubt.

APPENDIX I
The Lines in the South African Conference, 1981[1]

'1904 LINES'[2]

Union-Castle Line (British) ⎫
Clan Line (British)   ⎬ *B & C Group*
Houston Line (British)   ⎭
Ellerman & Bucknall Line (British)
Springbok Shipping Company (South African), *formerly* Springbok Line (South African), *formerly* Bullard, King (British)
Harrison Line (British)
Hall Line (British)

OTHER MEMBERS (WITH DATE OF ENTRY)

1911   P & O Line (British), *formerly* British India Line (British)[3]
1924   Deutsche Ost-Afrika Linie (W. German)[4]
       Nedlloyd Lijnen (Dutch), *formerly* Holland-Afrika Lijn (Dutch)
1925   Transatlantic (Swedish)
       Wilhelmsen (Norwegian)[5]
1926   CMB (Belgian), *formerly* Cie. Maritime Belge (Belgian)
1927   Lloyd Triestino (Italian), *formerly* Navigazione Linera Triestina SA and 'Italia'[6]
1930   Companhia Nacional de Navegacao (Portuguese)[7]
1932   Companhia Colonial de Navegacao (Portuguese)[8]

[1] *Source:* CAL. I am particularly grateful to Mr Don Small for assistance in the compilation of this Appendix.

[2] The Conference was reconstructed at the beginning of 1904 and a general Agreement between the members was drawn up for the first time (V. E. Solomon, *The South African Shipping Question, 1886–1914* (Cape Town, 1982), 111 ff.). It thus became customary within the Conference to regard 1904 as the year of its *de jure* foundation (even though the Conference was really founded in 1883), and to regard the '1904 Lines' as the founder members, or inner core.

[3] P & O's Agreement was terminated on 1 January 1982 at the Company's own request.

[4] DOAL's membership was terminated at the start of the Second World War and not resumed until 9 August 1951.

[5] The Wilhelmsen Line, though retaining Conference membership, ceased operations in 1979 and its rights were transferred to Transatlantic.

[6] After wartime separation, Lloyd Triestino was readmitted to the Conference in September 1948.

[7] Until 1969 CNN was only an Associate Member; in this year it became a Full Member.

[8] CCN was only an Associate Member, and in 1972 was expelled for starting a service in opposition to the Conference in alliance with another Portuguese line, EIN.

1935   Blue Star Line (British)[9]
1946   Chargeurs Réunis (French), *formerly* Cie. Maritime des Chargeurs
       Réunis (French)
       Cie. Générale Maritime (French), *formerly* Cie. Messageries Maritimes
       (French)
1950   South African Lines (South African)
       South African Marine Corporation (South African)
1970   Ignazio Messina (Italian)
1974   Overseas Containers (British)
1976   Jadranska Slobodna Plovidba (Yugoslavian)[10]
1980   Royal Swazi National Shipping Company (Swazi)
       Consortium Line (Spanish)
1981   Hellenic Lines (Greek)[11]

[9] A member in the Southbound trade only, but non-operative.
[10] An Associate Member only.
[11] Ceased trading in 1983.

APPENDIX II
The South African Merchant Fleet, 1947–1985

Year	Gross tons	Year	Gross tons
1947	129,264	1967	470,187
1948	168,648	1968	470,078
1949	175,109	1969	498,743
1950	175,743	1970	510,504
1951	158,846	1971	538,493
1952	140,395	1972	511,190
1953	119,986	1973	490,751
1954	127,227	1974	535,322
1955	160,623	1975	565,575
1956	166,802	1976	477,011
1957	176,628	1977	476,324
1958	194,032	1978	660,735
1959	236,135	1979	741,469
1960	245,413	1980	728,926
1961	261,183	1981	730,915
1962	232,636	1982	776,153
1963	231,154	1983	764,809
1964	303,329	1984	712,220
1965	302,308	1985	632,455
1966	398,664		

Source: Lloyd's Register of Shipping, *Statistical Tables* (annual).

APPENDIX III

Union-Castle, the SA Commercial Banks and the NFC: Deposits in and Remittances from 1950–1952 (£000)

	Jan.	Feb.	Mar.	Apr.	May	June	July	Aug.	Sept.	Oct.	Nov.	Dec.
1950												
Commercial Banks[a]												
Deposited	...	...	...	...	100	...	...	...	...	...	...	...
Remitted to UK	...	...	...	...	...	...	...	...	...	...	...	...
Running total	...	...	...	...	1230	...	...	...	...	...	...	...
NFC												
Deposited	—	350	300	200	250	200	—	—	—	—	—	—
Remitted to UK	—	—	—	—	—	—	—	—	—	—	300	200
Running total	—	350	650	850	1100	1300	1300	1300	1300	1300	1000	800
1951												
Commercial Banks												
Deposited	—	—	—	—	—	—	—	—	—	—	—	—

Remitted to UK	–	–	250	–	240	–	–	–	–	–	–
Running total	510	510	510	760	760	1000	1000	1000	1000	1000	1000
NFC											
Deposited	200[b]	–	–	–	–	–	–	–	–	–	–
Remitted to UK	–	–	–	–	–	–	–	–	–	500	–
Running total	1000	1000	1000	1000	1000	1000	1000	1000	1000	500	500
1952 *Commercial Banks*											
Deposited	–	–	–	–	–	120	–	–	–	–	–
Remitted to UK	–	–	250	–	–	–	–	–	–	–	–
Running total	510	510	260	260	260	140	140	140	140	140	140
NFC											
Deposited	–	–	–	–	–	–	–	–	–	–	–
Remitted to UK	–	–	500	–	–	–	–	–	–	–	–
Running total	500	500	500	–	–	–	–	–	–	–	–

[a] Standard Bank and Barclays D. C. & O., with the amount divided equally between each.
[b] Transferred from fixed deposits in the Commercial Banks which matured on 1 January 1950.
Source: Cayz. H., U-C DM.

APPENDIX IV

The Programme for the De-requisition of the Union-Castle Fleet Prior to the Negotiations for the Special Immigrant Service

Ship	Release Date	Date of First Sailing
*Capetown Castle*ᵃ	June 1946	Jan. 1947
*Carnarvon Castle*ᵃ	Jan. 1947	Jan. 1947
Warwick Castle (ex *Pretoria C.*)	Nov. 1946	Mar. 1947
Llandovery Castle	Sept. 1946	Mar. 1947
*Athlone Castle*ᵃ	Sept. 1946	Apr. 1947
Llanstephan Castle	Sept. 1946	May 1947
Durban Castle	Nov. 1946	June 1947
Llangibby Castle	Dec. 1946	July 1947
*Stirling Castle*ᵃ	Jan. 1947	Sept. 1947
*Winchester Castle*ᵃ	Apr. 1947	Nov. 1947
*Arundel Castle*ᵃ	Oct. 1947	Apr. 1948
Dunnottar Castle	Dec. 1947	July 1948

ᵃ Mail vessels.

Source: Appendix to Provision of Shipping for Emigrants to South Africa, 22 Jan. 1947, a brief provided for Mr Alfred Barnes prior to his interview on 23 Jan. 1947 with representatives of the South African government: PRO, MT 73/23.

APPENDIX V

The Composition of the SA Shipping Board

UNDER THE ACT OF 1929

Voting Members
Nominated by the Governor-General (but not from the public service or the SAR&H)   3
Nominated by ASSOCOM   1
Nominated by the FCI   1
Nominated by the SAAU   1
Non-Voting Members
Nominated by the Governor-General from the public service and the SAR&H   3
Total Membership   9

Source: SOUTH AFRICA. *Laws, Statutes, etc.* Shipping Board Act, No. 20 of 1929.

In 1965 the Act of 1929 was amended in order to allow the 'State President' (previously 'Governor-General') to nominate *one* voting member from the public service. This was presumably designed to bring the *de jure* position into line with the *de facto* one, since Dr Norval—a public servant—had been Chairman of the Shipping Board for the previous fifteen years: 6 No. 1066, Government Gazette Extraordinary, 24 Mar. 1965.

PROPOSED UNDER THE BILL OF 1955

Voting Members
Nominated by the Governor-General from the public service   2
Nominated by the Governor-General from the SAR&H   1
Nominated by the Governor-General from elsewhere   2
Nominated by 'commerce'   1
Nominated by 'manufacturing industries'   1
Nominated by 'agriculture'   1
Total Membership   8

Source: SOUTH AFRICA. Parliament. House of Assembly. Bills: AB 52 series. This Bill was formally withdrawn on 30 May 1955.

AS ENLARGED BY THE ACT OF 1976

Voting Members

Secretary for Commerce (Chairman)	1
Civil servants from the Departments of Industries, Customs & Excise, and Agricultural Economics and Marketing	3
SAR&H	1
PPECB	1
Organized commerce (ASSOCOM and the Afrikaanse Handelsinstituut)	2
Organized industry (FCI, the National Association of Automobile Manufacturers of South Africa, and the Steel and Engineering Industries Federation of South Africa)	3
The Chamber of Mines	1
SAAU	1
Total membership	13

Source: SOUTH AFRICA. *Laws, Statutes, etc.* Shipping Board Act, No. 74 of 1976.

APPENDIX VI
The Pretoria Formula

The Lines' request that a measure of flexibility be introduced into the so-called "Pretoria Formula" was carefully considered. Without affecting the underlying principles of the "Pretoria Formula", it was felt that over a period of a trade cycle the Lines should earn an average return on their capital investment (as represented by the written down estimated replacement cost of their vessels) of 5 per cent. per annum, after providing for depreciation at the rate of 4 per cent. per annum on the estimated replacement cost of their vessels, and that to achieve this a measure of flexibility is desirable. It was agreed that this matter would be the subject of further consideration at the next Annual Shipping Conference, and that much could be gained if consultation could take place in the meantime.

Source: CAL, De Waal Meyer to Bevan, 10 Nov. 1958.

APPENDIX VII

The Revised Pretoria Formula, 1960

DEPARTMENT OF COMMERCE AND INDUSTRY
Cor. Paul Kruger and Minaar Streets,
Private Bag 84,
PRETORIA.
9 August 1960.

John S. Bevan Esq.,
Chairman, South African Conference Lines,
Cayzer House,
2 & 4, St Mary Axe,
LONDON, E.C.3.

Dear Sir,
Following on the discussions Dr. A. J. Norval, Chairman of the South African Shipping Board, had with you in Pretoria and more recently in London, I have much pleasure in advising you that the Hon. the Minister of Economic Affairs has agreed to the following formula taking the place of the Pretoria Formula of 1955 to wit:

That the South African Conference Lines shall have the right to adjust freight rates, without prior approval, so as to yield up to 10 per cent during the upward swing of the trade cycle in order to realise *five* per cent on replacement value over the complete cycle or cycles, subject to the following provisions:

Paragraph (a) that the basis of the calculation of profit be confined to those goods and those shipping activities which constitute the main subject of the Conference Agreement;

Paragraph (b) that on the submission of an approved list, to which additions may be made from time to time, of essential plant and raw material requirements of the Union by the South African Shipping Board no increase in freight rates be made in respect thereof without prior approval on the distinct understanding that the freight on such a list does not, on an average, exceed 20% of the total southbound freight;

Paragraph (c) that the freight rates on exports of South African products, not subject to tramp competition, be increased above the level of existing tariff rates only with the approval of the Minister—the extent of such increases to be related to the exigencies of economic conditions ruling at the time;

Paragraph (d) that the freight rates on minerals, not subject to tramp competition, exported from the Union and subject to annual commodity-agreements between the Conference Lines and the shippers be increased above the level of existing tariff rates only after notification to the Shipping Board and with the approval of the Minister—the same to apply to the export of the agricultural or horticultural products exported under an annual freight agreement;

Paragraph (e) that the rate of depreciation on ships be fixed at 5% per annum to operate from the beginning of the year which will be taken as the basis for the Triennial Review to be held in Cape Town in January, 1962;

Paragraph (f) that advance payments on ships under construction, as well as the valuation of buildings and equipment, be excluded when determining the financial results for the purpose of freight rate adjustments, but interest on such advance payments to be added to the total cost of construction; and

Paragraph (g) that at the Triennial Shipping Conference the rates of freight operative under the Conference Agreement be reviewed, based on the submission of cost data as was done in 1958, and supplemented by cost data submitted annually by the Union-Castle Company.

I shall appreciate it to have your formal acceptance of the terms of the new formula.

Yours faithfully,
(Sgd) A. Kotzenberg.
SECRETARY: COMMERCE AND INDUSTRY

APPENDIX VIII

General Increases in Freight Rates[a] in the Europe–South Africa Trade: Northbound and Southbound, 1951–1985

Date of Introduction	Northbound[b] (%)	Southbound (%)
1. 7.51	10.0	10.0
1. 9.55	10.0	10.0
15. 2.57	5.0	5.0
1. 2.58[c]	2.5	2.5
1.11.60	—	7.5
1. 1.61/13.2.61	5.0[d]	—
1. 1.62	—	7.5
1. 4.64	7.5[e]	10.0
1. 4.65	—	10.0
1. 7.66	5.0[f]	5.0
1. 8.67	6.0[g]	7.5
1. 9.68[h]	10.0	15.0
2. 5.69	−5.0	—
1.10.70	7.5	12.5
15. 3.71	6.0	10.0
23. 8.71	12.5	12.5
30.10.72	7.5	7.5
26. 8.74	10.0	10.0
1. 8.75	10.0	10.0
27.12.76	15.0	15.0
1. 1.78[i]	28.8	28.8
1. 7.78	6.0	6.0
1. 1.79	15.0	15.0
1. 1.80	12.0	12.0
1. 1.81	14.0	14.0
1. 1.82	12.0	12.0
1. 1.83	7.5	7.5
1. 1.84	12.0	12.0
1. 1.85	8.0	8.0

[a] Excluding bunker and currency surcharges (and reductions in them), except where subsequently consolidated into tariff rates.

^b Excludes contract rates.

^c Consolidation of bunker surcharge introduced on 15 Feb. 1957.

^d On 1 Jan. 1961 there was a 5% increase on citrus and deciduous fruit, while remaining rates were increased by 5% on 13 Feb. 1961.

^e This increase did not apply to citrus and deciduous fruit, deboned beef and certain other sections of the tariff. However, citrus and deciduous fruit had been increased by 7.5% on 1 Nov. 1962.

^f Excluding perishables, which had been increased by 7.5% on 1 Apr. 1966.

^g This was announced as 7% 'with some exceptions', but since these exceptions included at least half of the total Northbound freights and were asked to bear significantly lower increases, 'in effect', as Lemon told the Lines on 8 May 1967, the increase was only '6% overall': CAL.

^h Consolidation of devaluation surcharges introduced on 1 Dec. 1967.

ⁱ Includes consolidation of bunker surcharge of 14.5%, which was initially introduced at 2.7% on 3 Dec. 1973.

Source: CAL.

APPENDIX IX

Changes in Northbound and Southbound Freight Rates in the Europe–South Africa Trade Since 1951: An Index Based on Rates in 1950

Date of Introduction	Northbound	Southbound
1950 (base year)	100	100
1. 7.51	110	110
1. 9.55	121	121
15. 2.57	127	127
1. 2.58	130	130
1.11.60	130	140
1. 1.61/13. 2.61	136	140
1. 1.62	136	150
1. 4.64	146	165
1. 4.65	146	181
1. 7.66	153	190
1. 8.67	162	204
1. 9.68	178	235
2. 5.69	169	235
1.10.70	182	264
15. 3.71	193	290
23. 8.71	217	326
30.10.72	233	350
26. 8.74	256	385
1. 8.75	282	423
27.12.76	324	486
1. 1.78	417	626
1. 7.78	442	664
1. 1.79	508	764
1. 1.80	569	856
1. 1.81	649	976
1. 1.82	727	1093
1. 1.83	782	1175
1. 1.84	876	1316
1. 1.85	946	1421

Source: Appendix VIII.

APPENDIX X

The Northbound Trade, 1964: Contract and Non-contract Cargo, and Perishables

	Freight tons	Freight earnings (£)
Contract Cargo		
Baled produce	114,942	2,386,827
Other commodities	717,015	4,122,635
	831,957	6,509,462
Non-contract Cargo		
(a) Subject to tramp competition	276,959	1,260,752
(b) Not subject to tramp competition	739,146	4,385,210
	1,016,105	5,645,962
Perishables	870,355	8,139,378
	2,718,417	20,294,802

Source: CAL, Secretariat notes.

APPENDIX XI

B & C Political Contributions, 1967–1984 (£)[a]

Year	British United Industrialists	Econ. League	Aims of Industry	L'pool Cons.	Cons. Party	Total[b]
1967	5,000	750	—	—	—	6,000
1968	5,000	750	—	400	—	6,400
1969	5,000	750	—	550	—	6,300
1970	5,000	750	—	550	—	6,300
1971	5,000	750	—	550	—	6,300
1972	—	1,105	—	550	—	1,655
1973	—	1,105	—	—	10,567	11,672
1974	—	1,000	5,250	—	21,700	27,950
1975	—	2,000	250	—	16,000	18,250
1976	—	2,000	—	—	22,045	24,045
1977	—	2,000	—	—	23,545	25,545
1978	—	2,000	—	—	23,605	25,605
1979	—	2,000	—	—	39,071	41,071
1980	—	3,109	—	—	43,525	46,634
1981	—	3,422	—	—	95,810	99,232
1982	—	3,714	—	—	40,175	43,889
1983	—	3,892	—	—	94,050	97,942
1984	—	3,892	—	—	97,900	101,792

[a] Excludes unpublished contributions to such organizations as UKSATA and the South Africa Foundation.

[b] Includes £250 to the Commonwealth Industries Association in both 1967 and 1968.

Source: B & C Annual Reports.

LIST OF SOURCES, AND SELECT BIBLIOGRAPHY

MANUSCRIPT SOURCES

British & Commonwealth Archives, Cayzer House, London
B & C Board Meeting Minutes, 1955–82; B & C Chairman's Statement, AGMs 1956–83; B & C Annual Report and Accounts, 1956–85; Cayzer, Irvine Directors' Minute Books, 1935–66; Clan Line Board Meeting Minutes, 1939–66; Union-Castle Directors' Meetings' Minute Books, 1942–64; Union-Castle Chairman's Statement, AGMs 1944–55; Union-Castle Annual Report and Accounts, 1944–64.

Cape Archives Depot, Cape Town
Cape Town Chamber of Commerce: Minutes, Secretary's correspondence, and miscellaneous papers, 1941–55.

Central Archives Depot, Pretoria
SA Immigration Council papers, 1947–8 (K201).

Europe South & South-East African Conference Lines, Conference Secretariat Archives, BP Centre, Cape Town
Minutes and transcripts of Conference–government negotiations (mainly duplicating those held in the London Conference Secretariat), 1944–77; miscellaneous correspondence and other papers, 1944–77.

Europe South & South-East African Conference Lines, Conference Secretariat Archives, Portland House, London
Joint Meeting Minutes, 7 Feb. 1958–18 Oct. 1977 (earlier ones now transferred to the National Maritime Museum, Greenwich); Minutes of weekly Southbound meetings, 1943–70; Minutes of all major negotiations (including some verbatim transcripts) between the Conference and the South African government, outsider lines, etc., 1944–77; Conference Chairman's correspondence, cable and telex traffic with the South African government (particularly the Secretary for Commerce and the Chairman of the Shipping Board), Conference representatives in South Africa, member lines, outsider lines, shippers, etc., including reports on discussions and negotiations in South Africa and elsewhere, 1944–77; Supporting Letters . . . to be read in conjunction with Ocean Freight Agreement operative from 1 Jan. 1967 to 31 Dec. 1976; Memorandum of Understanding between the South African Government, the Perishable Products Export Control Board and the South African Conference Lines regarding the introduction of a New Technique of Ocean Transport in the Trade between South Africa and Europe, 1974;

Union-Castle Agreement Book, No. 2, 1922–54; miscellaneous papers, 1939–77.

Luke Papers

Various speeches of W. E. Luke at UKSATA and South Africa Foundation meetings; Reports to BNEC, 1967–79.

National Maritime Museum, Department of Books and Manuscripts, Greenwich, London

South African Conference Lines: Joint Meeting Minutes, 3 Mar. 1933–18 Oct. 1957 (later ones remain with the Conference Secretariat).

Public Record Office, Kew

Post-war migration: Government Policy–South Africa (DO 35/1135); Emigration from the UK to South Africa, 1946–7 (MT 73/23 and MT 73/24).

PUBLISHED OFFICIAL SOURCES

'Agreement between the Government of the Union of South Africa, the Perishable Products Export Control Board and the Union-Castle Mail Steamship Company, Limited Relative to the ocean conveyance of goods between the Union of South Africa and certain United Kingdom and Continental Ports. Operative from 1st January, 1947, to 31st December, 1956.' ('Ocean Freight Agreement', signed 4 Apr. 1945)
'Agreement between the Government of the Union of South Africa, the Perishable Products Export Control Board and the Union-Castle Mail Steamship Company, Limited, (for and on behalf of the South African Conference) Relative to the ocean conveyance of goods between the Union of South Africa and certain United Kingdom and Continental Ports. Operative from 1st January, 1957, to 31st December, 1966.' ('Ocean Freight Agreement', signed 19 Aug. 1955)
'Agreement between the Government of the Republic of South Africa, the Perishable Products Export Control Board and the Union-Castle Mail Steamship Company, Limited, (for and on behalf of the South African Conference) Relative to the ocean conveyance of goods between The Republic of South Africa and Europe. Operative from 1st January, 1967, to 31st December, 1976.' ('Ocean Freight Agreement', signed 22 Aug. 1966)
'Agreement between the Government of the Republic of South Africa, the Perishable Products Export Control Board and the Conference Relative to the ocean conveyance of goods between the Republic of South Africa and Europe. Operative from 1st January 1977 to 31st December 1991.' ('Ocean Freight Agreement', signed 15 June 1977)
Committee of Inquiry into Shipping: Report, Cmnd. 4337, May 1970 ('The Rochdale Report').
SOUTH AFRICA: *Laws, Statutes, etc.* Shipping Board Act, No. 20 of 1929; No. 74 of 1976.
—— *Parliament. House of Assembly.* Bills: AB 52 series, Shipping Board Bill (1955).

BIBLIOGRAPHY   245

South African *House of Assembly Debates.*
South African Ocean Mail Service: 'Contract between the Government of the
 Union of South Africa and the Union-Castle Mail Steamship Company,
 Limited. Operative from 1st January, 1947, to 31st December, 1956.' ('Mail
 Contract', Pretoria, signed 4 Apr. 1945)
'South African Ocean Mail Service Contract between The Government of the
 Union of South Africa and The Union-Castle Mail Steamship Company,
 Limited. Operative from 1st January, 1957, to 31st December, 1966.' ('Mail
 Contract', Pretoria, signed 18 Aug. 1955).
South African *Senate Debates.*
South African Shipping Board: *Annual Report* (1944–69).
Union of South Africa, *Interim Report of the Shipping Commission* (Pretoria,
 1945).
—— *Interim (Final) Report of the South African Shipping Commission* (Pretoria,
 1947).
—— South African Railways, *Report of the Overseas Mission* (1946) (Johannesburg,
 31 Mar. 1947).
—— *Report of the Committee of Inquiry in Connection with the Shipping Service
 operated by the Railway Administration* (Pretoria, 1952).

PRINCIPAL NEWSPAPERS AND PERIODICALS

*Cape Times; Commerce & Industry; Fairplay; Financial Mail; The South African
Shipping News and Fishing Industry Review; The Times.*

SELECT BIBLIOGRAPHY

Barber, J. *South Africa's Foreign Policy, 1945–1970* (London, 1973).
—— *The Uneasy Relationship: Britain and South Africa* (London, 1983).
Berridge, G., *Economic Power in Anglo-South African Diplomacy: Simonstown,
 Sharpeville and After* (London, 1981).
Bennet, C., and Sharpe, K. E., 'Agenda Setting and Bargaining Power: The
 Mexican State versus Transnational Automobile Corporations', *World
 Politics*, 32.1, Oct. 1979.
Bower, P., *A Century of Service, 1883–1983: Europe/South & South East African
 Conference Lines* (Cape Town, 1983).
Brown, G., *In My Way* (Harmondsworth, 1972).
Cafruny, A. W., 'The Political Economy of International Shipping: Europe
 versus America', *International Organization*, 39.1, Winter 1985.
Castle, B., *The Castle Diaries, 1964–70* (London, 1984).
Christopher, Sir G. P., *Roots and Branches* (Liverpool and London, n.d.).
Chrzanowski, I., Krzyanowski, M., and Luks, K., *Shipping Economics and
 Policy: A Socialist View* (London, 1979).
Crossman, R., *The Diaries of a Cabinet Minister, 2, Lord President of the Council
 and Leader of the House of Commons, 1966–68* (London, 1976).
Davies, R., and O'Meara, D., 'Total Strategy in Southern Africa: An Analysis
 of South African Regional Policy since 1978', *Journal of Southern African
 Studies*, 11.2, Apr. 1985.

de Guingand, Major-General Sir Francis, *From Brass Hat to Bowler Hat* (London, 1979).

First, R., Steele, J., and Gurney, C., *The South African Connection: Western Investment in Apartheid* (London, 1972).

Geldenhuys, D., *The Diplomacy of Isolation: South African Foreign Policy Making* (Johannesburg, 1984).

Green, E., and Moss, M., *A Business of National Importance: The Royal Mail Shipping Group, 1902–1937* (London, 1982).

Grundy, K. W., *Confrontation and Accommodation in Southern Africa: The Limits of Independence* (Berkeley, 1973).

Ingpen, B. D., *South African Merchant Ships* (Cape Town, 1979).

Juda, L., *The UNCTAD Liner Code: United States Maritime Policy at the Crossroads* (Boulder, Colo., 1983).

Katzenellenbogen, S. E., *South Africa and Southern Mozambique: Labour, Railways and Trade in the Making of a Relationship* (Manchester, 1982).

Knorr, K., 'International Economic Leverage and its Uses', in Knorr, K. and Trager, F. N. (eds.), *Economic Issues and National Security* (Lawrence, Kan., 1977).

Loubser, J. G. H., 'Vervoerdiplomasie met Spesiale Verwysing na Suider-Afrika', *Politikon*, 6.2, Dec. 1979.

Lukes, S., *Power: A Radical View* (London, 1974).

Maasdorp, G. G., *Transport Policies and Economic Development in Southern Africa: A Comparative Study in Eight Countries* (Durban, 1984).

Middlemas, K., *Cabora Bassa: Engineering and Politics in Southern Africa* (London, 1975).

—— 'Independent Mozambique and Its Regional Policy', in Seiler, J. (ed.), *Southern Africa since the Portuguese Coup* (Boulder, Colo., 1980).

Mitchell, W. H., and Sawyer, L. A., *The Cape Run* (Lavenham, 1984).

Muir, A., and Davies, M., *A Victorian Shipowner: A Portrait of Sir Charles Cayzer, Baronet of Gartmore* (London, 1978).

Murray, M., *Union-Castle Chronicle, 1853–1953* (London, 1953).

Nicholls, G. H., *South Africa In My Time* (London, 1961).

Norval, A. J., *A Quarter of a Century of Industrial Progress in South Africa* (Cape Town, 1962).

Olson, R. S., 'Economic Coercion in World Politics', *World Politics*, 31.4, July 1979.

Ovendale, R., 'The South African Policy of the British Labour Government, 1947–51', *International Affairs*, 59.1, Winter 1982/83.

Reynolds, C., *Modes of Imperialism* (Oxford, 1981).

Serafetinidis, M., Serafetinidis, G., Lambrinides, M., and Demathas, Z., 'The Development of Greek Shipping Capital and its Implication for the Political Economy of Greece', *Cambridge Journal of Economics*, 5, 1981.

Schoeman, B., *My lewe in die politiek* (Johannesburg, 1978).

Sletmo, G. K., and Williams, E. W. Jnr., *Liner Conferences in the Container Age: U.S. Policy at Sea* (New York, 1981).

Solomon, V. E., 'The "Open Market" in South African Shipping: A Forgotten Controversy', *The South African Journal of Economics*, 47.3, 1979.

—— *The South African Shipping Question, 1886–1914* (Cape Town, 1982).

Spence, J. E., *Republic under Pressure: A Study of South African Foreign Policy* (London, 1965).

Stone, J., *Colonist or Uitlander? A Study of the British Immigrant in South Africa* (Oxford, 1973).

Sturmey, S. G., *British Shipping and World Competition* (London, 1962).

UNCTAD, *The Regulation of Liner Conferences*, TD/104/Rev. 1 (New York, 1972).

Vail, L., and White, L., *Capitalism and Colonialism in Mozambique: A Study of Quelimane District* (London, 1980).

Verburgh, C., *Ontwikkeling en vooruitsigte van die Suid-Afrikaanse handelskeepvaart* (Stellenbosch, 1966).

Yeats, A. J., *Trade Barriers Facing Developing Countries: Commercial Policy Measures and Shipping* (London, 1979).

Young, G., *Salt In My Blood* (Cape Town, 1975).

INDEX